Organising Labour in Globalising Asia

D1800131

This book offers wide-ranging insights into the organising capacities of workers in Asia today. Nine case studies examine workers' responses to class relations through independent unions, non-governmental organisations (NGOs) and more (dis)organised struggles.

Economic globalisation is generally held to have entirely negative consequences for labour organising, but this book reveals some of the openings for local activism that can arise from transnational production arrangements. In this way, *Organising Labour in Globalising Asia* challenges the conventional view that globalisation is the main determinant of labour's weakness and marginalisation in the region.

Covering 'second tier' industrialisers of East and South Asia – such as China, Thailand, Malaysia, the Philippines, Indonesia, India and Bangladesh – this interdisciplinary book will be of great interest to social scientists in the fields of Asian studies, politics, economics, political economy and more specifically in international labour studies.

Jane Hutchison is Lecturer in Politics and International Studies at Murdoch University, Australia.

Andrew Brown is Lecturer in Asian Studies at the University of New England, Australia.

The New Rich in Asia Series
Edited by Richard Robison and David S.G. Goodman

Organising Labour in Globalising Asia

**Edited by
Jane Hutchison and
Andrew Brown**

Asia Research Centre, Murdoch University

London and New York

First published 2001
by Routledge
11 New Fetter Lane, London EC4P 4EE

Simultaneously published in the USA and Canada
by Routledge
29 West 35th Street, New York, NY 10001

Routledge is an imprint of the Taylor & Francis Group

Typeset in Baskerville by Taylor & Francis Books Ltd
Printed and bound in Great Britain by MPG Books Ltd, Bodmin

British Library Cataloguing in Publication Data
A catalogue record for this book is available from the British Library

Library of Congress Cataloging in Publication Data
Organising labour in globalising Asia / edited by Jane Hutchison and
Andrew Brown
p. cm. – (New Rich in Asia)
Includes bibliographical references and index.
1. Labor movement–Asia. 2. Globalization. I. Hutchison, Jane, 1954–
II. Brown, Andrew, 1953– III. Series.
HD8653.5 .O74 2001
331.88'095–dc21   00–045946

ISBN   0–415–25059–5 (hbk)
ISBN   0–415–25060–9 (pbk)

Contents

Contributors

Andrew Brown is Lecturer in the School of Social Science at the University of New England, New South Wales.

Patricia Cahill is a Ph.D. candidate in Economics at Murdoch University, Western Australia.

Vedi R. Hadiz is Lecturer in the Department of Sociology, National University of Singapore.

Jane Hutchison is Lecturer in Politics and International Studies at Murdoch University, Western Australia.

Michael Pinches is Senior Lecturer in Anthropology at the University of Western Australia.

Rajah Rasiah is Associate Professor in Economics at Universiti Kebangsaan Malaysia.

Marilyn Rock is a Parliamentary Research Officer in Western Australia.

Sally Sargeson is Research Fellow at the Asia Research Centre, Murdoch University, Western Australia.

Stephen Sherlock is a Research Specialist at the Parliamentary Research Service, Parliament House, Canberra.

Preface

As the sixth and final volume of *The New Rich in Asia Series* on emerging social forces in Asia, this book is centred on the self-organising capacities of industrial workers. Unlike some other volumes on this topic, it is not restricted to the rise and operations of unions, but also covers workers' involvement in organisations not normally classified as 'industrial' – namely non-governmental organisations (NGOs) – as well as instances of activism where workers combine outside any formal body. This broad approach is consistent with labour organising being understood as the collective responses of workers to the various dilemmas they face through their incorporation into capitalist class relations.

The book is not written as a series of country-level reports on the state of Asian labour movements; instead, the nine main chapters are case studies of the self-organising capacities of different workers in defined local settings. Each of the studies nevertheless engages with disparate debates around the theme of labour's relative industrial weakness and political marginalisation in newly industrialising Asia. In this regard, a key theme is the impact of developments associated with economic 'globalisation'. Such developments are widely argued to have entirely negative consequences for labour as an independent social force. However, various studies in this book make it clear that the outcomes from facets of globalisation are more complex than this assessment would suggest. Indeed, in some cases it is shown that transnational production arrangements can generate openings for workers' local self-organising through the deepening of class processes in otherwise hostile environments.

Whereas much attention has been given to labour-organising capacities in the first 'newly industrialised countries' (NICs) of East Asia, the case studies in this volume are gathered from the 'second-tier' new industrialising countries of Asia – Thailand, Malaysia, Indonesia, the Philippines, China, India and Bangladesh. The first four of these countries were hit by the 1997 regional financial crisis – Indonesia most severely. Where relevant, the particular effects of this crisis are commented upon in the case studies; however, it has to be said this is not a book on labour and the crisis *per se*.

****

The first chapter, 'An introduction', gives the intellectual background-context to issues confronted individually in each of the nine case studies. First, the meaning of 'class' that informs this collection is explained. In brief, against common understandings of class as an actor in socio-economic and political conflicts, it is argued that class is better viewed as a relation and process that is the object of certain conflicts in capitalist societies. Second, normative assumptions behind certain approaches to labour organising are discussed. Assumptions as to what the real form of labour organising should or should not be have not only framed analyses of the course and significance of workers' activism in the region, they have also at times legitimated interventions against modes of organising which constitute labour as a social force beyond the workplace. This is especially so for various liberal approaches. Set against changes in the international order for capitalist development, the discussion is concerned to highlight connections between research and policy agendas which invariably shape expectations around the nature of labour organising in the region.

The remainder of the chapter then critically examines three broad areas of debate in relation to workers' perceived relative weakness as a social force in globalising Asia. These broad areas are: (1) culture and conflict, (2) states and political change, and (3) economic globalisation itself. In relation to each of these matters the possible openings for labour organising are particularly considered.

In the second chapter, Marilyn Rock's case study is of the rise of the Bangladesh Independent Garment-Workers' Union (BIGU) – highlighting its significance in a country where party-political affiliations have often contained independent labour organising. Against more general propositions about the impact of economic globalisation on labour-organising capacities, Rock makes the observation that transnational production arrangements have helped to generate a critical mass of women workers behind the formation of BIGU – their involvement in the union being as well a challenge to historical accounts of their cultural subordination. However, Rock argues that BIGU might not have been founded were it not for the active assistance of the Asia-American Free Labor Institute (AAFLI), an organisation well known for its interventions against 'political' unionism in East and South Asia. To this extent, Rock's study draws attention to the impact of international organisational links on the local organising capacity of these garment workers.

Sally Sargeson, in the third chapter, shows that young, female, migrant workers in a Chinese joint venture factory have not been utterly disempowered by changes to their employment conditions associated with economic globalisation. Rather, they have able to appropriate and subvert various discourses around the intensification of their labour at a time when competitive pressures were increasing on the factory, with the result that the local manager was pushed to end his much resented discriminatory treatment of these migrant workers from another province in China. Sargeson argues that competitive pressures on the factory arising from its insertion in transnational production arrangements, in combination with workers' own '(*dis*)organised' responses to these pressures, caused a deepening of class relations in this factory. While there were no immediate economic benefits for the workers involved, Sargeson states some gains in organising capacity were achieved under circumstances that are widely held to exemplify the structural conditions of workers' demobilisation.

In the fourth chapter, Jane Hutchison establishes positive connections between export-oriented production and trade union formation in the Philippine garments industry through a detailed survey of local subcontracting practices in the industry. What emerges is that, although many factors encourage the extensive putting-out of production, Philippine managers are regularly constrained in this practice by the quality demands of their overseas buyers and contractors. In the exporting sector, there are thus larger factories (meaning factories with large workforces in-house) and, for this reason, more opportunities for workers to form unions. However, circumstances influencing the pattern of unionisation in the garments industry must also be set against the broader political environment for labour organising in the Philippines. In this regard, Hutchison outlines the industrial relations system, as well as developments in civil society which have altered the climate for labour militancy in the 1990s.

In the fifth chapter, Rajah Rasiah considers the effects of the labour process on labour-organising capacities – this time in relation to male workers in Malaysia's Proton car industry. In so doing, he critically addresses the proposition that 'flexible specialisation' in production creates openings for more 'humane' worker–management relations and possibly greater workplace democracy. However, Rasiah begins by establishing that, in Proton, flexible specialisation techniques are in fact unevenly applied and do not include more inclusive modes of labour control. Further, given the continuities in political control, he observes that independent organising has not been enhanced, especially as (before the 1997 crisis) workers tended to be 'bought off' by relatively high wages. Subsequently, the in-house union has made some new efforts to tackle the problems facing workers in Proton that arise from falling demand.

In the sixth chapter, Vedi Hadiz continues to look at the organising capacities of new working classes in light export manufacturing – this time in Java. However, rather than focus on changing conditions in the labour process, he argues that the foundations for organising have been laid by developments in the workers' communities. As Suharto's 'New Order' labour laws were so restrictive, residential areas became important sites for labour self-organising. In addition, new workers needed the assistance of 'alternative organising vehicles' (like NGOs) to circumvent the constraints on independent unionism. Referring to economic and political changes associated with the 1997 financial crisis and fall of President Suharto, Hadiz remains pessimistic about the political openings for labour. While some laws have been relaxed, he notes that contestation in the political arena is confined to an elite with few links to organised labour.

In the seventh chapter, Andrew Brown looks at aspects of labour organising which have emerged as a consequence of growing problems associated with workplace health and safety issues, especially in the wake of the disastrous 1993 fire at the Kader Industries (Thailand) factory that claimed the lives of almost 200 workers. He suggests that, in the context of a weak, fragmented and politically isolated trade union movement, activism that aimed at improving health and safety standards has led to the forging of some new alliances in the country between labour and non-labour actors. Though not overly optimistic, Brown does suggest these struggles for improved health and safety may yet prove significant for ongoing attempts to rebuild an effective and independent organised labour movement in Thailand.

In the eighth chapter, Stephen Sherlock examines current difficulties facing the labour movement in Bombay. In so doing, he is critical of the view that the movement's problems mainly stem from the city's greater integration into the world economy. He rather blames, in part, organising strategies in the past that relied heavily on political patronage and state protection for industry and employment. Emerging labour market conditions in Bombay make organising more difficult, in that they involve a growth in small enterprises and a shift from manufacturing to services-based employment. However, Sherlock believes that the labour movement leadership has been ill prepared for this development in that its reliance on the state has shielded it from the difficult task of organising on the ground. In this context, he argues, the nationalist response of blaming globalisation has only added to the movement's current problems by encouraging the view that workers are powerless in the face of global capital.

In the ninth chapter, Patricia Cahill also looks at labour responses to economic globalisation in India, but this time at strike action workers and their unions took in opposition to the introduction of private capital to the telecommunications sector. Workers and unions in this sector have long been accused of acting as a self-serving labour aristocracy. However, Cahill disputes this claim from a number of positions, noting the broader class issues around privatisation that the workers' strike actions endeavoured to highlight. But, as other contributors to this volume have found, the catalyst for the campaign came not only from the existing union federation leadership, but also from a group of public interest advocates concerned about the government's broader economic liberalisation agenda. Cahill suggests it was these public interest advocates who helped to draw out the class dimensions of reputed new efficiencies from privatisation, so helping to galvanise the activism of local union organisers across the country.

Finally, in the tenth chapter, Michael Pinches explores the links between class and ethnic or national identities in the collective responses of Filipino migrant workers to their overseas employment experience. In so doing, he also draws attention to facets of labour organising that take place beyond the workplace and outside union structures. To begin with, Pinches explains how ethnicity is a marker of the low status of migrant workers in their host countries, and thus a source of social isolation and control. However, he argues that overseas employment remains an attractive option, despite the degradation involved, not just as an avenue to higher wages but also as a response to demeaning class relations in the Philippines. Meanwhile, migrant workers engage in acts of 'everyday' defiance overseas that are commonly centred on their identities as Filipinos and involve the support of other Filipino workers. As such, Pinches argues that ethnic or national identities are a powerful expression of workers' sentiments relating to class. This point is conversely reflected in his observation that calls from the Philippine middle class and elite for better state protection of migrant workers is often motivated by concerns to see their own ethnic and national status in the region safeguarded.

The chapters in this volume detail the organising capacity of workers in a range of national and local settings. As with all case studies, there is no claim to generalise in terms of the frequency of an occurrence across populations: instead the concern is to elaborate on specific processes in theoretical terms. This need is especially acute when it comes to assertions about the effects of economic globalisation on labour activism in Asia. At the industry, community or even factory levels, globalisation impacts on workers and their movements in a number of ways – both immediate and distant – but as often as not this impact is altered by national and local circumstances. Against the tendency to totalise globalisation, this volume aims to provide a diversity of accounts which are in keeping with the complexities of labour-organising capacities on the ground in Asia today.

Jane Hutchison and Andrew Brown

ACKNOWLEDGEMENTS

Richard Robison suggested we do this book, and we thank him for that. We are also grateful to our contributors for their encouragement and forbearance, and to our commissioning editors at Routledge, Victoria Smith and Craig Fowlie, the anonymous reviewers and all the production crew for their kind assistance. This book received financial and administrative support from the Asia Research Centre at Murdoch University – special thanks to Del Blakeway on that account. Finally, love and thanks to Andrew Adamson, Ingrid Wijeyewardene and Kestin and Angus Brown.

1 Organising labour in globalising Asia

An introduction

Jane Hutchison and Andrew Brown[1]

The historical experience of capitalist industrialisation in Western Europe led liberals and socialists alike to view labour organising as a normal – although not uncontested – occurrence. Despite differences in the social and political contexts of industrialisation, and in the timing and structure of that process, the struggles of Western European workers and their movements were widely accommodated within democratic frameworks, characterised by rights of association, systems of parliamentary representation and the rise of social safety nets (Geary, 1981; Katznelson and Zolberg, 1986). Thus labour organising came to be associated with the political inclusion of 'acceptable' expressions of labour dissent, sanctioned and enforced by the state and, in some cases, linked to parties contesting open national elections (Tilly, 1995). European liberals and socialists may have disagreed over the content and purpose of workers' organising, but they acknowledged and predicted its widespread occurrence in capitalist societies.

Labour movements were influential in shaping the core institutional arrangements of advanced capitalism in the twentieth century, but in the course of significant industrialisation in East Asia they have mostly been weak and marginalised.[2] To quote one influential commentator, in this part of the world 'rapid industrialisation has nowhere spawned effective trade unionism or enhanced worker participation in political or economic arenas' (Deyo, 1997: 210).[3] Deyo argues that where there have been noticeable improvements in the material standing of first- and second-generation workers in East Asia, these have been largely an outcome of changes in the labour market or in state policy, rather than a forced response to independent labour organising. The point Deyo makes is not that labour activism is entirely absent, but that when it occurs it is mostly fragmented and ineffective.

Not surprisingly, there are a variety of different – sometimes competing – explanations for the East Asian situation. In this chapter we cover a range of these under the three broad headings: *culture and conflict, states and political change,* and *economic globalisation*. By discussing general themes in the literature, the chapter introduces wide-ranging issues around labour's relative weakness as a social force which the case studies to follow look at in a more focused fashion. Throughout the volume, 'labour organising' is taken to mean workers' responses to class processes and relations that are collective and self-organised (or 'independent').[4] Accordingly, attention is not only given to formal unionism: labour activism through organisations not usually classified as 'industrial' – especially non-governmental organisations (NGOs) – is also examined, as well as the '(dis)organised' responses of workers outside any formally constituted body.[5]

'Class' is often de-centred from contemporary analyses of labour organising in Asia, with the result that little or no attempt is made to ground such analyses in an understanding of the peculiarities of capitalist employment relations (cf. Beresford and Kelly, 1993). This chapter thus begins by explaining the abstract understanding of class which informs this volume. Moving on to the normative dimensions of post-war writing on labour in Asia, the second part of the chapter mainly deals with moves in liberal thinking around the 'real' nature and purpose of labour organising and the place such thinking occupies in wider discourses on capitalist development and the changing international order. The discussion highlights how academic assessments of the direction and significance of worker organising can frame interventions to de-legitimate worker organising beyond the industrial arena.

The remainder of the chapter covers aforementioned factors behind the relative weakness and marginalisation of organised labour in East Asia. In this regard, we are especially critical of attempts to totalise phenomena like 'culture' and 'globalisation' as singular and self-evident in their consequences. Instead, we note their impacts are generally more contradictory than supposed and also contingent to the extent that they are shaped by other events and processes. An issue we stress is the enduring legacy of authoritarian politics at both state and civil-society levels.

On class

In this book, labour organising in Asia is examined through a series of local case studies; but these studies are linked by a particular theoretical appreciation of capitalist class relations in general (see Beresford and Kelly, 1993; Hess, 1998: 18). Here we specifically respond to suggestions that class is not a useful category of enquiry in Asia – either on the grounds that other social relations (familial, patron–client, ethnic and so on) are more dominant (De Guzman, 1993) or because the class attachments of East Asian workers are normally blocked or diluted by the desire for personal upward social mobility (Perry, 1996: 3). Pinches (in Chapter 10) makes reference to this last point when he notes that Filipino migrant workers can be dissuaded from resisting their harsh treatment by the prospect of some social advancement for themselves and their immediate families through earning higher wages overseas. But Pinches views this as a possible response *to class*, not as evidence for the relative absence of class. The distinction to grasp here is between class as a process or relation which is the object or source of conflict, and class as a relatively cohesive group which is the subject of conflict (Thompson, 1978; Wood, 1995). In this part of the chapter, we explain the distinction as it informs the approach to labour organising in this volume.

In thinking of class as a social group, a separation is often made between class structure and consciousness or 'between the "objective" and "subjective" dimensions of class' (Crompton, 1995: 48, 50).[6] Defined in objective or structural terms, classes are accordingly the individuals that share a common socio-economic location in the employment structure. But as a proposition about the making of history, classes of this type are only properly formed once the individuals within them are purposefully united as a relatively cohesive group. This 'subjective' dimension is essential because, in its absence, classes are just masses lacking social and political significance (Miliband, 1988: 23). This approach to class can be clearly seen in Sungsidh's (1989) work on Thai labour. He argues that class comes into play with the transformation of a 'scattered mass into an organised social group'; a process he understands as occurring in developmental stages, the final one being the emergence of class consciousness in 'opposition to other classes and the state' (Sungsidh, 1989: 4). However, when Thai workers do not behave as his model predicts, Sungsidh is forced to conclude that class is an inappropriate category of analysis because it cannot 'explain the empirical realities of social changes in Thailand' (ibid.: 9).

A problem with this approach to class is that too much emphasis is placed on workers' collective activism being an inevitable outcome of their shared objective location. To have real explanatory value in outlining 'the lines of demarcation in conflict producing processes' (Wright, 1985: 137), class as a 'subjective' entity must be isomorphic with a class structure that is theoretically significant. But this requirement only collapses the area of enquiry between structure and agency to such an extent that workers' struggles are reduced to 'a formula' (Katznelson, 1986: 7; Metcalfe, 1988: 15). As we have already seen with Sungsidh, deviations from the predicted course of 'true' labour activism can easily become a rationale for the abandonment of class analysis *per se*.

Yet, as Dow and Lafferty (1990: 4) state, 'classes are not actors'. Class is better understood as the processes by which 'surplus labour is pumped out of the direct producers' in capitalist societies (Marx, 1976: 927; Resnick and Wolff, 1981; Wood, 1995: 76). Accordingly, class conflict is that which occurs *over* class processes, rather than that *between* necessarily self-constituted groups (Therborn, 1983: 24; Dow and Lafferty, 1990). In these terms, it is still possible to speak of classes as socio-economic categories, so long as there is no concomitant assertion of 'a natural progression' from structural location to collective activism (Katznelson, 1986: 17–18). Approached in this way, the problem of *defining* class is removed as the matter of objective class boundaries becomes increasingly irrelevant. As such, class analysis has more affinities with the so-called 'labour process' literature than it does with theories of class structure *per se* (Stark, 1980; Mackenzie, 1982; Carter, 1995).

Through understanding class as a process, more attention can be paid to the ways in which workers are actually arrayed in the workplace and other social settings. To quote Wood:

> The links that connect [workers] ... are not defined by the simple assertion that class is structurally determined by the relations of production. It still remains to be explained in what sense and through what mediations the relations of production establish connections among people who, even if they occupy similar positions in production relations, are not actually assembled in the process of production.
>
> (Wood, 1995: 95–6)

In researching labour-organising capacities, factors like the 'proximity and durability of connections between particular groups of workers' (Tilly, 1995: 19; Lembcke, 1993) typically come to the fore. These spatial and temporal elements are, for example, covered in this volume by Hutchison and Hadiz (Chapters 4 and 6) in their endeavours to explain workers' aggregation in large factories and industrial communities respectively. But organising need not rely on physical proximity – Cahill (in Chapter 9) makes the point that telecom workers in India have been able to counter their dispersal by exploiting the access they have to the telephone system!

The presence or absence of labour organisations and the particular forms they take are factors that shape the nature of workers' responses to class relations (Rueschemeyer, Stephens and Stephens, 1992: 54). To this extent, they can be regarded as an explanatory variable as much as a target of research in this volume. But a point to stress here is that labour organisations have no fixed or 'real' relationship to conflicts over class. This can be attributed to the various ideologies at play in organisations of different kinds – but not completely. Rather, unions in particular are both 'a form of resistance to, and accommodation with, capital' (Hyman, 1987: 47). This is precisely because workers themselves are faced with all kinds of 'contradictory injunctions' in relation to class (Metcalfe, 1988: 197). In the words of Rueschemeyer, Stephens and Stephens:

> the interests of labor inevitably involve a whole array of partly contradictory goals because labor is never completely a commodity and the whole human being cannot be eliminated from the factor of production that is labor.
>
> (Rueschemeyer, Stephens and Stephens, 1992: 54)

This said, a review of the academic literature on factors behind labour-organising capacities in Asia must take account of the different normative views as to what 'real' organising involves – especially as this often has a bearing on what is being analysed and how. The next part of the chapter therefore moves to differences in academic thinking over the function of labour organising and the politics of this in relation to broader discourses on capitalist development and the international order.

Labour organising and development

Theories of labour organising are numerous (see Martin, 1989), but a key dispute persists over whether the motivations for worker activism are work-related or not. Involved in this are various disagreements over the goals of labour organising and the strategies used – whether 'real' organising is focused on improvements in wages and conditions through collective bargaining or whether it also entails campaigns beyond the factory in association with other organisations, political parties and social movements. In the liberal-pluralist perspectives on unionism that dominated analyses of comparative industrial relations in Asia and the rest of the developing world in the 1960s, these organising alternatives have been expressed in a range of definitional distinctions between 'economic' and 'political unionism'.[7]

Liberal-pluralist predictions about the course of labour organising went seriously awry in East Asia (rather than South Asia); however, they remain of contemporary interest as a set of ideas that are 'open for manipulation as a political totem' in international policy circles (Cohen, 1991: 6). Of course liberal-pluralists are not alone in this, but their thinking has a particular stature because of its long association with the foreign policy of the United States in the area of labour and capitalist development (Gershman, 1975; Sims, 1992). Here we outline the liberal-pluralist position in relation to general developments in labour organising in East and South Asia in the last four decades.

The liberal-pluralists' distinction between 'economic' and 'political unionism' is founded on their opposition to socialism. Writing on Asian labour movements in the 1960s, liberal-pluralists worked from the assumption – both American-centred and idealised – that economic unionism is an organic feature of advanced industrialised societies – a 'branch of the social tree' as Sufrin (1964: 17) once put it (see also Galenson, 1962; Millen, 1963; Kassalow, 1969; Sturmthal, 1972). This understanding was tied to the view that workers *qua* workers are but one of a number of interest groups that arise with the greater division of labour in advanced industrialised societies (Martin, 1989: 14–22). Institutionalised conflict and competition of this kind was not perceived as threatening, in fact quite the opposite: it was considered a sure measure of modernisation. By contrast, political unionism was held to be an 'extra-industrial' phenomenon (Mann, 1977: 11) – its embrace of a wider agenda being mostly attributed to the intrusion of socialist ideas and movements.

However, political unionism was also claimed to arise as a result of the different conditions prevailing in less industrialised countries – especially the relatively low levels of institutional specialisation that is evidenced by the 'overdevelopment' of the state *vis-à-vis* the private sector (Galenson, 1962; Sufrin, 1964). Further noted was the influence of anti-colonial and nationalist struggles on the character of new labour movements, prior to the onset of extensive industrialisation (Millen, 1963). After national independence, it was expected that labour movements in Asia and the rest of the developing world would remain 'political' through their incorporation into the government arena as power bases for parties and politicians (Sufrin, 1964: 22–3). In essence, the liberal-pluralist view was that different modes of labour organising arise at various stages in the modernisation process. In the relative *absence* of capitalist industrialisation, political unionism was claimed to prevail; thus economic unionism was closely tied to capitalist development (interpreted as modernisation).

Liberal-pluralists captured the 'political' character of many early Asian labour movements. But only in *South* Asia did state–labour relations take the 'inclusionist-corporatist' form after national independence that liberal-pluralists were predicting for the region as a whole (Siddique, 1989: 395). Elsewhere, in East Asia, political accommodations with workers' movements were brief, if they occurred at all. Although many unions in India and Bangladesh sustained close relations with various ruling and opposition parties (see Chapters 2, 8 and 9 in this volume), state-building in East Asia was largely predicated on the political *exclusion* of independent labour movements and/or their absorption into state structures.

Liberal-pluralists missed the mark in their forecasts for state–labour relations in East Asia, but their thinking was embodied in United States foreign policy and interventions to this end (Cohen, 1991: 6). In the context of the Cold War bipolar politics, political unionism was associated with communism and its variants, whereas economic unionism was held to help ease the social sedition that arises from workers' 'reasonable' demands being unmet (Millen, 1963: 5–6). United States policy support for economic unionism was also driven by the lobbying of domestic labour groups – notably the American Federation of Labor-Congress of Industrial Organizations (AFL-CIO) – to see the interests of American workers protected from competition from cheap labour through the 'strengthening [of] free trade unionism abroad' (Gershman, 1975: 3). But United States backing for the suppression of 'labour and left-wing groups' in fact 'helped to buttress what might otherwise have been vulnerable regimes', thereby facilitating the emergence of states with a relatively high level of autonomy or insulation from social forces (Stubbs, 1994: 370). Many early labour movements in the region may have been linked to radical forces, but their opponents were hardly democrats. Liberal-pluralist dualisms rationalised Cold War interventions in support of political arrangements that have subsequently featured the marginalisation of labour.

From the late 1960s, leading political scientists in the United States in fact abandoned liberalism to argue for political controls and social order as the essential foundations of economic development (Huntington, 1968). Soon afterwards, neo-liberal economists moved to push economic individualism and untrammelled markets to the centre of development policy agendas (Leys, 1996). With these changes in the development orthodoxy – partly reflecting a decline in the domestic political sway of organised labour in the United States – the idea that labour organisations play an unacceptable, 'distortionary' role in economic development gained more prominence (Freeman, 1993). Indeed, as the economic successes of Japan and the other East Asian newly industrialising countries (NICs) replaced communism at the centre of global-governance concerns, there emerged 'an intriguing, but unintended, convergence of views' among conservatives, neo-liberals and radicals that strong unionism is a barrier to competitive investment (Islam and Chowdhury, 1997: 83–4).[8]

However, in the 1990s, liberal thinking in international policy circles moved again, with bodies like the World Bank adopting a more 'institutional' position on states and markets, and on the function of labour organising (Freeman, 1993; Berger and Beeson, 1998). As such, the view of the World Bank (1995: 86) is now that plant-level, economic unionism can have 'positive effects on efficiency and equity' by forcing organisational and technological changes through demands for improved wages and conditions. This assessment appears closer to the position of the International Labour Organisation (ILO), which argues that unions can enhance productive efficiencies (Standing, 1992). Yet the shift is not as great as it seems, in that the World Bank's position remains more 'market-centred' than 'social-minded' in its intention to facilitate the operation and spread of markets, rather than to restrict their influence over social life (Sengenberger, 1994: 11). Meanwhile, the World Trade Organisation (WTO) continues to resist pressure from some quarters for the insertion into multilateral trade agreements of social clauses which would allow trade sanctions against countries that do not comply with core ILO conventions on basic labour rights and protection.[9]

In Chapter 9, Cahill addresses the World Bank's latest position on labour and development, arguing that it obscures the unequal socio-economic effects of policies to liberalise the Indian economy. From the standpoint of the telecommunications industry, she maintains that labour's political opposition to the entry of private capital in the basic network is equivalent to corporations' own lobbying of government over the same matter. Her further point is that policies to deregulate the labour market, which the World Bank promotes, will actually undermine the organising capacities of formal sector workers in India by increasing the size of the contingent, non-permanent workforce.

The neo-liberal 'Washington consensus' on globalisation and capitalist development thus currently defines the arena of legitimate labour organising largely according to the objectives of market enhancement. There is renewed support for economic, as opposed to political, unionism – only this time the international environment for debates over labour and development has changed with the passing of the Cold War and capitalism's dominance over 'rival systemic paradigms' (Berger and Beeson, 1998: 499). Labour unions are viewed as legitimate institutions, principally to the extent that they make a contribution to the goals of greater productive efficiency; to a much lesser extent they are viewed as significant vehicles for democratic representation and greater pluralism. Also sidelined in this thinking is the recognition that even the emergence of economic unionism in Asia is subject to ongoing political struggles: the dynamics of this being completely unexplored.

Scholars on the left have always been attentive to the politics of liberal approaches to labour organising. For example, bodies like the Asia-American Free Labor Institute (AAFLI) – an international arm of AFL-CIO – have been criticised for their pointed interventions in contests between rival labour organisations in various East and South Asian countries over a number of decades (Sims, 1992: 4). In supporting 'free unionism', AAFLI has been accused of in fact obstructing the efforts to contest political regimes that tightly control workers' ability to freely associate. Still, this organisation is cited as providing needed resources for worker organising in hostile environments (MacShane, 1992: 10). Rock, in this volume (Chapter 2), shows that this has been the case in the recent rise of the Bangladesh Independent Garment-Workers' Union (BIGU) in South Asia.

Against liberal perspectives on labour organising, some scholars on the left have taken a special interest in the speculated significant emergence of 'social movement unionism' in some parts of Asia (Lambert, 1990; Scipes, 1992, 1996; West, 1997). The term 'social movement unionism' is applied to labour organising 'whose demands include broad social and economic change' and 'whose constituencies spread far beyond the factory gates' – often through alliances with other social groups and movements (Seidman, 1994). While similar to Millen's (1963: 9) characterisation of political unionism as a 'broad-based' movement, the term sits within a quite different intellectual frame – one that specifically eschews liberalism's 'artificial separation between politics and economics' (Scipes, 1996: ix). Moreover, it is often aligned with contemporary attempts on the left to 'rethink the political' in association with the phenomenon of 'new social movements' (Scipes, 1992; Waterman, 1993). On this basis, social movement unionism is distinguished by viewing:

> workers' struggles as merely one of many efforts to qualitatively change society, with the workplace being neither the only site for political struggle and social change nor even necessarily the primary site.
>
> (Scipes, 1996: ix)

Explanations for the hypothesised emergence of social movement unionism in Asia tend to draw on dependency and world-systems theory on the nature and causes of the underdevelopment of countries. According to this perspective, workers' interests are inseparable from the larger struggle against national domination in the international economic order – their wages and conditions being an outcome of an unequal world system and the power of multinational corporations (MNCs) (Frank, 1980). The view that workers in Asia are disempowered by exposure to the global economy will be discussed in a later section of this chapter. For the moment, it is simply necessary to observe that writing on social movement unionism is closely associated with opposition to neo-liberalism and globalisation.

Beyond a concern with workers' *self*-organising, the case studies in this volume do not adopt a uniform position with regards to the 'real' nature of labour activism. This is because such judgements are contingent on the particular circumstances workers find themselves in, and on their own perceptions of what can and ought to be done. The discussion in this part of the chapter has aimed to highlight normative aspects of writing on Asian labour that have a connection to transnational political projects *vis-à-vis* globalisation and capitalist development (Coates, 1999). We have focused on liberal perspectives because of the dominant position they occupy in relation to this. In the next part of the chapter, we turn to some of the factors which have been cited more specifically to explain labour's general weakness as a social force in East Asia, beginning with the influence of culture.

Culture and conflict

It was formerly argued that Asian cultures obstruct capitalist industrialisation by blocking the uptake of modernising precepts like universalism, individualism and 'achievement motivation' (McClelland, 1964). However, as capitalist industrialisation proceeded in East Asia, these ideas underwent something of a reversal – many of the cultural traits previously seen as 'anti-modern' were reassessed as sources of the East Asian economic 'miracle' (Pye, 1985; Chung, Shepard and Dollinger, 1989). These include personalism, primary attachments to the family, group loyalty, deference to authority and a preference for social cohesion and harmony; in short, 'knowing one's place' in society. Although mostly attributed to Confucianism, such traits resonate more broadly with the idea that Asia as a whole is culturally distinct from the West (Pinches, 1999: 2). The 1997 financial crisis caused some reassessment of the contribution of 'Asian values' to economic development, but not particularly in relation to labour issues.

Whereas the classical position was that traditional values are superseded by modernisation, neo-culturalists assume that such values endure, despite structural change (see Wong, 1988). Thus, for example, traditional ways of interacting in the family are said to have a direct effect on employment relations in the modern firm – workers being 'treated like family members, who reciprocate with hard work as if they were family members' (Wilkinson, 1994: 192). Asian workers are claimed to identify more strongly with their employers and managers than their Western counterparts and so to be less likely to unite as a group over class-based issues.

The neo-culturalist perspective helped to foil the convergence thesis – the idea that societies become more alike as they industrialise – yet it is poorly equipped to explain variations in the organising capacities of workers in various countries and industries at different moments, especially running into problems when confronted with historical and contemporary evidence of labour activism in the workplace and the national political arena. A key problem is that this perspective gives culture an independent life of its own, treating it as something which is unaffected by broader social and political arrangements, and thus as something unchanging over time (Billig, 1994). There is also a marked tendency to overstate the homogeneity of Asian societies, ignoring inconsistencies in cultural precepts that are a reflection of social relations imbued with power and inequality (Pinches, 1999). Critics of the neo-culturalist position thus pay attention to the ways in which cultural precepts are often 'contested, resisted and recast' by the very social groups they appear to devalue and demobilise (Keesing, 1991: 46).

Along these lines, Hadiz (in Chapter 6) notes that Islamic principles and practices – often regarded as enforcing docility among young, female workers – can sometimes also be a vehicle through which these same workers in fact resist their harsh treatment by employers. In referring to the 'modernising' discourses of individualism and rational calculation – which are also assumed to hinder workers' collective resistance – Sargeson (Chapter 3) also observes that young, female workers in China were able to use these values tactically against their manager's discriminatory employment practices. Finally, Pinches (Chapter 10) shows how the class sentiments of Filipino migrant workers include ethnic and nationalist feelings that other commentators have considered antithetical to class solidarity. Although none of these studies pertain to Confucianism *per se*, they all serve to illustrate the general point that class conflicts are not necessarily overridden by what might seem to be opposite motivating principles. Indeed, alternative markers of social belonging and exclusion can be involved in workers' resistances to class in that they lay claim to their equal status with non-workers, so justifying their demands for better treatment.

Other critics of the neo-culturalists' approach pay greater attention to the construction of 'Asian values' by national political elites. In analysing the effects of cultural precepts deemed traditional, Lawson (1998) suggests the question to ask is: Who currently claims the authority to exercise political power from such axioms? In this way, she highlights the ideological and 'invented' aspects of so-called 'traditional values'. Rodan (1996a) adopts a similar position, arguing that 'Asian values' are a contemporary expression and instrument of conservative political thinking, within and outside the region. Far from 'Asian values' being a reflection of immutable East–West cultural differences, in the form in which they are currently deployed by national political elites, they serve as a discursive device to obscure wider conflicts over the nature of domestic social and political arrangements in the changing international order (Robison, 1996: 313). In the next part of this chapter, it is thus appropriate that we turn to the nature of state power and issues of political change in relation to labour-organising capacities.

States and political change

East Asian political regimes are by no means all the same, nor are they uncontested and unchanging, but liberal or social democratic forms of government have not characterised the political economy of development in this part of the world. Whether 'developmental' or 'predatory', states in the region have exhibited strong authoritarian tendencies in relation to various social forces, including labour (Deyo, 1987; Evans, 1989; Jenkins, 1991; Bell and Jayasuriya, 1995). With this in mind, the weakness of East Asian labour movements is widely explained by state intentions and capacities to obstruct the emergence of labour as an independent force through 'corporatist' and/or 'exclusionary' strategies (Frenkel, 1993: 312–13).

By comparison, state–labour relations in South Asia have been different. Most notably in India, their 'collaborative' or 'inclusionist' form has been shaped by a number of factors, including labour's place in the independence movement; electoral democracy; labour alliances with political parties; the influence of socialism over policy and legal protection for workers in the formal sector (Candland, 1995). Yet political incorporation in India has proved a simultaneous source of weakness and strength: on one hand it allows the labour movement a degree of influence over government policy, but on the other it also leaves the movement 'vulnerable to the electoral calculations of the political parties to which they are affiliated' (ibid.: 75). Sherlock (Chapter 8) is especially critical of this feature of the labour movement in Bombay, arguing that it has been an important cause of labour's difficulties in responding adequately to recent restructuring in the textile industry.

What factors, then, explain the political exclusion of labour in East Asia? One widely held view is that state–labour relations are a function of the pursuit of export-oriented industrialisation (EOI). The 'strong' version of this is that there is a *causal* link, as government restrictions on worker organising are specifically introduced 'for the purpose of pursuing export-led growth' (Haggard, 1989: 135–6).[10] Adopting this explanation in relation to Malaysia, Kuruvilla (1995) argues that state policies towards labour are a function of the 'needs' of a particular economic development strategy. As he notes, a test of this thesis is the timing of policy changes – a point which critics have taken up.

Opponents of the notion of a causal link between repressive state policies and EOI like to observe that government moves against labour organising mostly occurred *prior to* the commencement of EOI and were often a part of broader attempts to contain political oppositions and/or communism in the 1950s and 1960s (Haggard, 1989: 136; Deyo, 1997: 220). Deyo argues that 'organizational efforts during the subsequent emergence of an industrial proletariat' were thus 'pre-empted' by the rise of authoritarianism (ibid.: 199). Of course, the early marginalisation of labour was then itself a major factor behind the capacity of states to contain labour's self-organising through ensuing decades (Jenkins, 1991: 209–12). In Singapore, for example, state controls were increased with higher levels of foreign investment, but Rodan (1989: 84) notes that this 'was after and not before the political preconditions for a new economic strategy' were in place. In the Philippines, martial law and labour repression in the 1970s coincided with a significant expansion in export-oriented manufacturing, but the claim of a causal connection between these events (Villegas, 1988) is countered by President Marcos' purely political motivation in shutting down civil society (Hawes, 1992).

The assertion of a simple 'economic logic' to controls over labour organising is contradicted by the evidence of factors behind gaining, retaining and legitimating state power (see Collier and Collier, 1991). This is not to say there are no economic advantages from such moves; it is simply to say that such moves are not merely the result of rational economic choice.[11] What is especially significant is the timing of state-building and capitalist industrialisation in many East Asian countries which were, in part, an outcome of various realignments in the international order in the second half of the twentieth century (Stubbs, 1994; Deyo, 1997; Berger and Borer, 1997).

If authoritarianism has contributed to labour's marginalisation in many East Asian countries, what are the effects of uneven moves to further democratisation (Laothamatas, 1997)? Democratisation is always multifaceted, comprising a variety of changes at formal, constitutional and societal levels (Hassall, 1997). A substantive indicator of its progress is not simply the (re)introduction of 'free and fair' elections, but rather the achievement of rule that is marked by 'political accommodations' (Hewison, Rodan and Robison, 1993: 6). To what extent, then, has the political 'space' for independent labour organising been enlarged by the 'jagged wave' of democratisation in East Asia (Luckham and White, 1996)?

In response to this question, Deyo (1997: 208) observes that labour's potential as a social force in the region has generally been greater in the *lead-up* to political reforms, usually only to fall away again in subsequent periods of institutional consolidation. In Thailand, the Philippines, South Korea and (most recently) Indonesia, workers and their movements have been a part of successful mass mobilisations against authoritarian regimes; yet resultant reforms have not brought independent labour into significant new accommodations with the state. While there has been some significant easing of legal controls over workers' autonomous activism, this in itself has not substantially altered labour's political position. The labour movement in South Korea is undoubtedly the region's strongest (Ranald, 1999: 303–12), yet it still remains politically excluded (Shin, 1999: 40). Since the 1997 financial crisis, labour has been allowed 'to sit at the [political] table solely to ensure that the mass layoffs of Korea's unionized workforce are accomplished relatively smoothly' (Bernard, 1999: 202).

In large part, labour's political standing is an effect of its relative weakness as an independent social force – and the fact that it is therefore forced to rely on cross-sectional support from other sectors of civil society (Rueschemeyer, Stephens and Stephens, 1992: 59). Labour's inability to consolidate its standing after periods of crisis can be explained by changes to the socio-political landscape that invariably occur as different social sectors find their political aspirations are at variance after the initial reform process (ibid.: 76; Yun, 1997). In broad terms, it seems that workers and their movements are more readily brought into the political mainstream during periods of heightened opposition – when disparate forces are united behind the single cause of regime change. Indeed, in the case of South Korea, Koo (1996) argues that the emergence of an independent labour movement was greatly facilitated by the breadth and intensity of popular opposition to authoritarian rule over the years. However, following democratic reforms in the late 1980s, members of the middle class were more reluctant to support labour's militancy – preferring instead to see political change without much economic disruption (Yun, 1997: 165–6; Bernard, 1999: 196).

Most recently, in the case of Indonesia, Hadiz (in Chapter 6) notes that the fall of Suharto has eased some legal restrictions on labour organising, but early actions like recognising ILO conventions were largely directed at an international audience. Emergent political groupings have sometimes sought support from particular labour movements, but in general, Hadiz argues, the democratic transitions in Indonesia are being steered by elite and middle-class forces, with labour being still relatively marginalised from the process.

The point we make here is that some undermining of authoritarianism in various countries has not seen labour brought into significantly new political accommodations. This is partly a legacy of the political arrangements that preceded reforms – their enduring impact on social relations and the fact that the reforms have not necessarily upset socio-economic structures. Labour generally continues to find that its political influence is dependent on a fair degree of cross-sectional support in civil society, yet this support is itself often contingent on other factors, like regime legitimacy and the state of the economy. Brown (in Chapter 7) explains that political lobbying for improved worker health and safety standards in Thailand after the disastrous 1995 Kader factory fire has been mostly led by assorted community activists, as the existing labour movement remains weak and fragmented. Without cross-sectional interest in this matter – or without the earlier international and domestic media coverage of the fire – Brown suggests that labour alone would not have been able to make health and safety such a political issue.

With other chapters in this volume, Brown's case study raises the question of NGO involvement in the area of labour organising. Asian NGOs have been said to fill 'an institutional gap' in weak democracies by addressing the otherwise neglected issues of equitable resource delivery, social empowerment and sustainable development (Clark, 1992; Clarke, 1998). As vehicles of alternative development strategies, NGOs have been portrayed as working in isolation from government – this often being a normative viewpoint. However, in line with more considered political science perspectives on civil society (Rodan, 1996b; White, 1996), there have recently been more close analyses of the different ways in which NGOs are associated with state structures (Riker, 1995; Clarke, 1998). In addition, there is also greater academic and activist interest in NGOs and democratisation as vehicles for both the mobilisation of popular forces behind regime change and the deepening of democracy through grassroots representation in government (Silliman and Noble, 1998).

In association with 'new social movements', NGOs are often as well claimed to embody a 'new politics' that 'eschews the capture of state power and the centralising tendencies of Marxist–Leninist movements', while retaining 'the commitment to a structural transformation of society' (Clarke, 1998: 40). To this extent, NGOs are said to mark the decline of the left in civil society across much of East Asia (Hewison and Rodan, 1996). However, it is significant that NGOs are normally associated with those sections of the population that are most *marginalised* by capitalist industrialisation. Silliman and Noble (1998: 10) list these as: 'tenant farmers, women, indigenous peoples, and other poor and disadvantaged groups in the global South'. Urban NGOs have a record of involvement in the establishment of alternative income-generating projects, consisting of micro-enterprises, small-scale lending and cooperative direct-marketing arrangements. Attention to the concerns of new workers has been slower in coming and more limited – although this picked up in the 1990s (Eldridge, 1995: 109–10; Hadiz,

1997). The question to ask here is: What effects does NGO involvement in the labour arena have on workers' capacities to self-organise in the region?

Hadiz (in Chapter 6) observes that NGOs in Indonesia are often able to evade the legal strictures applying to independent unionism by organising beyond the workplace, in communities. This organising is typically done through the provision of financial resources, legal advice and industrial (and political) education programmes. Hadiz argues that NGO involvement contributed to a changed landscape for labour activism in the 1990s, but he is cautious nevertheless in predicting a direct connection between community organising and effective independent unionism in the future (see Hadiz, 1997: 135, 156). A difficulty he highlights is that labour NGOs are often run by student, middle-class, professional and/or religious activists, rather than by workers themselves. In Korten's (1990: 96) words, they are 'third-party' organisations. While this can be interpreted as evidence for cross-sectional support for labour issues, it is worth remembering that this is not necessarily the equivalent of workers' *self*-organising and empowerment (Hadiz, 1997: 156). This said, it is of course not the case that workers are all similarly positioned. For example, middle-class feminists can be shown to have played an important part in encouraging the activism and leadership of *women* workers in fledgling independent unions.

Of course, some of the domestic labour–NGO alliances have been matched by international NGO campaigns to encourage consumer boycotts of the products of companies with plants in various low-wage Asian countries. These campaigns have been accused of promoting protectionism against cheap imports, but, in addition to this, there are pertinent uncertainties as to the impact they may have on the organising capacities of Asian workers themselves. Campaigns directed at individual consumers mostly have publicity effects on the companies and governments concerned. In so doing, they help to create an environment in which labour standards appear on the international trade and investment agenda, but, in the absence of concomitant domestic political changes, there are few changes on the ground.

This part of the chapter has broadly considered the national political envi-ronment for labour organising in East (and South) Asia at state and societal levels. In addition to highlighting the significance of authoritarian tendencies in many countries, our aim has been to draw out areas which are currently less well discussed in the literature – these being labour's standing in civil society and the contributions of NGO involvement. The next and final section addresses the impacts of economic globalisation. In this regard, we especially focus on the effects of transnational production arrangements on worker activism through the deepening of class relations in production.

Economic globalisation

There is now a large and diverse literature on the subject of 'economic globalisation' (Hirst and Thompson, 1996; Gupta, 1997; Mittelman, 1997; Olds *et al.*, 1999). While interpretations of the phenomenon vary, it is not difficult to list a range of developments that are captured by the term. These include the closer integration of national economies; the undermining of nation-states; the rise of neo-liberalism; the introduction and rapid up-take of new information and communication technologies; the shift to 'knowledge-based' economies, and the spread of more 'flexible' production and employment systems. All of these developments might be variously linked, but it would be a mistake to imagine that they thereby constitute a fixed totality. In Jessop's words:

> Globalisation is generally better interpreted as the complex of many differ-ent processes than as a distinctive causal process in its own right. It is mis-leading to explain specific events and phenomena in terms of the process of 'globalisation', pointless to subsume anything or everything under the um-brella of 'globalisation', and unhelpful to seek to link anything and every-thing to 'globalisation' as if this somehow conveys more insight than an alternative rubric could.
>
> (Jessop, 1999: 19)

Critics point to the 'enduring national foundations' of globalisation to counter the perception that globalisation is a pre-constituted force, bearing down on once-sovereign nations (Zysman, 1996; Weiss, 1997; Moran, 1998).

With regards to labour, however, economic globalisation is often portrayed in a more limited fashion as 'multinationals constantly moving capital to where labour is cheapest, and taking little responsibility for the living standards of workers or their families' (Manning, 1998: 133). This scenario – Sengenberger (1992) calls it the 'low road' to international competition – is widely associated with the 'new international division of labour' (NIDL) thesis in which the greater mobility of capital is said to create a worldwide hiring pool for workers in manufacturing (and some services) (Fröbel, Heinrichs and Kreye, 1980; Ross and Trachte, 1990). The core argument of the NIDL thesis is that production will mostly be sited in countries and regions where labour is of an optimal type – cheap, abundant and unorganised. The employment of women on even lower wages is explained as a further employer strategy to substitute one set of workers for another (Elson and Pearson, 1980). According to the NIDL scenario, workers either lose their jobs or are forced to take cuts in their earnings and entitlements, work longer hours and accept more contingent forms of employment to stay on (Sengenberger, 1992: 144).

Winters (1996: 196–8) notes that international labour competition *per se* is not new; rather its form has changed and become more intensive through the emergence and expansion of transnational production arrangements from the late 1960s. First, international competition between workers is now more direct because it occurs through actual job substitution; second, it is now also more extreme in that the workers involved have greater disparities in their wages, employment standards and political rights. Winters argues that, while earlier competition between workers in different advanced industrialised countries saw labour gains through productivity-based bargaining, this latest version produces a 'race to the bottom' for wages, working conditions and organising capacities.

Both Hutchison and Sherlock (in Chapters 4 and 8) observe that the core themes of the NIDL thesis resonate easily with nationalist traditions in Asian labour organising, especially in so far as they focus attention on the activities of foreign corporations and institutions. But Sherlock shows that the NIDL scenario cannot explain the longer-term restructuring of the Bombay textile industry and, as such, is an obstacle to the formation of a more effective organising response. While Sherlock aims to move attention away from economic globalisation as *the* major factor behind labour's difficulties in Bombay, other studies in the volume deal more directly with the actual effects of the NIDL scenario on workers' activism. In particular, three studies indicate that transnational production arrangements have rather more mixed – in fact, sometimes positive – effects than literature on the topic generally suggests.

Rock, Sargeson and Hutchison (in Chapters 2, 3 and 4) all find that export-oriented production can be an enabling factor when it comes to women workers' collective activism in particular settings. In common, they describe how production for an overseas market can force a deepening of capitalist work relations through the closer management of product quality and labour productivity.[12] In a number of ways, the workers involved experience greater pressures to intensify their labour; however, at the same time (and often as a result of the same circumstances), they can also be in a better position to self-organise. These case studies echo Haiven, Edwards and Bélanger's (1994: 278–9) contention that the 'problem of labour' (getting work from workers) is not entirely obviated by the greater mobility of capital and that, at some point, negotiation is still required. National and industry circumstances have a great effect on whether or not workers are able to resist the pressures on them through unions and formal bargaining, or more (dis)organised actions.

These case studies are in keeping with other research showing that transnational production arrangements are not the principal factor accounting for labour's relative weakness as a social force in East Asia (Manning, 1998: 138; Lim, 1990; Sengenberger, 1994). But as well they go further in outlining some of the actual positive effects of such arrangements on the organising capacities of specified workers – although not so far as to endorse the view of the World Labor Research Working Group that the NIDL is 'a double-edged sword' that undermines labour movements in the advanced capitalist countries, only to increase new worker activism in capital-receiving regions (Silver, 1995: 181–3). Transnational production arrangements have certainly swelled the proletariat in Asia, but this is a necessary, not sufficient, condition for the rise of new labour movements.

Debates around labour and economic globalisation have tended to focus on the 'low road' scenario but, as Deyo (1997) and Rasiah (in Chapter 5) point out, there is a need to examine the effects of shifts to more capital- and technology-intensive forms of 'flexible production'[13] on East Asian labour. In Deyo's words:

Flexibility here refers to the ability quickly, efficiently and continuously to introduce changes in product and process. Such flexibility yields a superior capacity to respond to the intensified pressures of liberalised trade, world market volatility, market fragmentation, heightened demand for just-in-time production and continuous improvements in productivity and quality, and rapid technological change.

(ibid.: 214)

Flexible production is characterised as 'taking the wages out of competition' through the adoption of approaches to labour management which are centred on re-skilling the workforce, teamwork rather than job fragmentation and the possibility of 'strategic accommodations' with management based on mutual trust (Mathews, 1989: 38; Sengenberger and Pyke, 1991: 3). However, as with economic globalisation itself, the nature, scale, origins and consequences of new production systems are widely contested (Hirst and Zeitlin, 1991; Sayer and Walker, 1993: 191–223; Amin, 1994). In particular, there is disagreement over the extent to which they form a 'coherent totality' – with changes in marketing techniques, new technologies, altered employment relations and developments in industry policy all occurring in unison. Hirst and Zeitlin (1991) argue that the assumption of a necessary 'fit' between all these elements arises when the influence of certain 'strategic choices and political struggles' is ignored – contingent accommodations between competing interests in the past being mistakenly interpreted as universal imperatives for the future.

In his work on labour and industrial organisation in East Asia, Deyo (1997: 205) views 'flexible specialisation' as 'a condition for success under intensified global economic competition'. Yet, in line with Hirst and Zeitlin, he is keen to stress that the uptake of new production systems is shaped by prevailing institutional arrangements and political circumstances. He argues that the adoption of more flexible methods is facilitated when the state provides 'supportive social infrastructure' in the areas of training, education and research and development, and enforces basic labour standards (ibid.: 215). In Thailand and a number of other Southeast Asian countries, Deyo (1995) suggests that there has been a partial uptake of new production techniques, but that these changes have not been accompanied by concomitant shifts towards more 'humane' labour-management systems. Increases in wages and other benefits – when and where they have occurred – have not led to greater worker participation in the labour process. Indeed, 'improvements in compensation levels and working conditions are as often introduced to *avoid unions* as to foster long-term organisational changes' (Deyo, 1997: 216, emphasis added). Rasiah's case study of the Proton car firm in Malaysia (Chapter 5) draws similar conclusions. He observes that the introduction of 'flexible' systems has been uneven, largely due to the wider policy environment. With regards to labour-organising capacities in the firm, Rasiah is also keen to stress the enduring importance of the nature and role of the state.

In the literature on labour and globalisation, a dimension usually less ex-plored is the growing cross-border movement of fixed-term contract workers, male and female. From East and South Asia, migrant workers have mainly moved within the region and into the Middle East – some countries becoming noted exporters of labour, the Philippines especially (Gardezi, 1991; Stahl, 1992; Prasai, 1993). As available research indicates, migrant contract workers experience additional controls and hardships as a consequence of their legal-political standing as 'aliens' in their countries of employment (Gibson and Graham, 1986: 133–4; Cohen, 1991: 151–65; Aguilar, 1999). Not only are they typically barred from organising as workers, they are often further denied the basic rights and protections due to citizens of a country. Isolated from kin and community, migrant contract workers are widely subject to ethno-cultural labelling and discrimination (Aguilar, 1999: 320). No wonder, then, that such workers are often 'propelled into a re-appreciation of national identity and belonging' by their experiences of employment overseas (ibid.: 320–1). In his study of Filipino migrant workers, Pinches (in Chapter 10) examines responses such as these and their effects on workers' responses to their class experiences, abroad and in the Philippines.

Finally, there is yet another dimension to economic globalisation which is amply highlighted by the 1997 regional financial crisis. This is the influence of global money markets on the 'real economy' of many countries in the region. With regards to the crisis, dramatic falls in the value of a number of East – especially Southeast – Asian currencies caused sharp drops in economic activity, price hikes, lifts in unemployment and, hence, greater poverty (Haggard and MacIntyre, 1998; Bello, 1999). In this case, globalisation had its effects on workers via the damage done to national currencies and so to the financial underpinnings of investment. As a result, workers in various sectors and industries lost their jobs or continue to experience greater pressures on wages and working conditions (Hadiz, 1998).

This volume does not offer a general assessment of the impacts of the 1997 crisis on labour activism in the region, except to observe that workers' immediate responses have largely been an upshot of their existing capacities to organise. Hadiz (in Chapter 6) makes this point clearly in relation to Indonesia, where the crisis has been played out most dramatically. In the Malaysian Proton car factory, Rasiah (in Chapter 5) notes that the existing in-house union has found its earlier isolation from the Transport Equipment Workers Union makes it more difficult to respond to new pressures on the workforce. On the other hand, Bello (1999: 442) believes that the crisis has fuelled nationalist sentiments in the region which may revive 'mass politics with a class edge'. To this extent, labour-organising capacities may be influenced by changes to the socio-political landscape, although this will be affected by other factors, not least the longevity of the crisis.

No small collection of case studies can hope to comprehensively cover all facets of economic globalisation as they impact on labour-organising capacities in Asia.[14] However, in their detailed examination of the processes at work in a specific locale, the studies in this volume are an important corrective to approaches that argue low levels of effective unionisation are primarily the products of globalisation as an undifferentiated totality (Hess, 1998: 17). From here we argue that there is a further need for empirical research into the impact of developments associated with globalisation on labour in Asia. A strength of the case-study approach is that it enables the more careful disaggregation of 'global', 'national' and 'local' processes as they are experienced by particular groups of workers.

Conclusion

This introduction has covered the broad intellectual context in which the chapters have been written – a context which has tended to play down the significance of class and to concentrate on the theme of labour's weakness and marginalisation in the region. On the first point, we have made a case for linking labour organising to class as a process or relation. Thus, instead of limiting enquiry to the search for theoretically privileged forms of labour organising (as providing evidence for the existence or otherwise of class conflict), the task is one of investigating the various, changing forms of activism through which workers in Asia are registering their opposition to a range of capitalist processes and imperatives. On labour's general weakness as a social force, we have discussed key areas of explanation that focus on a host of factors associated with the timing and nature of capitalist industrialisation in Asia, especially in relation to domestic state-building and changes in the international order. In this way, we have introduced themes that the case studies to follow pursue in more detail.

Notes

1 Our thanks to Richard Robison, Garry Rodan and the contributors to this book (especially Michael Pinches) for their comments on this chapter.
2 'East' Asia is used for Northeast and Southeast Asia, as distinct from South Asia. The studies in this collection cover both East and South Asia; however, this introduction is focused on the literature on labour-organising capacities in East Asia, as it is here that debates over labour, states and international competitiveness have been particularly vigorous and relevant to workers in other parts of the world.
3 This quotation applies to Southeast Asia. For similar comments on Northeast Asia, see Deyo (1989). South Korea is the only possible exception to this generalisation (see Kim, 1993; Ranald, 1999).
4 'Independent' does not denote the absence of voluntary alliances with other sectoral groups or organisations; simply, the term means that workers' responses are not directly controlled or managed by 'external' forces, including the state.
5 The term '(dis)organised' is Sargeson's in Chapter 3.
6 Crompton (1995: 54) lists other paired terms for this 'structure–agency' distinction in class theory. One often used by Marxists is the 'class-in-itself' and 'class-of-itself' separation.
7 There are other terms used, but these are the essential ones.
8 The radicals who concur with this view have generally been those who argue that this situation arises from globalisation, particularly the heightened mobility of capital. However, on the centre-left, there has also been the alternative position espoused – that labour unions can be a catalyst for productive efficiency in the economy of a nation. See Standing (1992) and, for a more critical assessment, Coates (1999).

9 On the grounds that social clauses are a retaliatory and protectionist response to new competition from the developing world on the part of Western nations (particularly the United States), many East and South Asian governments and labour organisations are opposed to their introduction (see Charnovitz, 1987; Raghavan, 1996).

10 We are here interested in the association between state policies and EOI – other scholars have written on the effects of EOI on labour-organising capacities in terms of how 'different types of industrialization affect the capital–labour relationship' (Bjorkman, Lauridsen and Marcussen, 1988; Deyo, 1989: ch. 6).

11 As previously noted, neo-liberals and radicals have both often made this assumption (see Islam and Chowdhury, 1997: 83–4).

12 Note that here we stress economic globalisation's effects on the nature of class relations at the point of production.

13 Other related terms are 'flexible specialisation' (Piore and Sabel, 1984); 'lean production' (Womack, Jones and Roos, 1990) and 'neo-Fordism' (Aglietta, 1979) – see also Sayer and Walker (1993).

14 On the nature of case-study research, see Yin (1994).

Bibliography

Aglietta, Michel (1979) *A Theory of Capitalist Regulation: The US Experience*, London and New York: Verso.

Aguilar, Filomeno V. (1999) 'The triumph of instrumental citizenship? Migrations, identities and the nation-state in Southeast Asia', *Asian Studies Review* 23, 3: 307–36.

Amin, Ash (1994) 'Post-Fordism: Models, fantasies and phantoms of transition', in Ash Amin (ed.) *Post-Fordism: A Reader*, Oxford and Cambridge, MA: Blackwell, pp. 1–39.

Bell, Daniel A. and Jayasuriya, Kanishka (1995) 'Understanding illiberal democracy: A framework', in Daniel A. Bell, David Brown, Kanishka Jayasuriya and David Martin Jones (eds) *Towards Illiberal Democracy in Pacific Asia*, New York: St Martin's Press, pp. 1–16.

Bello, Walden (1999) 'East Asia: On the eve of the great transformation?', *Review of International Political Economy* 5, 3: 424–44.

Beresford, Melanie and Kelly, Di (1993) 'Industrial relations in ASEAN and other capitalist countries', *Economic and Industrial Democracy* 14: 89–107.

Berger, Mark T. and Beeson, Mark (1998) 'Lineages of liberalism and miracles of modernization: The World Bank, the East Asian trajectory and the international development debate', *Third World Quarterly* 19, 3: 487–504.

Berger, Mark T. and Borer, Douglas A. (1997) 'Introduction: The rise of East Asia: Critical visions of the Pacific Century', in Mark T. Berger and Douglas A. Borer (eds) *The Rise of East Asia: Critical Visions of the Pacific Century*, London and New York: Routledge, pp. 260–87.

Bernard, Mitchell (1999) 'East Asia's tumbling dominoes: Financial crisis and the myth of the regional model', in Leo Pantich and Colin Leys (eds) *Global Capitalism Versus Democracy: Socialist Register 1999*, Woodbridge: Merlin Press and New York: Monthly Review Press, pp. 178–208.

Billig, Michael (1994) 'The death and rebirth of entrepreneurism on Negros Island, Philippines: A critique of cultural theories of enterprise', *Journal of Economic Issues* XXVIII, 3: 659–78.

Bjorkman, Maja, Lauridsen, Laurids S. and Marcussen, Henrik Secher (1988) 'Types of industrialization and the capital–labour relation in the Third World', in Roger Southall (ed.) *Trade Unions and the New Industrialization of the Third World*, London and Newark, NJ: Zed Books, pp. 59–80.

Candland, Christopher (1995) 'Trade unionism and industrial restructuring in India and Pakistan', *Bulletin of Concerned Asian Scholars* 27, 4: 63–78.

Carter, Bob (1995) 'A growing divide: Marxist class analysis and the labour process', *Capital and Class* 55: 33–55.

Charnovitz, Steve (1987) 'The influence of international labour standards on the world trading regime: A historical overview', *International Labour Review* 126, 5: 565–84.

Chung, Chen H., Shepard, Jon M. and Dollinger, Marc J. (1989) 'Max Weber revisited: some lessons from the East Asian capitalistic development', *Asia-Pacific Journal of Management* 6, 2: 307–22.

Clark, John (1992) 'Democratising development: NGOs and the State', *Development in Practice* 2, 3: 151–62.

Clarke, Gerard (1998) 'Non-Governmental Organizations (NGOs) and politics in the developing world', *Political Studies* 46: 36–52.

Coates, David (1999) 'Labour power and international competitiveness: A critique of ruling orthodoxies', in Leo Pantich and Colin Leys (eds) *Global Capitalism Versus Democracy: Socialist Register 1999*, Woodbridge: Merlin Press and New York: Monthly Review Press, pp. 108–41.

Cohen, Robin (1991) *Contested Domains: Debates in International Labour Studies*, London and New Jersey: Zed Books.

Collier, Ruth and Collier, David (eds) (1991) *Shaping the Political Arena: Critical Junctures, the Labor Movement and Regime Dynamics in Latin America*, Princeton: Princeton University Press.

Crompton, Rosemary (1995) 'The development of the classical inheritance', in Patrick Joyce (ed.) *Class*, Oxford and New York: Oxford University Press, pp. 43–55.

De Guzman, A. (1993) ' "Katas ng Saudi": The work and life situation of the Filipino contract workers of Saudi Arabia', *Philippine Social Sciences Review* 51, 1–4: 1–56.

Deyo, Frederic C. (1987) 'State and labor in East Asia', in Frederic C. Deyo (ed.) *The Political Economy of the New Asian Industrialism*, Ithaca and London: Cornell University Press, pp. 182–202.

—— (1989) *Beneath the Miracle: Labor Subordination in the New Asian Industrialism*, Berkeley: University of California Press.

—— (1995) 'Human resource strategies and industrial restructuring in Thailand', in Stephen Frenkel and Jeffrey Harrod (eds) *Industrialization and Labor Relations: Contemporary Research in Seven Countries*, Ithaca: Cornell University Press, pp. 23–36.

—— (1997) 'Labour and industrial restructuring in South-East Asia', in Garry Rodan, Kevin Hewison and Richard Robison (eds) *The Political Economy of South-East Asia: An Introduction*, Melbourne: Oxford University Press, pp. 205–24.

Dicken, P. (1992) *Global Shift: The Internationalisation of Economic Activity*, 2nd edn, London and New York: Paul Chapman.

Dow, Geoff and Lafferty, George (1990) 'From class analysis to class politics: A critique of sociological interpretations of class', *Australian and New Zealand Journal of Sociology* 26, 1: 3–35.

Eldridge, Philip J. (1995) *Non-Government Organizations and Democratic Participation in Indonesia*, Kuala Lumpur: Oxford University Press.

Elson, Diane and Pearson, Ruth (1980) *The Latest Phase of the Internationalisation of Capital and Its Implications for Women in the Third World*, Brighton: Institute of Development Studies, University of Sussex.

Evans, Peter (1989) 'Predatory, developmental and other apparatuses: A comparative political economy perspective in the Third World state', *Sociological Forum* 4, 4: 233–46.

Frank, Andre Gunder (1980) 'Third World manufacturing export production', *The South East Asian Economic Review* 1, 2: 83–105.

Freeman, R.B. (1993) 'Labour market institutions and policies: Help or hindrance to economic development', *Proceedings of the World Bank Conference on Economic Development*, Washington, D.C.: World Bank.

Frenkel, Stephen (1993) 'Variations in patterns of trade unionism: A synthesis', in Stephen Frenkel (ed.) *Organized Labor in the Asia-Pacific Region*, Ithaca: ILR Press, pp. 309–46.

Fröbel, Folker, Heinrichs, Jurgen and Kreye, Otto (1980) *The New International Division of Labour*, Cambridge: Cambridge University Press.

Galenson, Walter (1962) *Labor in Developing Countries*, Berkeley: University of California Press.

Gardezi, Hassan N. (1991) 'Asian workers in the Gulf States of the Middle East', *Journal of Contemporary Asia* 21, 2: 179–94.

Geary, Dick (1981) *European Labour Protest, 1848–1939*, New York: St Martin's Press.

Gershman, Carl (1975) *The Foreign Policy of American Labor*, Beverly Hills and London: Sage Publications with The Centre for Strategic and International Studies, Georgetown University.

Gibson, Katherine and Graham, Julie (1986) 'Situating migrants in theory: The case of Filipino migrant construction workers', *Capital and Class* 29: 130–49.

Gupta, Satya Dev (ed.) (1997) *The Political Economy of Globalization*, London: Kluwer Academic Publishers, pp. 13–40.

Hadiz, Vedi R. (1997) *Workers and the State in New Order Indonesia*, London and New York: Routledge.

—— (1998) 'Reformasi total? Labor after Suharto', *Indonesia* 66: 109–24.

Haggard, Stephen (1989) 'The East Asian NICs in comparative perspective', *Annals of the American Academy of Political and Social Science* 505, September: 129–41.

Haggard, Stephen and MacIntyre, Andrew (1998) 'The political economy of the Asian economic crisis', *Review of International Political Economy* 5, 3: 381–92.

Haiven, Larry, Edwards, P.K. and Bélanger, Jacques (1994) 'Globalization, national systems and the future of workplace industrial relations', in Jacques Bélanger, P.K. Edwards and Larry Haiven (eds) *Workplace Industrial Relations and Global Challenge*, Ithaca: ILR Press, pp. 275–84.

Hassall, Graham (1997) 'Democracy in Asia revisited', *Asian Studies Review* 21, 2–3: 2–18.

Hawes, Gary (1992) 'Marcos, his cronies and the Philippines' failure to develop', in Ruth McVey (ed.) *Southeast Asian Capitalists, Southeast Asian Program*, New York: Cornell University Press, pp. 145–60.

Hess, Michael (1998) 'Unions and economic development: An overview', in Michael Hess (ed.) *Labour Organisation and Development: Case Studies*, Canberra: NCDS Asia Pacific Press, pp. 1–29.

Hewison, Kevin and Rodan, Garry (1996) 'The ebb and flow of civil society and the decline of the Left in Southeast Asia', in Garry Rodan (ed.) *Political Oppositions in Industrialising Asia*, London and New York: Routledge, pp. 40–71.

Hewison, Kevin, Rodan, Garry and Robison, Richard (1993) 'Introduction: Changing forms of state power in Southeast Asia', in Kevin Hewison, Richard Robison and Garry Rodan (eds) *Southeast Asia in the 1990s*, Sydney: Allen and Unwin, pp. 2–8.

Hirst, P. and Zeitlin, J. (1991) 'Flexible specialization versus post-Fordism theory: Evidence and policy implications', *Economy and Society* 20, 1: 1–55.

Hirst, P. and Thompson, G. (1996) *Globalisation in Question*, London: Polity Press.

Huntington, Samuel P. (1968) *Political Order in Changing Societies*, New Haven: Yale University Press.

Hyman, Richard (1987) 'Strategy or structure? Capital, labour and control', *Work, Employment and Society* 1, 1: 25–55.

Islam, Iyanatul and Chowdhury, Anis (1997) *Asia-Pacific Economies: A Survey*, London and New York: Routledge.

Jenkins, Rhys (1991) 'The political economy of industrialization: A comparison of Latin America and East Asian newly industrializing countries', *Development and Change* 22: 197–231.

Jessop, Bob (1999) 'Reflections on globalisation and its (il)logic(s)', in Kris Olds, Peter Dicken, Philip F. Kelly, Lily Kong and Henry Wai-chung Yeung (eds) *Globalisation and the Asia-Pacific: Contested Territories*, London and New York: Routledge, pp. 19–38.

Kassalow, Everett (1969) *Trade Union and Industrial Relations: An International Comparison*, New York: Random House.

Katznelson, Ira (1986) 'Working-class formation: Constructing cases and comparisons', in Ira Katznelson and Aristide R. Zolberg (eds) *Working-Class Formation: Nineteenth-Century Patterns in Western Europe and the United States*, Princeton, NJ: Princeton University Press, pp. 1–41.

Katznelson, Ira and Zolberg, Aristide R. (eds) (1986) *Working-Class Formation: Nineteenth-Century Patterns in Western Europe and the United States*, Princeton, NJ: Princeton University Press.

Keesing, R. (1991) 'Asian cultures?', *Asian Studies Review* 15, 2: 43–50.

Kim, Hwang-Joe (1993) 'The Korean union movement in transition', in Stephen Frenkel (ed.) *Organized Labor in the Asia-Pacific Region*, Ithaca: ILR Press, pp. 133–61.

Koo, Hagen (1996) 'Work, culture and consciousness of the Korean working class', in Elizabeth J. Perry (ed.) *Putting Class in its Place: Worker Identities in East Asia*, Berkeley: Institute of East Asian Studies, University of California, pp. 53–76.

Korten, David C. (1990) *Getting to the 21st Century: Voluntary Action and the Global Agenda*, West Hartford: Kumarian Press.

Kuruvilla, Sarosh (1995) 'Industrialization strategy and industrial relations policy in Malaysia', in Stephen Frenkel and Jeffrey Harrod (eds) *Industrialization and Labor Relations: Contemporary Research in Seven Countries*, Ithaca: ILR Press, pp. 37–63.

Lambert, Rob (1990) 'Kilusang Mayo Uno and the rise of social movement unionism in the Philippines', *Labour and Industry* 3, 2–3: 258–80.

Laothamatas, Anek (1997) *Democratization in Southeast and East Asia*, Singapore: Institute of Southeast Asian Studies.

Lawson, Stephanie (1998) 'Confucius in Singapore: Culture, politics and the PAP State', in Peter Dauvergne (ed.) *Weak and Strong States in Asia-Pacific Societies*, St Leonards: Allen and Unwin, pp. 114–34.

Lembcke, Jerry (1993) 'Class formation and class capacities: A new approach to the study of labor and the labor process', in Berch Berberoglu (ed.) *The Labor Process and Control of Labor: The Changing Nature of Work Relations in the Late Twentieth Century*, Westport and London: Praeger, pp. 1–19.

Leys, Colin (1996) *The Rise and Fall of Development Theory*, London: James Currey, Bloomington: Indiana University Press and Nairobi: East African Educational Publishers.

Lim, Linda Y.C. (1990) 'Women's work in export factories: The politics of a cause', in Irene Tinker (ed.) *Persistent Inequalities: Women and World Development*, New York and London: Oxford University Press, pp. 101–19.

Luckham, Robin and White, Gordon (eds) (1996) *Democratization in the South: The Jagged Wave*, Manchester and New York: Manchester University Press.

Mackenzie, Gavin (1982) 'Class boundaries and the labour process', in Anthony Giddens and Gavin Mackenzie (eds) *Social Class and the Division of Labour*, Cambridge: Cambridge University Press, pp. 63–86.

MacShane, Denis (1992) 'Asia: The next frontier for trade unions', *The Pacific Review* 5, 1: 1–12.

Mann, Michael (1977) *Consciousness and Action Among the Western Working Class*, London: Macmillan.

Manning, Chris (1998) 'Does globalisation undermine labour standards? Lessons from East Asia', *Australian Journal of International Affairs* 52, 2: 133–47.

Martin, Ross M. (1989) *Trade Unionism: Purposes and Forms*, Oxford: Clarendon Press.

Marx, Karl (1976) *Capital*, vol. 1, London: Penguin.

Mathews, John (1989) *Tools of Change: New Technology and the Democratisation of Work*, Sydney: Pluto Press.

McClelland, David (1964) 'Business drive and national achievement', in Amitai Etzioni and Eva Etzioni (eds) *Social Change*, New York: Basic Books, pp. 165–78.

Metcalfe, Andrew (1988) *For Freedom and Dignity: Historical Agency and Class Structures in the Coalfields of NSW*, Sydney: Allen and Unwin.

Miliband, Ralph (1988) *Marxism and Politics*, Oxford: Oxford University Press.

Millen, Bruce (1963) *The Political Role of Labor in Developing Countries*, Washington, D.C.: The Brookings Institute.

Mittelman, James H. (ed.) (1997) *Globalization: Critical Reflections*, Boulder: Lynne Rienner Publishers.

Moran, Jonathan (1998) 'The dynamics of class politics and national economies in globalisation', *Capital and Class* 66: 53–83.

Olds, Kris, Dicken, Peter, Kelly, Philip F., Kong, Lily and Yeung, Henry Wai-chung (eds) (1999) *Globalisation and the Asia-Pacific: Contested Territories*, London and New York: Routledge.

Perry, Elizabeth J. (1996) 'Putting class in its place: Bases of worker identities in East Asia', in Elizabeth J. Perry (ed.) *Putting Class in its Place: Worker Identities in East Asia*, Berkeley: Institute of East Asian Studies, University of California, pp. 1–10.

Pinches, Michael (1999) 'Cultural relations, class and the new rich of Asia', in Michael Pinches (ed.) *Culture and Privilege in Capitalist Asia*, London and New York: Routledge.

Piore, M. and Sabel, C. (1984) *The Second Industrial Divide*, New York: Basic Books.

Prasai, Surya B. (1993) 'Intra-Asian labor migration', *Asian Survey* 33, 11: 1,055–70.

Pye, Lucian W. (with Pye, Mary W.) (1985) *Asian Power and Politics: The Cultural Dimensions of Authority*, Cambridge, MA: Belknap Press.

Raghavan, Chakravarthi (1996) 'Barking up the wrong tree: Trade and social clause links', *Third World Economics* 129: 11–15.

Ranald, Patricia (1999) 'Analysing, organising, resisting: Union responses to the Asian economic crisis in East Asia, South Korea and the Philippines', *Journal of Industrial Relations* 41, 2: 295–325.

Resnick, Stephen and Wolff, Richard (1981) 'Class structures in developing societies', in W. Ladd Hollist and James N. Rosenau (eds) *World System Structure: Continuity and Change*, Beverly Hills: Sage, pp. 243–317.

Riker, James V. (1995) 'Contending perspectives for interpreting government–NGO relations in South and Southeast Asia', in Noeleen Heyzer, James V. Riker and Antonio B. Quizon (eds) *Government–NGO Relations in Asia: Prospects and Challenges for*

People-Centred Development, Kuala Lumpur: Asian and Pacific Development Centre and Basingstoke: Macmillan Press, pp. 15–55.

Robison, Richard (1996) 'The politics of "Asian values" ', *The Pacific Review* 9, 3: 309–27.

Rodan, Garry (1989) *The Political Economy of Singapore's Industrialisation: National State and International Capital*, Kuala Lumpur: Forum.

—— (1996a) 'The internationalisation of ideological conflict: Asia's significance', *The Pacific Review* 9, 3: 328–51.

—— (1996b) 'Theorising political opposition in East and Southeast Asia', in Garry Rodan (ed.) *Political Oppositions in Industrialising Asia*, London and New York: Routledge, pp. 1–39.

Ross, Robert and Trachte, Kent (1990) *Global Capitalism: The New Leviathan*, Albany: State University of New York Press.

Rueschemeyer, Dietrich, Stephens, Evelyne Huber and Stephens, John D. (eds) (1992) *Capitalist Development and Democracy*, Cambridge: Polity Press.

Sayer, Andrew and Walker, Richard (1993) *The New Social Economy: Reworking the Division of Labor*, Cambridge, MA: Blackwell.

Scipes, Kim (1992) 'Social movement unionism and the Kilusang Mayo Uno', *Kasarinlan* 7, 2–3: 121–62.

—— (1996) *KMU: Building Genuine Trade Unionism in the Philippines, 1980–1994*, Quezon City: New Day Publishers.

Seidman, Gary (1994) *Manufacturing Militance: Workers' Movements in Brazil and South Africa, 1970–1985*, Berkeley: University of California Press.

Sengenberger, Werner (1992) 'Intensified competition, industrial restructuring and industrial relations', *International Labour Review* 131, 2: 139–54.

—— (1994) 'International labour standards in a globalized economy: The issues', in Werner Sengenberger and Duncan Campbell (eds) *International Labour Standards and Economic Interdependence*, Geneva: International Institute for Labour Studies, pp. 3–15.

Sengenberger, Werner and Pyke, Frank (1991) 'Small firm industrial districts and local economic regeneration: Research and policy issues', *Labour and Society* 16, 1: 1–24.

Shin, Doh C. (1999) *Mass Politics and Culture in Democratizing Korea*, Cambridge and New York: Cambridge University Press.

Siddique, S.A. (1989) 'Industrial relations in a Third World setting: A possible model', *The Journal of Industrial Relations* 31, 3 (September): 385–401.

Silliman, G. Sidney and Noble, Lela Garner (1998) 'Introduction', in G. Sidney Silliman and Lela Garner Noble (eds) *Organizing for Democracy: NGOs, Civil Society and the Philippine State*, Honolulu: University of Hawai'i Press, pp. 1–25.

Silver, Beverly J. (1995) 'Labor unrest and world-systems analysis: Premises, concepts and measurement', *Review* 18, 1: 7–34.

Sims, Beth (1992) *Workers of the World Undermined: American Labor's Role in US Foreign Policy*, Boston: South End Press.

So, Alvin Y. (1990) *Social Change and Development: Modernization, Dependency and World-System Theories*, Newbury Park, London and New Delhi: Sage Publications.

Stahl, C.W. (1992) 'South–North migration in the Asia-Pacific region', *International Migration* 29, 2: 163–93.

Standing, Guy (1992) 'Do unions impede or accelerate structural adjustment? Industrial versus company unions in an industrialising labour market', *Cambridge Journal of Economics* 16: 327–54.

Stark, David (1980) 'Class struggle and the labour process', *Theory and Society* 9, 1: 89–130.

Stubbs, Richard (1994) 'The political economy of the Asia-Pacific region', in Richard Stubbs and Geoffrey R.D. Underhill (eds) *Political Economy and the Changing Global Order*, London: Macmillan, pp. 366–77.

Sturmthal, Adolf (1972) *Comparative Labor Movements: Ideological Roots and Institutional Development*, California: Wadsworth Publishing Company.

Sufrin, Sidney C. (1964) *Unions in Emerging Societies: Frustration and Politics*, Syracuse: Syracuse University Press.

Sungsidh Piriyarangsan (1989) 'The formation of a workers–strategic group: An analysis of the labor movement in Thailand (1958–1976)', Ph.D. thesis, University of Bielefeld.

Therborn, Göran (1983) 'Why some classes are more successful than others', *New Left Review* 138: 37–68.

Thompson, E.P. (1978) 'Eighteenth-century English society: Class struggle without class?', *Social History* 3, 2: 133–66.

Tilly, Charles (1995) 'Globalization threatens labor's rights', *International Labor and Working-Class History* 47: 1–23.

Villegas, Edberto M. (1988) *The Political Economy of Philippine Labor Laws*, Quezon City: Foundation for Nationalist Studies.

Waterman, Peter (1993) 'Social movement unionism: A new union model for a new world order?', *Review* 16, 3: 245–78.

Weiss, Linda (1997) 'Globalization and the myth of the powerless state', *New Left Review* 225: 3–27.

West, Lois A. (1997) *Militant Labor in the Philippines*, Philadelphia: Temple University Press.

White, Gordon (1996) 'Civil society, democratization and development', in Robin Luckham and Gordon White (eds) *Democratization in the South: The Jagged Wave*, Manchester and New York: Manchester University Press, pp. 178–219.

White, Gordon (ed.) (1998) *Developmental States in East Asia*, London: Macmillan.

Wilkinson, Barry (1994) *Labour and Industry in the Asia-Pacific: Lessons from the Newly-Industrialized Countries*, Berlin and New York: Walter de Gruyter.

Wilson, D. (1962) *Politics in Thailand*, Ithaca: Cornell University Press.

Winters, Jeffrey A. (1996) *Power in Motion: Capital Mobility and the Indonesian State*, Ithaca and London: Cornell University Press.

Womack, J., Jones, D. and Roos, D. (1990) *The Machine that Changed the World*, New York: Rawson Associates.

Wong, Siu-Lun (1988) 'The applicability of Asian family values to other sociocultural settings', in Peter L. Berger and Hsin-Huang Michael Hsiao (eds) *In Search of an East Asian Development Model*, New Brunswick, NJ: Transaction, pp. 134–54.

Wood, Ellen Meiksins (1995) *Democracy Against Capitalism: Renewing Historical Materialism*, Cambridge: Cambridge University Press.

World Bank (1995) *Workers in an Integrating World*, New York: Oxford University Press.

Wright, E.O. (1985) *Classes*, London: Verso.

Yin, Robert K. (1994) *Case Study Research: Design and Methods*, 2nd edn, Thousand Oaks, London and New Delhi: Sage Publications.

Yun, Seongyi (1997) 'Democratization in South Korea: Social movements and their political opportunity structures', *Asian Perspective* 21, 3: 145–71.

Zysman, John (1996) 'The myth of a "global" economy: Enduring national foundations and emerging regional realities', *New Political Economy* 2: 157–84.

2 The rise of the Bangladesh Independent Garment-Workers' Union (BIGU)

Marilyn Rock

The establishment of an export-oriented garments industry in Bangladesh in the late 1970s prompted the creation of a first-generation female industrial labour force (McCarthy and Feldman, 1983; Kabeer, 1991). Significantly, this labour force was mainly composed of young, unmarried women – a group traditionally subject to very rigid forms of control through the socially sanctioned norms of *purdah* or female seclusion. But, since the mid-1980s, Bangladeshi women garment workers have been active in attempts to form unions in their industry. Despite some successes, their initial endeavours in this regard were both difficult and disappointing: difficult in the sense that factory owners harbour a hostile attitude towards attempts to organise, with instant dismissal being the outcome for workers identified as unionists; disappointing in the sense that their efforts were frequently used for the vocal extension of party political matters. However, in 1994, a new *independent* union – the Bangladesh Independent Garment-Workers' Union (BIGU) – was formed with the stated aim of promoting the industrial interests of members themselves. Such has been the popularity of this union that both employers and state officials have expressed concern that its emergence and expansion poses a potential threat to the survival of the garment industry – an industry which played a leading role in the initial industrialisation process in Bangladesh, emerging as the country's only billion-dollar manufacturing export industry.

The formation and popularity of BIGU – through which garment workers have found a voice and attempted to express their interests – is significant at three levels. First, it challenges perceptions that Bangladeshi women are rendered quiescent by the competitive conditions of their employment and by cultural notions of female propriety, showing instead how elements of the labour process and the experience of harsh working conditions can interact to promote collective action. Second, the independence of the union represents a move away from 'political unionism' which, hitherto, has been a pivotal component in the history of labour organising in Bangladesh. However – and this is the third point – the circumstances of BIGU's establishment also illustrate the vital role that local non-governmental organisations (NGOs) and international labour organisations – in this case the Asia-American Free Labor

Institute (AAFLI) – may have to play in forwarding independent unionism in a country like Bangladesh.

This chapter begins with a critical discussion of the literature, which emphasises only the *obstacles* to Bangladeshi women workers organising in the export garments sector. Following this, there is an overview of the history of labour organising in Bangladesh (formerly East Bengal) which draws particular attention to the factors encouraging the rise and persistence of politically affiliated unionism. Finally, this chapter documents the emergence of BIGU, discussing in some detail the domestic and international factors and events that have encouraged its formation, as well as those that constantly threaten to weaken (if not destroy) it.[1]

Theorising women workers in export factories

The 'new international division of labour' (NIDL) thesis (Fröbel, Heinrichs and Kreye, 1980) has had a strong influence on the way in which women workers in export factories are theorised. This thesis stresses a model of economic globalisation in which capital from major First World countries is attracted to production sites in the Third World that are low cost, principally because of the ready availability of very low-paid, acquiescent workers. From this labour pool, it is claimed that employers particularly prefer young unskilled or semi-skilled *female* workers, as they will work for the lowest wages and endure a higher intensity of work (ibid.: 347–8). While agreeing that the feminisation of the workforce is encouraged by international competition, feminist scholars prefer to emphasise the fact that women workers have historically been less militant, largely because of their place and socialisation in patriarchal societies (Lim, 1978; Elson and Pearson, 1981; Heyzer, 1986).

According to the NIDL thesis, labour-organising capacities are weakened by transnational production arrangements. But in the Bangladesh garments industry the demands of overseas markets are important in shaping the labour process in ways that *promote* labour organising.[2] Here, a significant number of manufacturers are forced to keep production centralised so as to maintain constant monitoring and surveillance over quality standards that are crucial for attracting and maintaining export contracts. The limitations that international markets place on managers are also a factor in encouraging unionisation among the women workers, in that they result in their aggregation in particular sites. Thus this case study will show that the effects of economic globalisation on levels of unionisation in export-oriented manufacturing are more complex and dynamic than is generally supposed by the NIDL thesis.

However, above and beyond their location in export factories, women workers in Bangladesh are often said to face specific cultural constraints on their activism – most notably from Islamic notions of female propriety which relegate them to positions of invisibility and passivity (Dil, 1985; Mannan, 1989; Ahmed, 1991). Before explaining the industrial and political environment in which BIGU has emerged, it is necessary for me to qualify these claims. In much of the writing on women in Bangladesh, the notion of 'separate spheres' has been prominent – central to which is the institution of *purdah* (White, 1992: 22–5). When viewed in essentialist terms, this notion denotes a number of polarities which divide society into sex-segregated spheres. However, as the example of women workers in the export garments industry shows, such divisions are never static; rather, they 'are constantly shifting, being reworked and redefined by economic, political and ideological forces' (Stivens, 1998: 4). Furthermore, the convergence of gender relations and class means that options open to Bangladeshi women vary considerably across the socio-economic order, depending on their relationship to the means of production and their place within the distribution nexus (Kabeer, 1988).

Purdah as a practice has altered with changing economic and political circumstances. For instance, the feminisation of the manufacturing workforce in Bangladesh has been associated with the deepening of capitalist relations in agriculture and a deteriorating family wage (Feldman, 1993: 224). As a result, many poor rural families are now compelled to allow their female members to take up employment outside the home in order to improve their chances of collective survival. Concomitant with these socio-economic developments, successive governments have introduced policies to expedite the creation of an abundant source of cheap female labour.

As a direct outcome of the United Nations' 1975 International Year of Women and the 1976–85 Decade of Women, a Ministry of Women was established in 1976 and a policy was announced which introduced a 10 per cent quota for women in public-sector employment. This professed commitment to the cause of women and development was then incorporated into the Second Five-Year Plan (1980–5). But, given the high demand for such jobs, it is argued that this provision merely acted to *restrict* the hiring of women (Khan, 1993: 46–60). The New Industrial Policy of 1982 and the Revised Industrial Policy of 1986 – both fundamentally concerned with the strategy of export promotion – assumed that women would *a priori* be the favoured workforce, on the grounds that it is established practice internationally for women to do 'women's work' in export factories. However, because tailoring has traditionally been a *male* occupation in Bangladesh, NGOs had to offer programmes to train women for work in export factories (and provide dormitories and hostels for young, single women in urban centres). In addition, the state legitimated new forms of cultural expression of appropriate female behaviour, such as living away from the family group, unaccompanied travel on public transport and the wearing of non-traditional forms of dress (Feldman, 1992: 116–23).

Yet there have been obvious tensions and contradictions inherent in government policy towards women's participation in the public sphere. These were brought home in the mid-1980s with the resurgence of the Islamic fundamentalist party, the Jamaati-I-Islami, which sought to adopt more conservative practices, including the observance of *purdah*. Rather than contest these demands, the Ershad regime endeavoured to co-opt the growing strength of the Jamaati-I-Islami by seeking to make Islam the state religion through the passage in 1988 of the Eighth Amendment to the Constitution (ibid.: 125–6). This amendment, which meant that women – especially those working in the industrial sector – would have difficulty in observing restrictive Islamic practices, elicited a particularly strong response from Bangladeshi women themselves. In itself, this was evidence of the emerging confidence and politicisation of women, arising from their increasing integration into development policies. In sum, as Naila Kabeer puts it, various political regimes 'have sought to promote an Islamic identity in Bangladesh, with some of the attendant rhetoric of female seclusion and propriety'. Yet at the same time, they have often 'sought to champion women and development programmes with [their] very different rhetoric of women's emancipation' (Kabeer, 1991: 141).

When the export garments industry was first established in Bangladesh, women workers were largely controlled and disciplined on the factory floor by the perpetuation of *purdah* – incorporating the socialised norms of hard work, compliance and subordination – and, more significantly, by the fear of losing their jobs. This intensification of work though has subsequently become a source of daily conflict between workers and management. The resulting collective activism of female garment workers challenges scholarship that predicts their isolation and acquiescence. In addition, it marks an important break with existing modes of 'political unionism' in Bangladesh. So as to better understand the significance of BIGU for unionism in the country, the following section provides some historical background to the rise of organised labour and the part it came to play in national politics.

Historical background

Bangladesh as East Bengal under British rule

As in other parts of British-ruled India, an urbanised industrial working class first began to emerge in East Bengal (now Bangladesh) in the late nineteenth century. In response to low wages, strikes soon became common, but the majority of these were spontaneous and held without the aid of any formal organisation. There was no organised labour movement in East Bengal until early in the twentieth century. By contrast, West Bengal was a centre of remarkable advancement in the organisation of labour under the British; so much so that, with the Partition of Bengal in 1905, the labour movement gained an important further impetus when political leaders took up the cause of industrial workers (Ahmad, 1978: 8). Nationalist representatives realised that support from a labour force concentrated in the cities was a vital asset to the political struggle for independence; hence, they actively sought to broaden their political base by the inclusion of socio-economic issues. In this way, the labour movement became an integral part of the nationalist movement and ever since then trade unions have been steeped in party politics in Bangladesh and India (Ramaswamy, 1979; Nurullah, 1993: 17–22).

As the labour movement developed amid nationalist agitation, the colonial state sought to co-opt it by assuming a direct role in structuring labour activism and, through a remarkable range of labour laws enacted in the 1920s and 1930s, organised labour in India gained a new 'legal' status. These laws were to later furnish the foundation for the labour legislation, institutions and practices of the post-colonial state in Bangladesh (Rahman, 1986).

Bangladesh as East Pakistan under Pakistani rule

As a consequence of the termination of British rule in 1947, two new sovereign states of India and Pakistan were created. Although the East Bengalis had successfully pressed their claim to become the eastern wing of Pakistan, it was not long before tensions between East and West Pakistan came to the surface. The uneven rate of economic development in the country saw Bengali nationalism re-ignited: this time not against the British but against the uncompromising greed of the landlord–bourgeois bloc in West Pakistan (Ali, 1975; Karim, 1994).

All the forms of exaction imposed by the ruling class in West Pakistan were magnified in East Bengal: industrial wages were lower, working hours were longer, consumer prices were higher and the rate of unemployment was always greater (Nations, 1971). By 1954, labour unrest had reached an unprecedented high, impelling the government to announce a new, more liberal labour policy a year later. However, as these developments did not include the right to strike, worker dissatisfaction escalated and, in the context of political action for Bengali independence, the imposition of martial law was declared in 1958. Although martial law was certainly a setback for the labour movement, strike activity continued well into the 1960s. The state subsequently realised that class conflict could not be resolved by suppression alone and a revised labour policy was announced, under which the right to strike was bestowed on the working class, albeit for economic purposes (Nurullah, 1993: 28–9).

During this time, industrial workers formed 'the vanguard' of the broader independence struggle (Ahmed, 1984: 82). By the end of the 1960s, a rising tide of popular support for a complete break with Pakistan was apparent as an alliance of workers, students and intellectuals – mediated by the Awami League Party – was formed. Following the nine-month War of Liberation in 1971, the state of Pakistan disintegrated and the People's Republic of Bangladesh emerged shortly after – with the Awami League in government. The nascent state was then confronted with difficulties of reconstructing a neglected and war-torn economy, and gaining acceptance as a nation-state within the global economy.

The state and labour in post-colonial Bangladesh

Economic policy under the Awami League regime (1972–5) was directed towards the establishment of a 'just and egalitarian society', in which 'measures of nationalisation would be combined with new arrangements to ensure workers' participation in the management of industries' and their sharing 'in the fruits of increased production' (cited in Islam, 1988: 91). Nonetheless, these proclaimed ideals belied the reality of state capitalism. Workers soon realised that formal political independence did not mean a new social and economic reality; rather, they remained part of the old system and became subject to increasing social differentiation and further impoverishment. The existing relations of production were reproduced by the post-colonial state in which power was articulated through an unstable three-way alliance between the military, the bureaucracy and a 'trade-oriented' bourgeoisie who 'used state resources for [their] personal benefit and played no role in the development of the productive forces' (Alam, 1994: 55).

The socialist rhetoric and radical policy initiatives of the regime attracted criticism from foreign donors and international financial institutions whose financial assistance was vital to economic development.[3] In the context of a worsening economic and political situation, a military coup ushered in the regime of General Zia Rahman (1975–81), who claimed a more 'pragmatic appreciation' of economic and social reality. The new industrial policy announced in December 1975 aimed to facilitate the pursuit of export-oriented industrialisation (EOI) through a programme of selective privatisation and the promotion of private-sector investment (Humphrey, 1992: 46–62). But this policy shift was implemented with caution rather than conviction, as the Zia government wanted to avoid an escalation in worker militancy in a public sector already beset by labour unrest.

In 1982 there was a second military coup. This time, with the political left substantially weakened, General Ershad signalled further EOI through privatisation and private-sector development under the 1982 New Industrial Policy and the 1986 Revised Industrial Policy (ibid.: 63–97). However, the very limited resources available continued to be granted to favoured business cronies, who then used them to augment political and personal coffers. '[O]ne of the most centralised and corrupt [governments] in the history of Bangladesh' (Kochanek, 1993: 53), the Ershad regime was toppled by an urban-based mass movement in late 1990. Then, in a convincing victory, the right-wing Bangladesh Nationalist Party (BNP), led by Begum Khaleda Zia (the widow of General Zia), came to power in one of the first free elections held in Bangladesh for twenty years.

The roots of the policy commitment to EOI and denationalisation of selected industries are grounded in the regimes of Zia Rahman and Ershad, but the new BNP regime was concerned to speed up this process. Together with the increasing use of 'conditionality' imposed by the World Bank and International Monetary Fund (IMF), the reform process was accelerated by allowing greater concessions to foreign capital and granting 'full operational freedom to the private sector' (Kamaluddin, 1991: 45). To this end, the Industrial Policy of 1991 further liberalised the trade sector, with the state assuming a more supportive (rather than regulatory) role in the industrial sector. Overall, within this policy framework, a mushrooming of export garment factories took place, as garment firms from countries like South Korea, Taiwan, Hong Kong and China – whose quotas were being used up – took advantage of Bangladesh as quota-free territory (Kaye, 1986).

Since the mid-1970s, industrial workers have been active in resisting the economic reform process. Worker militancy has not reversed or even substantially modified state economic policy; nonetheless, it has slowed down the pace of reform to the extent that the labour movement is often singled out as responsible for the low level of economic growth. Although labour militancy has been a persistent problem for the state in post-colonial Bangladesh, the officially sanctioned labour movement has become a vehicle for dominant interests because of its links with political parties. This was reinforced by a 1977 government regulation requiring that each political party have a labour front of its own (Nurullah, 1993: 42–3). Consequently, numerous trade unions were formed with the sole purpose of strengthening and broadening the base of support of the political parties. In so far as the growth of unionism has been motivated by political interests, it has done little to effect any real change in the material conditions of the Bangladeshi working class (Bhuyan, 1986). Not surprisingly, under these circumstances inter-union rivalries are also a significant feature of labour relations in Bangladesh, with incumbent governments encouraging such rivalry to serve political ends.

In sum, after independence, organised labour in Bangladesh changed from an integral force in various anti-colonial and nationalist struggles to a co-opted instrument for the realisation of dominant interests – and hence arguably an *impediment* to workers improving their circumstances. But, in 1984, there was an important development: a new umbrella organisation – the Sramik Karmachari Oikya Parishad (SKOP) or United Front of Workers and Employees – was formed to represent the trade union movement as a whole (Rahman, 1994: 57–62). After its formation, SKOP played an increasingly controversial and significant role in industrial relations, extracting benefits such as wage revisions and the introduction of a national minimum wage for both public and private sectors. In addition, SKOP identified privatisation and redundancy issues as critical matters on which the labour movement should be consulted and, if possible, their agreement obtained. In this respect, as one leading labour figure put it:

> SKOP has emerged as a vital body for the workers of Bangladesh because it represents the only platform through which the working class can articulate a unity of interests.
>
> (interview with Rahman, 1996)

Nevertheless, the formation of SKOP has not substantially altered the reality of politically affiliated trade unionism. Although the larger trade union federations – especially those with permanent links with the three major political parties – ostensibly have the capacity to favourably influence policies for their membership, 'it is a moot point … whether they can adopt policies independently of the parties which are in the interest of workers' (Rahman, 1994: 43). It was in this context that women workers in the export garments industry began to organise from the mid-1980s.

The export garments industry

There were only a few industrial units producing garments for export in Bangladesh when, in 1976, a collaboration between a civil servant-turned-entrepreneur, Noorul Quader, and the South Korean conglomerate, Daewoo Corporation, provided a vital 'catalyst' to the expansion and success of the garment export sector in Bangladesh (Rhee, 1990). By the 1980s, factories were being set up almost on a daily basis in the major cities so that, by 1987, the number had reached 700 enterprises employing some 250,000 workers. A decade later, there were an estimated 2,000 export garment factories employing around 1.4 million workers – approximately 85 per cent of whom are female (BGMEA, 1996).

The labour process in garment manufacture is marked by: the expectation by management that workers will work up to fourteen hours (more during peak periods) a day, seven days a week; the maintenance of an intensity of work to meet production targets; the imposition of harsh forms of discipline and supervision; and the almost total absence of adequate facilities and ventilation.

These facets of the labour process – together with the payment of very low wages[4] and, on occasion, no payment at all – have meant that for some time the women workers have felt the need to organise for improvements in the process of producing garments for export (Hossain and Brar, 1988). This feeling is often articulated in the form of a deep resentment of and consciousness about their dismal working conditions and low pay, which they view as an affront to both their dignity and sense of justice. However, rather than return to their villages or dependent status within the household, in the 1990s women workers have been attempting to carry out their desire to organise. Their increasing politicisation and capacity to resist is epitomised by a remark made by an official of a Bangladeshi NGO: 'They are a determined and militant bunch of workers – they do not want sympathy or tears, just hard-fought efforts to improve their lot' (interview with Akhter, 1994).

Initially, the garment export workers were hesitant to articulate their grievances to management; consequently, 'underground' activities ensued whereby workers would meet out of working hours at parks and cinema halls to discuss the possibility of forming trade unions. At the same time, other forms of organising were occurring. Given the limited outreach of the labour movement in Bangladesh for women workers, it has been useful for them to interact with organisations whose work falls in line with the general objectives of trade unions: these include relevant NGOs, women's groups and human rights groups. These institutions offer such diverse facilities as libraries, seminars and discussions on the rights of women as citizens and workers which have played a crucial educative role in extending the arena of struggle for the garment export workers.

In particular, a category of grassroots organisations has emerged in Bangladesh to focus on issues of class and gender, reflecting a shift away from the previous preoccupation with the manifestations of poverty. The primary objectives of these NGOs is to promote an understanding among proletarian poor women about the nature of their collective oppression and to impart to them their organisational capacity to resist (Kabeer, 1988: 116–17).

In spite of the ambiguities surrounding the notion of NGOs empowering Third World women (Kabeer, 1994), in Bangladesh they have made a substantial contribution by involving women from destitute backgrounds in numerous income- and employment-generating activities (Kabir, 1987; White, 1992: 14–16).[5] In relation to the garments export sector, many local NGOs have played a pivotal role in providing garment workers with information about their exploitative working conditions. For instance, Steps Towards Development, Working Women, Women for Women and UBINIG (Alternative Policy Research for Development) have conducted extensive research into women and export-oriented industrialisation, with the aim of raising debate at the policy level as well as the popular level. In this context, the working conditions of garment workers have been targeted as a particular area of concern and various programmes provided to assist these workers with health issues, worker rights and organising activities (interview with Akhter, 1994). In the main, these grassroots NGOs concentrate on fostering new forms of collective awareness and association among female garment workers.

Of particular note among international NGOs is the role the Asia-American Free Labor Institute (AAFLI), an international arm of the American Labor Federation–Congress of Industrial Organizations (AFL–CIO). AAFLI has been operating in Bangladesh since 1973, working with a number of trade union federations largely in the capacity of imparting skills relating to all aspects of running a trade union. In addition, AAFLI has provided assistance in the development of social projects such as health care and apprenticeship training and, when asked to do so, has helped in the formation of trade unions – for example, the Bangladesh Cha Sramik Union (National Union of Tea Workers) and the Bangladesh Railway Employees League.

AAFLI has also assisted female garment workers to unionise. Although eighty-one plant-level unions had been legally formed between 1984 and 1991 with the assistance of NGOs and existing trade union structures, the majority of these did not survive due to repressive retaliatory measures taken by management (interviews with Khan and Lokollo, 1996). However, with the assistance of AAFLI, BIGU was formed in 1994 and has since become the largest, most successful garment union in Bangladesh. While AAFLI is an international arm of the AFL–CIO – an organisation identified historically as anti-communist and as supporting the global economic and political status quo (Sims, 1992: 1–20) – it nonetheless has played a vital role at the local level in Bangladesh. As Beth Sims notes:

labor organizations in the Third World desperately need material assistance
... to support their activities. In addition, they benefit from educational
services, given the complex economic and political factors they must take
into account during negotiations and organizing campaigns.

(ibid.: 11–12)

This is precisely the assistance the female garment workers required in helping
them to organise an alternative and completely independent garment workers'
union.

Initially, much of the garment workers' struggle took the form of partaking in
ongoing political campaigns, demonstrations and rallies, which yielded few
actual material gains. Although a minimum wage was declared for the garment
workers in 1985 – mostly through the work of SKOP – and agreements have
supposedly been reached regarding the right to organise and adherence to the
labour laws of Bangladesh (interviews with Amin, 1995; Hossain, 1996), in
reality these have not produced any real change as they have not been
implemented by employers. The working conditions of the garment export
workers have remained the same, largely because of the persistent problem of
industrial relations being highly politicised. As already pointed out, strong
alliances exist between trade unions and political parties, and the garment
workers claim many union officials are 'political animals' who use workers to
impress their federation leaders and affiliated political parties in an attempt to
gain entry into formal political life (interview with Akhter and Yeasmin, 1996).
Indeed, it is argued that most strikes in Bangladesh are called by opposition
political parties rather than by trade unions fighting for better pay and working
conditions (Al-Faisal, 1995; Kamaluddin, 1995). It is precisely this situation that
has caused general disillusionment among the export garment workers, who
claim they merely provide an impressive vocal addition to party political matters.
While many rallies and demonstrations of protest are held and charters of
demands lodged, this is essentially where the activities of the official unions
cease. Furthermore, accusations that union organisers are either 'making deals
with management' or 'shaking down the owners and screwing the workers' are
common (interview with Sigelakis, 1996). In an attempt to remedy the apparent
failure of existing trade union structures to redress worker grievances, BIGU was
formed – independent of any formal political affiliation.

The Bangladesh Independent Garment-Workers' Union (BIGU)

Although BIGU is perceived by its members as a genuine union, formed by the
workers for the workers, in truth the union would not have materialised had it
not been for the vital assistance of the quasi-NGO/international labour
organisation, the AAFLI. A prominent human rights lawyer in Bangladesh,
Fawzia Karim Firoze, recounts how she became actively involved in the legal
counselling of garment workers to ensure they have access to the legal system

and can avail themselves of coverage under the relevant labour laws. In 1992, she set up a human rights programme at AAFLI's headquarters in Dhaka: many garment workers attended and related the most horrific stories of intimidation and victimisation, as well as the continual abuse of their statutory rights as industrial workers. It was soon realised there was an urgent need for a legal programme tailored solely to the needs of these workers. More importantly, it was acknowledged that a new trade union organisation was required; one that would commit itself to assisting and educating these workers, rather than using them as 'political fodder'. After two years of running this human rights programme, steps were taken to organise in a massive way and, on 16 December 1994, the founding conference of BIGU was held.

Currently, BIGU is the largest garment union in Bangladesh, covering well over 500 garment factories in the main industrial centres of Dhaka and Chittagong, with a membership of just over 50,000 workers. So successful has the union been that:

> Now, we don't really have to go out and organise as there has been and continues to be a positive response – it is tremendous – members just keep coming. At first, one worker would come, then maybe two or three, now they come in big groups and one factory leads to other factories and BIGU just keeps growing.
>
> (interview with Firoze, 1996)

Undoubtedly, the reasons behind BIGU's apparent success are its intention to stay outside state-sponsored unionism and its constitutional requirement that all union officials must either be currently working or have worked in the garments export sector for a cumulative period of a minimum of five years. This provision ensures that union officers are actual garment workers rather than politically inspired professional trade-union leaders who have never worked a day in a garment factory. Similarly, to reflect the feminised nature of the workforce in garment production, at least nine of the fifteen positions must be held by women (BIGU, 1994: 5–6).

In BIGU's two district offices in Dhaka, a number of services are readily available to garment workers. Each centre offers both legal and medical assistance, with lawyers and doctors in attendance in the evenings. BIGU also runs classes to educate workers on their statutory rights and to teach them basic English and literacy skills so that they can make sense of the paperwork often thrust at them by management for signing. For instance, as factory time-cards are usually printed in English, many garment workers have been cheated out of their rightful earnings because the cards state that workers are in attendance from 8 AM until 4 PM when, in most cases, they work late into the night. Once the workers have signed these cards, they have no recourse to industrial action.

Another unscrupulous practice prevails whereby workers are often asked to sign or place a thumb mark on a piece of paper – at times a blank sheet – under some kind of pretence about what it concerns, only to discover they have signed a voluntary termination agreement. Under the law, they cannot then collect their termination benefits because they are deemed to have voluntarily resigned. Similarly, workers often sign papers claiming they have received benefits due to them. In fact, BIGU officials continually stress to the workers not to sign anything before bringing it to the attention of the union's lawyers. However, this is difficult as garment workers are generally forced or coerced into signing such papers. Nonetheless, as they gradually realise the implications, more and more workers are taking a stand against management in such situations. Every member of BIGU is issued with a copy of the union's constitution, as well as a *Handbook on Worker Rights for Garment Workers* in which workers are clearly and succinctly informed of their entitlements under the labour laws of Bangladesh. BIGU has also established its own publication – *Voice of the Worker* – which is a vital adjunct to the ongoing educative process of alerting garment workers to their rights and the services BIGU has to offer (interview with Sigelakis, 1996).

As the majority of garment workers had very little or no knowledge about their rights as industrial workers, the strategy of educating them has been integral to the process of class formation and trade union organisation. This was expressed by BIGU's press secretary in the following press statement:

> We endured many problems in organising the workers. With a largely female workforce that has been kept passive by the culture and tradition in Bangladesh, and kept ignorant by poverty and the lack of educational opportunities … the workers were hard to educate about their rights.
>
> (Akhter, 1995: 2)

The educative strategy has been a resounding success, with over 16,000 workers having directly participated in educative programmes. In addition to education, another pivotal strategy of BIGU is the actual use of the labour laws to address the industrial issues facing the garment workers; that is, BIGU lawyers are filing cases and using the Labour Courts instead of relying on rallies and demonstrations of protest. In this respect, it is worth noting that Labour Court records indicate there were hardly any cases concerning women workers before the 1990s. However, in 1992 there was a significant 'upsurge' in cases filed with the Court, coinciding with the commencement of Firoze's work with the export garment workers. There have subsequently been further increases in the number of cases, as additional lawyers have been appointed to cope with the workload. The cases filed by BIGU lawyers mostly concern illegal termination and the non-payment of wages; of these, approximately 65 per cent are settled informally as owners realise they are in clear violation of labour law. In fact, as it is a criminal offence under the Minimum Wages Ordinance (1961) to withhold wages without reasonable cause, factory owners prefer to settle out of court rather than face a potential prison sentence. Of the remaining cases, roughly 15 per cent fell outside the scope of the law and could not be pursued; about 25 per cent were contested in court – in virtually all contested cases, BIGU has prevailed. With BIGU having secured some notable victories, it is claimed that the situation can only improve (interview with Firoze, 1996).

Having fulfilled the statutory requirements for trade union formation, BIGU in 1996 applied for registration as a single national trade union instead of as a federation – involving the separate registration of each affiliated factory union – so that collective bargaining could take place for the industry as a whole. This application was made on the basis of the following arguments: under International Labour Organisation (ILO) Conventions 87 and 98,[6] BIGU has the freedom to choose the form of labour organisation it prefers; there already exist in Bangladesh two national trade union bodies: one for the tea plantation workers and one for the inland water workers; as all garment workers are covered by the same Minimum Wages Ordinance, it is logical to have in place a single national trade union.

However, BIGU's application was refused on the grounds there was no provision under the Industrial Relations Ordinance (1969) that would allow for the registration of a national union. Subsequently an appeal was lodged by BIGU, citing the precedent set by the two existing national labour bodies, but once again the application was refused. The reasoning given was that the tea plantation and inland water workers' unions were established prior to 1979, when there was no formal registration process. Yet another appeal was lodged with the Labour Appellate Court, but this also failed. However, in 1997 BIGU was successful in gaining registration – as a national federation rather than an independent union. By 1999, it had twenty-four affiliated factory unions.

In sum, the emergence of BIGU as a competing organisational vehicle represents a widespread dissatisfaction with the officially sanctioned and politically affiliated trade unions in Bangladesh, which had achieved very little by way of meeting the demands of the export garment workers. However, the form that BIGU will take remains the subject of an ongoing struggle in Bangladesh: key issues are whether it will be legal or illegal; whether it will be allowed to bargain with peak employer groups; and what the range of issues will be that it can legitimately speak on. For this reason, it is important to examine some of the responses domestic and international forces have launched against BIGU and its activities.

Responses to the organising activities of BIGU

To begin with, BIGU members and officials continued to be subject to threats, labour law violations and attacks that made organising very difficult. This problem was nowhere more evident than in the Palmal Group of fifteen garment factories – owned by the Vice President of the BGMEA, Nurul Haque Sikder – many of which have been named in legal cases filed by BIGU. In particular, the Palmal Knitwear Factory, which produces garments for the retail outlets of Sears and J.C. Penney in the United States, has been singled out for its treatment of BIGU activists and members. A factsheet compiled by BIGU (1995) lists a number of beatings by *mastans* (thugs armed with guns), illegal dismissals, blacklistings and falsifications of documents that have occurred at that site. Similarly, in an international labour publication – under the heading 'Repression made to order' – the International Textile, Garment and Leather Workers' Federation (ITGLWF) reports death threats against BIGU unionists to the extent that a management representative said: 'If it is necessary to kill workers, they will be killed, but there will not be a trade union in this factory' (cited in *Free Labour World*, 1996: 7).[7]

BIGU offices have also come under attack at various times. One of their district offices in Dhaka was the target of a particularly vicious onslaught. On the night of 10 November 1995, the Malibarg district office in Dhaka was brutally attacked by thirty *mastans* with Molotov cocktails and batons. They pistol-whipped union officers and held the union's lawyer at gunpoint, ripping off her sari and soaking her with petrol before attempting to set her alight. Offices were ransacked, windows smashed and an attempt was made to torch the building; on leaving the premises, the *mastans* fired shots into the air and warned BIGU to cease its activities (*Free Labour World*, 1996: 6).

This particular attack provoked considerable controversy, both nationally and internationally. For instance, the ITGLWF was quick to condemn the incident and, in a letter to Prime Minister Begum Khaleda Zia, the ITGLWF General Secretary, Neil Kearney, called for 'an immediate and thorough investigation into the attack and for swift action to bring these criminals to justice'. Kearney continues with the warning:

> This incident is further evidence that some people in the garment industry are prepared to go to criminal extremes to protect their vested interests. Such actions will damage the standing of Bangladesh in the eyes of the world and will harm its reputation as a trading partner.
>
> (ITGLWF, 1995: 1–2)

Indeed, Kearney invited the employers group – the BGMEA (some of whose members' enterprises have been involved in court cases brought by BIGU) – to condemn publicly the attack and to support demands for action.

Given the central place that the export garments industry has in the Bangladeshi economy, it is not surprising that steps have also been taken to ensure that the women workers are brought into the fold of state-controlled unionism. However, just as BIGU's rise was made possible by the intervention of AAFLI, efforts to counter its influence have also involved various international forces. In particular, the International Confederation of Free Trade Unions (ICFTU) – an historical rival of AAFLI[8] – granted its four affiliated federations in Bangladesh US$45,000 and is providing organisers with cars for the sole purpose of organising the export garment workers.[9] Although this is not unusual in the sense that the ICFTU engages in Third World development and labour programmes, it is pertinent to note that it does so 'with the aim of pre-empting left-wing advances and preventing unstructured labour revolts' (Munck, 1988: 122).

The coordinator of this campaign is Nazrul Islam Khan, who is not only the president of one of the largest right-wing trade union federations affiliated to the ICFTU – the Bangladesh Jatiyatabdi Sramik Dal (BJSD) – but is also secretary to the right-wing Bangladesh Nationalist Party (BNP). BIGU is alerting their membership to the ICFTU-funded campaign, as it is easy for the organisers of the four affiliates to identify which garment factories have BIGU unions. Once these have been identified, there is a danger that moves will be made to 'snap them up' by finding a 'stooge' or some charismatic person in each factory to encourage the workers to be part of the 'big four'. 'This would be tragic, as it would foil two years of hard work for BIGU' (interview with Sigelakis, 1996).

Nevertheless, BIGU's successful organising strategies have seen other garment unions 'getting their act together', as they have come to realise that the garment workers want a more concerted effort in the representation of their legitimate grievances. Consequently, these unions are filing more cases with the Labour Courts instead of relying on mere political point-scoring through media coverage of worker demonstrations and rallies. As a result, it is claimed, management is not dismissing workers as readily as before: they now realise the very real threat of being taken to court and forced to make out-of-court settlements (interview with Khan, 1996).

On the other hand, it is also claimed that trade-union organising and related activities in the export-oriented garment sector in Bangladesh has led to segregation – that is, momentum has developed for setting up small factories, as owners of large factories are now increasingly subcontracting to escape the problem of trade unionism, especially BIGU. Furthermore, it is alleged that some large factories are closing down under the guise of financial difficulty, but in fact largely as a consequence of the organising activities of BIGU; after a short period of time, such factories often re-open with a complete new workforce. These closures have culminated in the loss of employment for many of the industry's workers, as well as the loss of statutory entitlements due to them when a factory closes down (interview with Karmaker, 1996).

At the same time, BIGU's relationship with AAFLI has implicated the union in an alleged 'conspiracy' to ruin the Bangladeshi garments export industry through the controversial issue of child labour. From early 1995, numerous articles appeared in the nation's print media accusing AAFLI of being used and funded by vested interests in the West to bring to international attention the use of child labour in Bangladesh's export-oriented garment industry. Included in these allegations was the frequent claim that AAFLI's child-labour campaign was motivated by United States 'protectionism', aimed at destroying the garments export sector by making Bangladeshi garments 'costlier'.[10] This controversy over child labour has to be understood in the context of the passage of the Child Labor Deterrence Act – a bill proposed in 1992 by US Senator Tom Harkin in response to pressure from NGOs, especially the Child Labor Coalition in the United States. This bill proposed to make it illegal for overseas factories that employed children under the age of 15 to export their products to the United States, which would cause a crisis for the manufacturers of garments in Bangladesh: more than 50 per cent of the country's garment exports go to the United States. In response to the introduction of the Harkin Bill, many member garment manufacturers of the BGMEA laid off thousands of child workers (Economist Intelligence Unit, 1995: 17). With the impending passage of the legislation through Congress in 1995, BGMEA members prepared to get rid of their remaining child workers with no plans for support or rehabilitation. This threat mobilised a coalition of international agencies concerned about the negative consequences of the Harkin Bill. Rather than safeguarding the welfare of child workers, the effect of the US legislation would be to force these children – mainly girls – into more undesirable forms of work, such as prostitution.

The principal participants in the negotiations that followed were UNICEF, the ILO, the BGMEA and the US Embassy, and a Memorandum of Understanding (MOU) signed on 4 July 1995. Included under the terms of the MOU was the stipulation that appropriate provision be made for dismissed child workers to be placed into schools and for the families of these displaced young workers to be compensated for the loss of income (interview with Lokollo, 1996). Without going into the complexities of the prolonged negotiations leading up to the MOU (involving at times vigorous opposition from the BGMEA), AAFLI's role in the child-labour issue appears to have been no more than advisory. Specifically, AAFLI publicly took the position that if BGMEA members paid the legally prescribed minimum wage, paid overtime, provided nurseries and other facilities for the workers as required by the labour laws of Bangladesh, then adult workers would not be forced to send their children to work. As a result of this stance, AAFLI (and indirectly BIGU) fell victim to BGMEA's vilification campaign for bringing to attention their flagrant violations of the country's labour laws. However, the last thing the garment workers in Bangladesh want is the collapse of the industry: they seek nothing more than their statutory rights as industrial workers. This is clearly expressed in a BIGU press statement, released in response to allegations that the union was involved in calling for an international boycott of Bangladeshi garments:

> The garment industry is our lifeblood and we want nothing more than to see it thrive and to see workers share in the fruits of this industry.
>
> (*Almujadded*, 1995)

In all of the above reactions to the activism of BIGU, the Bangladeshi state has tolerated a general relaxation of the country's labour laws and the unscrupulous behaviour of many garment enterprise owners, so that the industry might flourish and continue to increase foreign-exchange earnings for the country. Together with the reality of state-sponsored unionism and continued political use of the export garment workers, the formation of BIGU appeared to be the only solution to the plight of these workers. This is clearly articulated in the following statement:

We knew that having our own union was the only chance we had to change our lives for the better. We knew that no one could help us unless we took the first step of helping ourselves The government of Bangladesh has looked the other way for years while the garment industry violated the labour laws … Part of the reason for this is a policy that sounds good – the government wanted the industry to grow and relaxed the laws to allow this to happen. There is another, perhaps more important, reason: many high officials in the government own garment factories and are enjoying the enhanced profits attributable to the lack of enforcement of the laws.

(Akhter, 1995: 2)

Conclusion

While there can be little doubt that the emergence of BIGU has shaken up labour relations in Bangladesh's garment industry, its longer term future is unclear. BIGU's capacity to withstand those oppositional forces bent on either totally destroying it or greatly restricting its operations will obviously depend on the unity of its members, the skill of its leadership and the continued financial and other assistance it is able to tap into. Certainly the road ahead will continue to be littered with economic and political obstacles. Nonetheless, while one must be cautious, it is important to recognise that some significant gains have been made. For the experience of struggle among the rank-and-file and BIGU's leaders has been invaluable in providing a basis for the future enhancement of self-organising.

Significantly, BIGU covers an industry whose low labour-organising potential is often attributed to its export-orientation and female-dominated workforce. However, this chapter has shown that production for export can have enabling effects on labour-organising capacities by promoting the spatial concentration of workers. It is only in this context that AAFLI has been able to provide much-needed legal and other assistance to the emerging union. While many employers have reacted to the union's formation by upping their levels of subcontracting, it is important to note that this is not specifically a forced response to globalisation. Difficult as organising is, production for export has been a foundation of recent formal activism by women workers in this industry. In this regard, the rise of BIGU has also been an important event in the story of women's more general socio-cultural status in Bangladesh.

Notes

1 This chapter is based on research I conducted during various field trips to Bangladesh between 1994 and 1996. For the most part, conversations I had with garment workers constituted a general forum of complaint in which the workers spoke of their long working hours, the lack of a weekly day-off so they could visit their family or village, the lack of facilities in the factories (including meal rooms, creches, ventilation and adequate bathrooms), low wages and the withholding of wages. I was always impressed by their obvious militancy and resolve to address these matters.

2 On this point, see also the chapters in this volume by Hutchison and Sargeson.

3 As with many other developing countries, Bangladesh has become heavily dependent on aid for development expenditure which, Rehman Sobhan argues, has compromised its political sovereignty by granting aid-givers unacceptable political dominance (Sobhan, 1990: 1). In addition, external financial assistance has become critical to the development of an industrial capitalist class 'whose entire fortunes are intimately tied up with access to external resources in the name of development' (Sobhan, 1989: 100).

4 An international comparison of garment workers' wages reveals that they vary

> from a high monthly wage of US$384 in Sweden, US$228 in Taiwan, US$114 in Hong Kong, to a low scale of US$63 in Pakistan, US$55 in India [and] US$29 in Bangladesh.
>
> (Hossain, Jahan and Sobhan, 1990: 38)

5 International organisations, such as the International Labour Organisation (ILO), the United Nations Children's Fund (UNICEF) and the United Nations Development Programme (UNDP) have also played prominent roles in the garments export industry in Bangladesh. The Women's Development Unit of UNICEF is particularly widely involved in training programmes for women in the field of skill development, including the skills required for export-oriented garment manufacture. Also, in association with the Bangladesh Garment Manufacturers and Employers Association (BGMEA), the Ministry of Labour and Manpower and Bureau of Manpower, Employment and Training, the ILO and the UNDP undertook a five-year training programme in the early 1990s with 'the immediate objectives [being] to establish a permanent institutional capacity for the training of middle management personnel, supervisors, technicians, skilled workers and trainers' (UNDP/ILO, 1995: 1). Even though these positions are mostly filled by males in the garment factories, female garment workers were encouraged to take up this training to enhance their chances of promotion.

6 ILO Conventions Nos 87 and 98 were ratified by the Pakistani state in 1948 and 1949 respectively. The former concerns the Freedom of Association and Protection of the Right to Organise, while the latter concerns the Right to Organise and Collective Bargaining.

7 For an account of other garment export factories in Bangladesh implicated in the persecution of the organising activities of BIGU, see ICFTU (1997).

8 As Gary Busch writes:

> The disaffiliation of the AFL–CIO in 1968 had a profound effect on Asian union development. It eliminated a source of funds for the ICFTU and created a rival body to interact with Asian labour, the AAFLI.
>
> (Busch, 1983: 131)

9 The source of this information cannot be divulged as anonymity was requested. However, I was able to sight a copy of a letter sent to the ICFTU affiliates in Bangladesh informing them of the programme.

10 See, for example, *Almujadded* (1995), *Daily Star* (1995), *Holiday* (1995), *Khabar* (1995) and *Financial Express* (1996).

Bibliography

Ahmad, Kamruddin (1978) *Labour Movement in Bangladesh*, Dhaka: Inside Library.

Ahmed, Alia (1991) 'The role of socio-economic structures and policies in determining the status of women in Bangladesh', *Women and Fertility in Bangladesh*, New Delhi: Sage, pp. 73–101.

Ahmed, Moudud (1984) *Bangladesh: Era of Sheikh Mujibur Rahman*, Wiesbaden: Franz Steiner Verlag.

Akhter, Nazma (1995) BIGU press release, Dhaka, November.

Alam, A.M. Quamral (1994) 'State and capital accumulation: The problems of capitalist transformation in Bangladesh', *South Asia* XVII, 1: 43–55.

Al-Faisal, Mahmud (1995) 'A pioneer labour leader speaks: Bangladesh Industrial Workers', *Dhaka Courier* 11, 42 (19 February): 21.

Ali, Tariq (1975) 'Pakistan and Bangladesh: Results and prospects', in Robin Blackburn (ed.) *Explosion in a Subcontinent: India, Pakistan, Bangladesh and Ceylon*, Harmondsworth: Pelican, pp. 293–346.

Banaji, Jairus (1977) 'Capitalist domination and the small peasantry: Deccan districts in the late nineteenth century', in special issue of *Economic and Political Weekly* August: 1,375–404.

BGMEA (Bangladesh Garment Manufacturers and Employers Association) (1996) *Newsletter* 7, 1 (January).

Bhuyan, M. Sayefullah (1986) 'Trade union movement', in S.R. Chakravarty and Virendra Narain (eds) *Bangladesh*, vol. 2, *Domestic Politics*, South Asia Studies Series 13, New Delhi: South Asian Publishers, pp. 160–9.

BIGU (Bangladesh Independent Garment-Workers' Union) (1994) *BIGU Constitution*, photocopied English translation, Dhaka: BIGU.

—— (1995) *Fact Sheet on Palmal Knitwear Factory*, Dhaka.

Busch, Gary (1983) *The Political Role of International Trade Unions*, London: Macmillan.

Dil, Shaheen F. (1985) 'Women in Bangladesh: Changing roles and sociopolitical realities', *Women and Politics* 5, 1 (Spring): 51–67.

Economist Intelligence Unit (1995) *Country Report: Bangladesh* 3rd quarter: 17–18.

Elson, Diane and Pearson, Ruth (1981) 'Nimble fingers make cheap workers: An analysis of women's employment in Third World export manufacturing', *Feminist Review* 7 (Spring): 87–107.

Export Promotion Bureau (1994) *Exports From Bangladesh: 1972–73 to 1993–94*, Dhaka.

Feldman, Shelley (1992) 'Crisis, Islam and gender in Bangladesh: The social construction of a female labour force', in Lourdes Beneria and Shelley Feldman (eds) *Unequal Burden: Economic Crises, Persistent Poverty and Women's Work*, Boulder: Westview Press, pp. 105–30.

—— (1993) 'Contradictions of gender inequality: Urban class formation in contemporary Bangladesh', in Alice W. Clarke (ed.) *Gender and Political Economy: Explorations of South Asian Systems*, Delhi: Oxford University Press, pp. 215–45.

Fröbel, F., Heinrichs, J. and Kreye, O. (1980) *The New International Division of Labour*, Cambridge: Cambridge University Press.

Heyzer, Noleen (1986) *Working Women in South-East Asia: Development, Subordination and Emancipation*, Philadelphia: Open University Press.

Hossain, Hameeda, Jahan, Roushan and Sobhan, Salma (1990) *No Better Option? Industrial Women Workers in Bangladesh*, Dhaka: University Press.

Hossain, Najmul and Brar, Jagjit S. (1988) 'The garment workers of Bangladesh: Earnings and perceptions towards unionism', *Journal of Business Administration* 14, 4 (October): 385–402.

Humphrey, Clare (1992) *Privatization in Bangladesh: Economic Transition in a Poor Country*, Asian edn, Dhaka: University Press.

ICFTU (International Confederation of Free Trade Unions) (1997) 'Bangladesh', *Annual Survey of Violations of Trade Union Rights*, Brussels: ICFTU, pp. 68–71.

Islam, Syed Serajul (1988) *Bangladesh: State and Economic Strategy*, Dhaka: University Press.

ITGLWF (International Textile, Garment and Leather Workers' Federation) (1995) 'Action to end reign of terror in garment industry urged', press release, Brussels, 23 November.

Kabeer, Naila (1988) 'Subordination and struggle: Women in Bangladesh', *New Left Review* 168 (March–April): 95–121.

—— (1991) 'Cultural dopes or rational fools', *European Journal of Development Research* 3, 1 (June): 133–60.

—— (1994) *Reversed Realities: Gender Hierarchies in Development Thought*, London: Verso.

Kabir, Khushi (1987) 'Non-government organisation in Bangladesh: Strategies and approaches', *Association of Development Agencies in Bangladesh* XIV, 3 (May–June): 38–46.

Kamaluddin, S. (1991) 'NIP in the bud: Bangladesh aims to boost private industry', *Far Eastern Economic Review* 15 August: 45–6.

—— (1995) 'Striking at the economy: Can the country afford its agitating politicians?', *Far Eastern Economic Review* 28 September: 34.

Karim, Nehal (1994) *Exploitation, Domination and Alienation: The Genesis of Bangladesh*, Dhaka: Osmania Library.

Kaye, Lincoln (1986) 'All dressed up but … : Bangladesh is unlikely to fill its new US garment quotas', *Far Eastern Economic Review* 16 October: 68–9.

Khan, Salma (1993) *The Fifty Percent: Women in Development and Policy in Bangladesh*, Dhaka: University Press.

Kochanek, Stanley (1993) *Patron–Client Politics and Business in Bangladesh*, New Delhi: Sage.

Lim, Linda (1978) 'Multinational firms and manufacturing for export in less-developed countries: The case of the electronics industry in Malaysia and Singapore', Ph.D. thesis, University of Michigan.

McCarthy, Florence and Feldman, Shelley (1983) 'Rural women discovered: New sources of capital and labour in Bangladesh', *Development and Change* 14, 2: 211–36.

Mannan, M.A. (1989) *Status of Women in Bangladesh: Equality of Rights Theory and Practice*, Research Report no. 113, Dhaka: Bangladesh Institute of Development Studies.

Munck, Ronaldo (1988) *The New International Labour Studies: An Introduction*, London: Zed Books.

Nations, Richard (1971) 'The economic structure of Pakistan: Class and colony', *New Left Review* 68 (July–August): 3–26.

Nurullah, S.M. (1993) *Industrial Relations: Trade Unions and Role of Government in Bangladesh*, research paper, The Hague: Institute of Social Studies.

Rahman, Ferdausur (1986) 'Bangladesh', *Evolution of Labour Legislation in Asia*, Hong Kong: Documentation for Action Group in Asia (DAGA), pp. 121–32.

Rahman, Masihur (1994) *Structural Adjustment, Employment and Workers: Public Policy Issues and Choices for Bangladesh*, Dhaka: University Press.

Ramaswamy, E.A. (1979) 'Politics and organized labour in India', in R. Cohen, P.C.W. Gutkind and P. Brazier (eds) *Peasants and Proletarians: The Struggles of Third World Workers*, New York: Monthly Review Press, pp. 286–302.

Rhee, Yung Whee (1990) 'The catalyst model of development: Lessons from Bangladesh's success with garment exports', *World Development* 18, 2: 333–46.

Sims, Beth (1992) *Workers of the World Undermined: American Labor's Role in US Foreign Policy*, Boston: South End Press.

Sobhan, Rehman (1989) 'Bangladesh and the world economic system: The crisis of external dependence', in Hamza Alavi and John Harris (eds) *South Asia: Sociology of Developing Societies*, Houndmills: Macmillan, pp. 100–11.

—— (ed.) (1990) *From Aid Dependence to Self Reliance: Development Options for Bangladesh*, Dhaka: Bangladesh Institute of Development Studies and Dhaka University Press.

Stivens, Maila (1998) 'Theorizing gender, power and modernity in affluent Asia', in Krishna Sen and Maila Stivens (eds) *Gender and Power in Affluent Asia*, London: Rout ledge, pp. 1–34.

UNDP (United Nations Development Programme)/ILO (International Labour Organisation) (1995) 'An overview of the UNDP/ILO project BGD/85/153', Dhaka.

White, Sarah (1992) *Arguing with the Crocodile: Gender and Class in Bangladesh*, Dhaka: University Press.

Articles

Almujadded (1995) 'Conspiracy going on to destroy garment industry', press release, 15 November.

Daily Star (1995) 'Garments' billion dollar gamble', 25 May.

Financial Express (1996) 'BGSF demands ban on AAFLI activities', 8 February.

Free Labour World (1996) 'Repression made to order', 7 June.

Holiday (1995) 'Garments disputants return to negotiating table', 2 June.

Khabar (1995) 'Garment industry: Demand to take action against AAFLI and Rosaline', 29 January.

Interviews

Akhter, Farida (1994) Executive Director, UBINIG (Alternative Policy Research for Development), Dhaka, January.

Akhter, Nazma and Yeasmin, Lovely (1996) General and Press Secretary and Organiser, BIGU (Bangladesh Independent Garment-Workers' Union), Dhaka, February.

Amin, Amirul Haque (1995) General Secretary, National Garment Workers' Federation, Dhaka, January.

Bashar, Abul (1996) President, National Workers' Federation, Dhaka, February.

Firoze, Fawzia Karim (1996) President, Bangladesh National Women Lawyers' Association, and BIGU lawyer, Dhaka, February.

Hossain, Abul (1996) President, Bangladesh Garment Workers and Employees' Federation, Dhaka, February.

Karmaker, Ranjan (1996) Coordinator, Steps Towards Development, Dhaka, February.

Khan, Anisuddin (1996) General Secretary, Bangladesh Free Trade Union Congress, Dhaka, February.

Lokollo, Hans J. (1996) Deputy Director, International Labour Office, Dhaka, January.

Rahman, Mukhlesur (1996) President, Bangladesh United Workers' Federation, Dhaka, February.

Sigelakis, Lydia (1996) Country Representative, Asian-American Free Labour Institute, Dhaka, February.

3 Assembling class in a Chinese joint venture factory

Sally Sargeson

This chapter argues that participation in transnational manufacturing and the establishment of labour market conditions that are intended to facilitate economic globalisation need not have wholly negative consequences for labour. Instead, these circumstances may actually provide some workers with new opportunities to educate and organise themselves around improvements in their working conditions. Certainly, this is what I observed among young women workers in a joint venture factory in Zhejiang province in China. In the course of outlining their story, I shall trace in one factory the intersections between processes of globalisation, national policy development and local conflicts over class.

First, consider the picture many scholars draw of the impact of globalisation on manufacturing workforces. We are told that, pressured by the threat of capital flight to sites boasting lower waged, more compliant labour forces, workers have little choice but to accede to the demands of transnational firms (Broad, 1995; Gough, 1992). Two demands that are of specific concern to my case study are (1) workers' acceptance of productivity-based wage schemes and greater employer flexibility in hiring and task allocation, and (2) marked reductions in the role unions play in representing workers' interests (Liemt, 1992; Thomas, 1995). Both these developments are held to be inimical to workers because they contribute to the intensification of pressures on productivity, the individualisation of employees and the political disempowerment of organised labour (Bryan, 1995; Western, 1995).

Workers' apparent inability to resist their exploitation, individualisation and the erasure of their public voice is often explained by related factors operating at the national and local level. Governments eager to attract new overseas investors and discourage established businesses from leaving, provide an ideological and regulatory environment conducive to global capital accumulation (Bryan, 1995; Piven, 1995). Notably they implement indigenised brands of neo-liberal economic policy, propagate a meritocratic ideology, introduce legislative and coercive measures to eliminate inflexibilities in national labour markets and constrain the activities of labour organisations. These measures are legitimated and popularised as providing 'freedoms', 'choices' and 'opportunities for advancement' (Strinati, 1990). Meanwhile, at the enterprise level, corporate models of management that tie workers' lifelong employment and material interests to the market success of the enterprise are further thought to militate against labour organising.

Workers' vulnerability has also been traced to the composition and character of workforces in transnational manufacturing. The preponderance of temporarily employed migrants, outworkers and subcontractors certainly encourages feelings of marginality, job insecurity and isolation (Castells, 1979; Cohen, 1991). However, Deyo (1984) suggests that these effects are compounded by gendered socialisation which reduces the career motivation and collective orientation of many unskilled young women workers in labour-intensive manufacturing. Still other studies point to sectoral and workplace divisions along ethnic and racial lines (Balibar and Wallerstein, 1991; AMRC, 1995; Lee, 1995) and to workers' reliance on patronage within firms and external support networks rather than labour organisations. All of these factors are considered obstacles to workers developing an awareness of common problems and acting cooperatively to remedy them.

Yet, in the course of conducting ethnographic research in a Chinese joint venture factory, I found that (at the precise moment when the enterprise was threatened with the removal of production to cheaper, more disciplined locations offshore) young, non-unionised, migrant female workers were able to mount a covert campaign to eliminate divisions between local and migrant employees. More importantly, a key aspect of this campaign was their positive utilisation of what are usually thought to be mechanisms of workers' disempowerment. Specifically, the migrant workers appropriated a meritocratic, productivist discourse to justify their tactics to one another and to prompt management to eliminate the pay and promotion system that set local workers apart from migrants in the factory. Moreover, during their campaign these workers said that the absence of a trade union granted them advantages of invisibility and tactical flexibility, and reduced the degree of commitment, coordination and risk-taking required of them.

The workers' actions resulted in no immediate material gains; on the contrary, they assisted in the introduction of an employment system designed to intensify the productivity of their labour. Yet, by their actions, they made gains in consciousness-raising and organising. The workers reconstructed political allegiances in the factory, thereby establishing the possibility of future renegotiations with management over the terms of their participation in transnational manufacturing. In short, they began assembling class relations in place of those based on workers' place-of-origin.

In pursuing the argument that globalisation has not had entirely debilitating effects on these Chinese workers, I shall begin by critically examining two influential sets of assumptions about ideological hegemony and the practice of labour politics. This will be followed by an outline of government moves to construct the conditions that allow Chinese firms to participate in the global economy, conditions that are shown to have been crucial to the expansion of the case-study enterprise: Jinshagang factory.[1] The major part of this chapter then examines the organisation of production and pay schemes in this particular factory, workers' resistance to those schemes and the consequent restructuring of the factory's production regime. It concludes by discussing how struggles over workplace organisation and wages in a transnational manufacturing site can have both narrow economic *and* broader political aims and consequences – for workers as well as their employers.[2]

Theorising workers' tactics

In the explanations of workers' disempowerment *vis-à-vis* globalisation sketched above, two important propositions are made. The first is that the control of labour by states and capital is facilitated by ideological hegemony; the second is that this control is further underpinned by political regulation and the ineffectiveness of labour organisations. Both these propositions tend to cast workers as the victims of structural changes wrought by states and capital.

As a concept, 'ideological hegemony' denotes the ideas and symbols which persuade and organise people to support existing relations of accumulation and domination (Gramsci, 1971: 375–7; Thompson, 1990; Giddens, 1991: 22). By a variety of means, workers are encouraged to believe that market competition is a fair and healthy mechanism by which to allocate wealth and labour. Of course, they do not necessarily concur with, much less internalise, such ideas: numerous studies show that new workers draw on counter-hegemonic ideas, structures and practices from their folk cultures in response (Taussig, 1980; Ong, 1987; Nash, 1989). However, it is often concluded that these cultural complexes invert, rather than efface, existing political-economic hierarchies. For example, in her study of Bolivian tin miners, June Nash observes that, instead of inspiring substantive change, the workers' culture may have actually strengthened relations of ownership and domination in that it

> provided the myths that justified the polarized wealth and cultivated a desire on the part of workers to become a part of that dominant group.
>
> (Nash, 1989: 318–19)

Similarly, Elizabeth Perry (1996: 3) argues that East Asian workers display much more interest in achieving higher social status and escaping from the working class into the ranks of officialdom, the intelligentsia or the bourgeoisie, than they do in contesting the structures and institutions that subordinate them as workers.

Ultimately, these studies highlight the effectiveness of ideological hegemony. In so doing, they assume nothing exists between this and revolutionary class consciousness (Wood, 1995: 105). But if evaluations of the counter-hegemonic potential in workers' cultures continue to rely on a fixed, essentialist notion of what 'really' comprises proletarian opposition, it is likely they will miss workers' efforts to appropriate hegemonic ideologies in ways that do not directly oppose the bourgeoisie but nevertheless do alter workers' identities and their relations with one another. In other words, they will ignore important processes by which workers forge collectivities.

Scholars often also assume that, in order to be potent, labour politics must be conducted by independent proletarian organisations which mirror in size, structure and modes of operation the other organisations and institutions that order and govern societies. For example, Deyo concludes that strong union leadership and broad participation in formally constituted unions are essential to effective labour activism. He finds that in their absence in Asia's export industries: 'where protest does take collective forms ... it occurs among small isolated groups, with minimal organisation and little chance of success' (Deyo, 1984: 283). The implication of the belief in unions as workers' only effective means of protection and emancipation, combined with the recognition that those same organisational vehicles are unable to deal with contemporary global challenges, is that workers have no viable means by which to resist their individualisation and the intensification of exploitation (Gough, 1992; Larochelle, 1992; Western, 1995).

But even apparently 'unsuccessful' attempts at mutual education, collective organisation and resistance are critical to the development of labour activism and therefore ought not to be passed over – especially in countries where the experience of wage labour is relatively new. Why assume that unions – which are the outcomes of prior struggles – are the essential instigators of worker activism? Formal labour organisations are visible and, consequently, readily susceptible to regulation, repression and sabotage. In situations where a repressive state has co-opted trade unions, might not workers draw on other forms of association? If, as in China, unions are integral to the state's strategies for controlling labour, informal patterns of organisation and *ad hoc* tactics of resistance might sometimes be more suitable vehicles for workers' struggles.

Certainly, Elizabeth Perry (1993; 1995) has convincingly demonstrated that in China in the early twentieth century, labour fragmentation, the absence of formal labour unions and the formation of exclusive, vertically aligned, non-proletarian associations did not preclude agitation by workers to improve their conditions and incomes. China's manufacturing workforce has historically been characterised by a high degree of activism by groups formed around ethnicity, place-of-origin, gender, occupation and the snobberies associated with job and enterprise status (Perry, 1997).[3] However, in the contemporary era, despite the integration that is currently taking place between Chinese and global capital, Perry (1995: 325) suggests that workers in China will remain blinkered by 'traditional' patterns of resistance, particularistic affiliations and a concern with place, face and status. In short, their activism will not take collective forms. Yet my observations suggest that even organising that appears to centre on place-of-origin might actually aim to educate workers politically and pave the way for more inclusive arrangements.

As I show in the following section, the Chinese state and employers have devised a coherent set of strategies designed to facilitate economic growth. They have targeted the shopfloor as a site that must be known and managed, and have isolated Chinese workers as a subject group upon which they wish to impose their will. To this end, they have propagated a neo-liberal meritocratic ideology, have undertaken labour market reform, have implemented laws and regulations governing the organisational forms and repertoire of actions available to workers both outside and inside the workplace, and have developed state-of-the-art methods for managing stringent production regimes, including using place-of-origin as a basis for organisational hierarchies and wage systems.

Workers have responded to these strategies by deploying what De Certeau (1984) describes as 'tactics'. Tactics are 'a way of using' – the manner in which the less powerful, at critical points in time, put systems of knowledge and management to use in ways not intended by their makers, with a view to subversion or carving out a space which they can manoeuvre in. The tactics I observed workers in Jinshagang factory adopting did not focus on the construction of a site exterior and opposed to the hegemonic discourses of neo-liberalism and meritocracy, labour market policies or managerial practices of state and employers. Nor did they involve attempting to develop or seek assistance from unions, for to do so would have been self-defeating. Rather, their tactics were created from *within* those discourses, policies and practices, and carried out in an apparently (dis)organised, clandestine manner. Their objective, and the end result of their actions, was to foreground workers' common experiences of production and exploitation over the local/migrant definitions that had previously underpinned management's control of the labour process and divided workers. In this way, they established a basis for worker solidarity using tools forged by their employers and the state.

Strategies for globalising China

In 1978, the Chinese government decided to increase the country's level of interaction with the world economy. The profound consequences of this decision are illustrated by the increase in levels of foreign investment and lending to China, and by the remarkable growth of China's exports. China is now the second most popular destination in the world for foreign direct investment and has one of the largest foreign debts among low- and middle-income countries (Lardy, 1995; *Beijing Review*, 14–20 December 1998). Between 1978 and 1996, the value of China's exports grew more than fifteenfold (PRC State Statistical Bureau, 1997). Foreign-invested firms and export-oriented rural enterprises involved in labour-intensive light manufacturing have been at the forefront of this growth in trade (Kueh, 1992; Lardy, 1995). Moreover, despite the Chinese government's attempts to encourage export growth in more capital-intensive, technologically advanced industries, between the mid-1980s and 1990s labour-intensive manufactures actually came to represent an increasingly large proportion of all China's exports (*Beijing Review*, 18–24 September 1995; PRC State Statistical Bureau, 1995; Zhu, 1995).

Chinese firms' participation in global processes of production, exchange and capital accumulation has been facilitated by a range of government policies.

Various new kinds of private property rights have been created and many formerly publicly owned businesses have been leased or sold (Gao, 1996). New laws protecting copyright and contracts have been promulgated, exchange and tariff rates have been adjusted, banking and credit reformed, pricing deregulated, and obstacles to the repatriation of foreign profits have been dismantled (Leong, 1997). Of greater relevance to this study, however, are the strategies that central and local governments have adopted to ensure that plentiful, compliant labour will attract foreign investors to China, thereby facilitating the growth of China's domestic export-oriented industries (Casati, 1991; Murray, 1994; Zhu, 1995). Most significantly, they have overseen the development of a competitive labour market, regulated relations between employers and workers, and created an ideological climate that is conducive to capitalist relations of production and accumulation.

In transforming labour power into a marketable commodity, administrative and legal barriers to geographical and job mobility are being dismantled. This has allowed approximately 200 million rural residents to find a livelihood in the non-agricultural sector.[4] The labour allocation role once played by government Labour Bureaux has largely been eliminated, as have the permanent jobs they dispensed. Workers are now employed directly by enterprises for contractual periods and can be fired for breach of contract or 'in times of severe business difficulties' (*Zhongguo laodong bao*, 26 January 1993; *Survey of World Broadcasts*, 17 December 1994). These moves have paved the way for mass lay-offs in the inefficient, overstaffed state-owned sector of the economy (*Gongren ribao*, 8 June 1992; *Zhongguo laodong bao*, 20 November 1992). In 1998, approximately 12 million urban employees were made redundant (*Beijing Review*, 23–9 November 1998). The growing number of urban unemployed have been told, in very clear terms, that in the future they will have to compete against some 130 million rural residents for jobs (*Zhongguo laodong bao*, 7 May 1992; *Zhejiang ribao*, 26 October 1992).

The formation of a competitive labour market in the context of a massive surplus of semi- and unskilled labour is fundamental to the government's strategy of restraining wage levels and disciplining labour, as this report makes clear:

> To check fundamentally the expansion of consumption funds, and check the continuous rise of the aggregate wage level, we must utilize our 'unlimited supply of labor' … Forming a labor market and labor mobility will not only create a direct check on wage increases through employment competition. It will also help lower people's expectations and self-evaluation, thus indirectly checking wage increases through the 'upward emulation' mentality.
> (Chinese Economic System Reform Research Institute, 1987: 19–20)[5]

The labour force is also strictly regulated by legislative and institutional means. Strikes are prohibited, unless a workplace is proven to be unsafe. Labour arbitration committees, established since 1986 to mediate the rising number of illegal strikes and disputes (Jiang, 1995), are said to be hampered by the intervention of interested government departments and are accused of sometimes acting in collusion with employers (*Zhongguo laodong bao*, 16 May 1992; *Fazhi ribao*, 8 October 1992; *Baokan wenzhai*, 24 November 1992; *Gongren ribao*, 5 March 1993). Otherwise, public security personnel have been used to intimidate and imprison protesting workers (*Survey of World Broadcasts*, 3 April 1996).

Union organisations are the main institutional means by which the government constrains part of the labour force. All legitimate trade unions in China are integrated into the All China Federation of Trade Unions (hereafter ACFTU), which is under the control of the Communist Party and government.[6] Independent trade unions are thus banned. Those that have been formed have been brutally repressed and their leaders gaoled.[7] In the post-Mao era, the ACFTU has begun to recruit members outside the state sector and adopt a more independent position relative to the Party and government (Chan, 1993). However, between 1990 and 1996, the total number of union branches declined and, despite the addition of approximately 85 million people to the non-agricultural labour force, union membership remained virtually stagnant (PRC State Statistical Bureau, 1997: 94, 735). The ACFTU's own research moreover shows that even relatively privileged urban workers in the state sector do not believe the union possesses either the will or the capacity to defend workers' interests (Wu and Guo, 1989; *Gongren ribao*, 1 July 1992, 25 February 1993). Rather, it is widely held that the union's brief is to propagandise Party policy and inculcate in workers attitudes that will be serviceable in a globalised economy. Such a view is informed by ACFTU statements applauding the virtues of a competitive spirit, self-reliance, hard work and productivity, and of an understanding of the efficiency, fairness and freedom of contractual relations:

> In reality contract jobs help guarantee the position of workers as masters, because if workers' remuneration is not equitable then they can negotiate, and if negotiations are unsatisfactory then they can leave.
>
> (*Zhongguo laodong bao*, 1 December 1992)[8]

However, even the limited degree of protection and representation afforded urban employees by the ACFTU and non-union organisations such as Workers' Congresses[9] is not available to most employees of the export-oriented, foreign-invested, township and village enterprises that are at the cutting edge of China's integration with the global economy. Few of these have any form of representative labour organisation (AMRC, 1995; Lau, 1995). Yet it is these enterprises which most frequently have been found to have disregarded safety standards, withheld wages, extended working hours beyond the legal maximum and imposed illegal penalties on workers in the pursuit of high profits (Anonymous, 1992; *Gongren ribao*, 18 February 1993; Chan, 1995; Jiang, 1995). In 1994, when the ACFTU launched a membership drive and began to popularise collective-bargaining procedures among foreign and joint venture employees, many local governments moved to restore confidence among investors and enterprise managers by promising to prohibit the formation of union cells and repress any 'social unrest' caused by ACFTU organisers (Chan, 1995; *EIU Business China*, 29 May 1995; *Agence France Presse*, 14 March 1996).

The government has also tried to ensure that labour remains cheap and quiescent by launching a propaganda campaign that promotes market-determined meritocratic principles as the most just and efficient criteria for recruitment, wage-setting and promotion. The state-owned media daily repeats the message that in all 'fair' wage systems there are direct causal links between workers' improved productivity and the profitability of enterprises, and between enterprise profitability and higher incomes for workers (*Hangzhou ribao*, 21 May 1992). The piece-rate and quota-contracting wage systems found in capitalist countries and in foreign-invested and rural enterprises – purportedly based on supply-and-demand signals and on 'scientifically' established methods of evaluation – are held up as models to be emulated in all sectors of the economy (*Zhongguo laodong bao*, 12 May, 18 June 1992; *Gongren ribao*, 7, 9 July 1992). News reports abound with detailed accounts of workers who have been rendered unemployed because of their enterprise's failure to adapt to the law of the market and implement a meritocratic system of promotion and wage payments (*Gongren ribao*, 11 June 1992, 17 February 1993).

Despite the government's espousal of allowing individual productivity, enterprise profitability and the market to determine wage levels, it has carefully monitored wages and, on a number of occasions, has intervened to curb rises. For example, in August 1990 the government imposed a cap on the salaries of Chinese nationals employed in foreign-invested enterprises so as to limit wage pressures in the state sector (Casati, 1991: 17). Before the introduction of China's first ever minimum-wage standards, under the Labour Law of January 1995, Chen Gang (legal director for the Ministry of Labour) hastened to reassure businesses that local governments would set minimum-wage levels that were appropriate to 'local economic conditions'. Therefore they need not fear the new standards would 'eat up their profits' (*Survey of World Broadcasts*, 17 December 1994).

In creating these labour market conditions, regulatory institutions and the ideology of a market-determined meritocracy, the Chinese government has established an environment that is conducive to global production, the extraction of surplus value and accumulation. But is Dick Bryan (1995: 6) correct to suggest that the only winner in this situation can be capital? Not all the workers I observed at Jinshagang factory think so. Indeed, some have expressed enthusiasm about the possibilities – political as well as material – opened up by domestic market reforms and their participation in transnational production (Geng and Li, 1989; *Gongren ribao*, 28 February 1993). Jinshagang factory is in many ways representative of the sorts of factories that are at the forefront of China's globalisation. Thus an examination of developments within it helps to illuminate some of the reasons for workers' optimism.

Jinshagang: Globalising a local factory

Jinshagang Electronic Components Factory is located in a wealthy suburban village on the outskirts of Hangzhou, the capital of Zhejiang province. The original factory was established in 1978 as a village-owned collective – the land and a building provided by the village government, with equipment and technical support coming from a research institute which had built on village land. The factory was contracted to Mao Senlin, who is still its managing director.

The factory's short history mirrors China's swing from autarky towards globalisation. Initially, the factory used locally produced components to assemble electronic calculators for the domestic market. However, within a few years competition from cheaper, more sophisticated imports forced the factory to switch to the production of simple school laboratory equipment. In 1985, Mao Senlin was introduced to a representative from the Japan-based Toshiba corporation, who was searching for a contractor to take over the assembly of components from a state factory that could not meet deadlines and quality requirements. Within a matter of months, Jinshagang had become a 'captive component supplier' for Toshiba.[10] Toshiba provided the factory with equipment and materials, and the factory switched its entire production routine to the assembly of electric plugs and switches. While the bulk of the factory's business still lies with Toshiba, it has signed two additional contracts to produce greeting cards and plastic clothes bags for Japanese firms. These companies also provided all the equipment necessary to manufacture their products. All output is exported to Japan, either for sale or for further assembly and re-export from Japan.

Subcontracting to Japanese companies has proven to be profitable and the firm has grown markedly. A new building was constructed in 1991, but within a year this was already unable to accommodate the growing volume of production. Two subsidiary factories were thus established. Nevertheless, in late 1992 the factory had to subcontract some of the simpler assembly work to another factory in a nearby town in order to cope with increased demand. In the space of seven years, the value of annual sales had increased from a few hundred thousand yuan to more than 13 million yuan, and the in-house workforce had increased from the original 25 staff and workers to more than 600.

In 1992, Mao Senlin moved to try to increase and consolidate his family's stake in the collectively owned business. On the strength of his successful management of the factory, Mao Senlin renegotiated the future payment of dividends to the village government. Payment was fixed at 50 per cent of the 1992 profits, plus an increase of 10 per cent per annum. Mao Senlin was given the right to distribute the remainder of profits as he pleased (including the right to set all salaries and bonuses) and to make all decisions about reinvestment and expansion. As the office manager remarked, this effectively resulted in the factory becoming a semi-private[11] firm:

The Maos didn't own the capital to begin with, but over time they began to use it as their own. They are worth millions now.

Despite its rapid growth and these changes to property rights in the factory, the Maos were still concerned about the long-term viability of the business. Mao Senlin's son, Mao Jian, who manages Jinshagang factory, told me at the end of 1992 that his Japanese clients had warned them that, if their rising prices were not offset by improved product quality, they would redirect equipment and future orders to Vietnam. The Maos feared that if they insisted on improvements in product quality, workers might then respond by demanding wage rises. Of course, this could flow on to higher (and therefore less competitive) production costs. The first means by which manager Mao tried to maintain low production costs was to convert the factory into a joint venture firm,[12] in order to become eligible for a three-year tax holiday:

> If I am to inherit [*sic*] this factory and just continue to sell our processing facilities, I might not be able to keep going. At the moment we are doing fairly well. But compared to other places in Southeast Asia – Taiwan, Malaysia – we can't possibly compete with them because of their high quality and technology. And now Vietnam and the Philippines represent an even greater threat to our labour-intensive industries because they are even cheaper than we are … We can still offer fairly cheap labour for a few more years if we don't have to pay tax, and that will give us time to grow and diversify.

Mao's concern that workers would react to management demands for quality improvements by pressing for higher wages seems odd. After all, many of the conditions that supposedly disempower workers – international competitors, mobile capital, pro-business national and local governments, no union, and an insecure migrant workforce surrounded by a massive reserve army of labour – were present in this factory. His reaction, however, illustrates the point that employers cannot be assumed to have an entirely 'free hand' over their employees, even when those employees lack formal means for organising (Haiven, Edwards and Bélanger, 1994: 278–9). Mao *was* concerned and tried to pre-empt any demands for higher wages. The second ingredient in Mao's plan to ensure the future of 'his' factory therefore involved the introduction of a new promotion and payment system for local employees to boost both productivity and product quality. This suggests that relations between groups of workers, as well as between managers and workers, have implications for the conditions under which globalisation proceeds.

The local politics of paying for global production

From its foundation, employees of Jinshagang factory had been allocated to positions according to the manager's own perception of their 'trustworthiness and loyalty to the factory'. All original supervisory and office staff were village residents who had close kinship or social connections with the Mao family. As the factory expanded and migrant workers began to be recruited, local residence became the principal criterion for promotion from the production line into supervisory positions. In 1992, local recruits were appointed to technical jobs or lower-level management positions within a few months of their arrival.[13] All but four of the thirty-eight managerial, supervisory and technical jobs at Jinshagang were thus held by local residents.[14]

As is the case with most export-oriented light manufacturing in China, all of the factory's labour-intensive production work was done by more than 570 young, female migrant workers, or 'outsiders' (AMRC, 1995; Lau, 1995; Lee, 1995). These women, who mostly came from rural areas in the neighbouring provinces of Anhui and Jiangxi, had relied on place-of-origin and kinship networks to help them find jobs in Hangzhou's competitive labour market. Their reasons for coming to the city were primarily economic: average individual incomes in their places-of-origin were approximately half what they could earn at Jinshagang factory (PRC State Statistical Bureau, 1996: 303).[15] Once recruited, their commitment to factory work was further secured by their payment of a 200-yuan bond – equivalent to almost a month's wages.

The factory's pay system similarly established local residence as the principal division in the workplace. The salaries of local employees were not linked to individual productivity, as was the case for the migrants. Instead, they reflected rank in the management hierarchy and the annual profits of the firm. All local employees received a fixed monthly wage. The managing director and factory manager both received 1,000 yuan per month, while the lowest level supervisory staff (small group leaders) received 250 yuan per month.[16] In addition to their fixed wage, all locals received an annual Spring Festival cash bonus. In 1992, the managing director received 470,000 yuan, the factory manager received more than 20,000 yuan and small group leaders received between 3,000 and 5,000 yuan. The differentials in position and pay that were determined by local residence were strongly resented by migrant employees:

> It's okay for *them*! They get a lot each month and their jobs are much lighter than ours are. They don't have to sit still in their chairs from morning till night, chafing their fingers on pieces of wire. The locals get all the easy jobs and all the money, while we outsiders do all the hard work. At least with capitalism, you get paid in the same way, for hours worked or items produced. Not because of where you come from or who you know.

Despite the *de facto* privatisation of the factory, local employees' knowledge that the factory had begun with collective funding and their experiences of automatic promotion and profit-sharing encouraged them to continue to view the factory as a collective village firm and to behave as they thought part-owners should. They exercised constant surveillance over migrant workers on the shopfloor, monitoring their rate and quality of output. When nagging them to increase productivity or pay more attention to quality, they stated that this would help boost factory profits and thereby result in improved working conditions, better food in the canteen or the possibility that they would be given an extra (unpaid) day's holiday at Spring Festival. They refused to allow migrant workers to chat with their neighbours or to move freely about the workshops. When talking about or giving orders to workers, the locally hired employees spoke loudly and in an authoritative, brusque manner and (as this excerpt from my field notes indicates) they attempted to publicly shame workers who had produced substandard articles:

> *Group leader, holding up a few greeting cards and turning to face other workers on the shop floor:* Look at this! Really, what an idiot! I've told her so many times and she still can't get it right! How can you be so stupid? Stop work immediately before you ruin any more materials. Come with me!

In contrast to the collectivist ethos fostered among local employees by their preferential treatment and profit-linked wages, migrant workers' pay was structured in such a way as to simultaneously maximise output, ensure product quality, individualise workers and set them in competition with each other. Their pay principally comprised piece-payments and a bonus. This resulted in total monthly incomes of between 170 and 220 yuan. Workers appealed to management to improve piece-payments several times between 1989 and 1992. However, the two wage-adjustments that were made barely compensated for inflation.

Migrant workers' monthly bonus payments were linked to their achievement of stringent quality norms. Workers were required to check the quality of each batch of components they received from upstream. If a worker found a mistake, they could claim the piece-payments of the worker who had last handled the components. If they did not detect the mistake and it was found by the next worker downstream, both would not only lose their piece-rates to the third worker, but their monthly bonus payments would also be reduced. Workers sometimes tried to resist the individualising effects of this quality system by hiding mistakes. In doing so, they risked loud abuse and fines if discovered by local supervisors, who rightly perceived the concealment of mistakes as an attempt to prioritise worker solidarity over enterprise profitability. A final aspect of the factory's divisive remuneration system was that, at Spring Festival, migrant workers only received small gifts instead of the sizeable cash bonuses given to locals.

Not surprisingly, the different roles accorded local and non-local workers and the discriminatory wage scheme that operated at the factory fuelled regional and modernist prejudices that predated the interaction of these particular groups of people at Jinshagang factory. Local workers described migrants as primitive intruders in their modern, industrialised urban community:

> They are peasants, these people. Not workers. Everyone knows Anhui people are quite uncivilised. Not like us.

Nevertheless, they acknowledged the advantages to be gained from employing these intruders:

> They certainly know how to work hard, these peasants! Not like city people who work in factories, who will just do a few minutes' work then wander off to chat with a friend.

Migrant workers similarly identified the principal boundary in the factory as being that between locals and migrants. But from their perspective, the defining characteristics of those on the other side of that boundary were not territory or modernity, but rather locals' performance of surveillance, coercive and extractive functions for management in return for rewards of money and power:

> The locals make a lot more money than we do. We do all the work that makes their profits, but we get nothing! If they aren't telling us what to do, how to work faster and make fewer mistakes, counting what we have made, checking it, threatening to reduce our bonuses, they don't even talk to us!

Migrant workers frequently complained that because local employees functioned as management's ever-present eyes and ears on the shopfloor, they were unable to organise collectively to pressure management to improve their pay and conditions. But migrant production workers were not only prevented from engaging in collective action by being surrounded by, and pitched against, local supervisors. Production workers were set apart by their own diverse origins and the fact that the new arrivals among them were grateful just to be given a job, a dormitory bed and a minimal wage. City jobs were hard to come by, any bed in the city was better than none and even a minimal wage was considerably more than they could earn in their home villages.

Merit and (dis)organised tactics

Migrant workers' dissatisfaction over the operation of this divide-and-rule strategy came to a head in late 1992 when, in response to the threats made by the factory's Japanese clients, the manager insisted that workshop supervisors improve product quality and productivity. These pressures were, in turn, transmitted via local small group leaders to production workers.

At first, when migrant workers heard through their supervisors that the future of orders was being linked to stricter quality requirements, they simply grumbled that this was just another production campaign:

> Always quality, quality, quality! Overtime, overtime, overtime! Deduct for this and deduct for that!

Over a period of a few weeks, however, it became obvious to them that this threat was being taken seriously by all levels of the factory hierarchy. In an atmosphere of impending crisis, workers developed a coherent set of tactics to pressure manager Mao to overturn the pay and promotion system that set locals against migrants. Yet they were never formally organised. Indeed, when migrant workers did begin to utilise these (dis)organised tactics, several told me that they actually benefited from not being coordinated in any formal sense. They reasoned that, as members of the ACFTU, they would have had to put their fate in the hands of a salaried urban official who was responsible to local Party and government heads. The manager, they knew, was a Party member and on very close terms with not only the village government leader, but also heads of the district government's Bureaux of Labour and of Industry and Commerce. They did not believe they would be given a fair hearing by these networks of powerful urbanites: 'They wouldn't listen to young female outsiders like us!'

Further, for them to engage in independent public agitation, it would have been necessary to gather together to devise a plan of action, draw up a list of complaints and demands, and present these to the manager and perhaps even the local Labour Bureau. They said they simply could not expect their fellow migrants to bear the risks involved:

> If we want to change anything we have to be united. But that's the problem: getting everyone to act together! Some of the girls have just arrived and paid their 200-yuan bond. It's probably the first time they have ever been in the city, so they are very timid. They are helping to support their families in the villages. Some have lost their homes in floods, and they are sending money back to rebuild their houses. They'd be frightened they would get fired and lose their bond if they complained.

If they were not formally organised and publicly agitating, the dissemination of ideas and canvassing of support could take place in a non-threatening environment. Moreover, their presentation of demands to management could remain oblique and anonymous.

The women workers' first tactic was mutual education, the construction of shared meanings and the generation of a supportive environment. At night in their tiny, crowded dormitory rooms – while they shared washing facilities or sat cross-legged on their bunks earning a few more yuan by assembling components they had brought back – the longest-serving workers gave voice to their anger over the manager's failure to promote capable workers and improve wages. They told newcomers how rude and arrogant local employees had been toward them, and how – despite their incompetence – locals were paid large annual bonuses. Aloud, they read excerpts from the daily newspapers about enterprises where pay had risen as a result of the introduction of productivity-linked systems and lamented that manager Mao had not implemented an 'objective' and 'fair' pay system at Jinshagang. They unfavourably compared the factory's discriminatory promotion and pay scheme, in which people got more or less money depending on their place of residence, to the 'more work, more pay' systems which operated in 'real foreign enterprises'. They concluded that Hangzhou bosses, in league with overseas capitalists, were 'sucking the blood of us migrant workers'. Together, they reclaimed their self-esteem and spoke to their common feelings of alienation and exploitation by singing popular songs about the life of rural migrants in China's cities:

> I'm a young person in the city
> Exhausted by the crowds streaming by
> I'm thirsty for the quiet village life
> I need gentle rays of sunlight
>
> Forget all the begging I do to get by
> Forget the troubles of everyday living
> Forget each and every cold face looking
> Forget every bitter tear flowing
> (Chang Kuan, 'City People'; full translation in Jones, 1992)

Workers' second tactic was simply to fail to turn up at work, even at the cost of forfeiting their 200-yuan bond. Increasingly, when workers found local supervisors' criticism or ridicule intolerable, they responded with their own invective, destroyed their tools and materials, and fled from the workshop. Their friends in the dormitory and relatives and fellow villagers eased their exit by providing them with temporary lodgings and introductions to other workplaces. Gossip about workshop 'incidents' unsettled locals and migrants alike, and the high attrition rate began to adversely affect production schedules.

Finally, the manager's opinion box began to fill up with letters from anonymous individuals protesting the 'old-fashioned', inequitable wage system in the factory. These letters of complaint were all couched in what the manager considered to be an appropriately respectful vocabulary. They congratulated the manager on having achieved such success with 'his' factory and predicted that, in the future, his obvious talent for business would bring even greater success. The manager also said he felt persuaded by the sound economic logic displayed by the writers of these letters. They reasoned that, given that the village had a small population which was fully employed, Jinshagang factory's future growth would inevitably entail the recruitment of yet more migrant labour. As the contributions made by migrants towards factory profits became more significant, the factory would find it beneficial to fully utilise the talents and productivity of these people. To this end, they urged the factory manager to implement a 'modern', 'scientific' incentive scheme that did not discriminate on the basis of place-of-origin, but instead impartially rewarded productivity, quality and initiative.

The manager was annoyed that, at a time when quality improvements were essential to the future of the business, local employees' high-handed manner towards migrants appeared to be contributing to an increasing incidence of upheaval and attrition among the workforce:

The outsiders all know that the locals get more than they do. They keep complaining that it is inequitable, that the income gap isn't fair because they work harder than the locals. They say that [wage] distribution really should be according to 'more work, more pay' [...] As a business, I have to think about what sort of contribution workers will make in the future, focus more on the workers who are really productive. We really should pay both locals and outsiders what they are worth, so that people making the same contribution towards profit earn the same amounts.

Mindful of the demands of his Japanese clients and the difficulties of meeting tight schedules with truculent, absconding workers, the manager responded by introducing a promotion and pay system in which output and quality were the twin standards by which all employees were evaluated. Henceforth, factory staff and workers would equally be eligible for annual bonuses pegged to their documented achievement of output and quality targets. For the first time ever, the monthly wages of local supervisors were linked to quotas which stipulated personal output, as well as targets for group productivity and achievement of quality standards. Promotion to supervisory positions would no longer be open only to locals, but instead would be offered to all outstanding workers.

On the pay day following implementation of the new promotion and wage scheme, several workshop supervisors discovered to their horror that they had received less than some of the workers they superintended. Two small group leaders were threatened with demotion. Most of the local staff sulked:

> It's not enough! I hate him! Almost everyone hates him now. The whole factory is full of angry faces. Haven't you noticed? Normally, around Spring Festival, everyone looks happy and excited, but instead we are all in a bad mood.

The immediate effect was shock at the callousness and lack of community loyalty shown by the manager in assessing local residents 'by the same criterion as dirty kids from Anhui'. Within a week, however, they had resigned themselves to being treated as members of China's growing mass of 'hirelings'. Although they still spoke of the factory workforce as comprising locals and migrants, their words suggested that they no longer had any illusions that the factory was a collective in which they were part-owners:

> He can do whatever he likes to any of us now – deduct our wages and bonuses, fire us, anything!

Moreover, they began to view their migrant colleagues in a new light. As we sat in the cold factory warehouse over which she presided, Gu's conversation reflected the changing attitudes of her fellow villagers:

> Lots of Hangzhou people make jokes about people who come from Zhuji,[17] or even worse, Anhui, making them out to be ridiculous. But some of those people are hard working and clever. It's just that because they come from poor areas they haven't had the same sorts of opportunities as we have. I don't think they should be discriminated against, treated with contempt. That sort of attitude will become less prevalent as time goes on, with further reform and competition, and more people moving around looking for work.

In sum, the socio-spatial boundary between local and migrant employees was being effaced, and replaced by class-based divisions between owner-managers and wage-workers.

Migrant workers' campaign to have the wage and promotion system at Jinshagang replaced by one which solely rewarded individual productivity and quality should not be viewed simply as a bid for higher wages. The migrant activists were conscious of the fact that such a change was unlikely to result in any immediate wage gains. Certainly, in the short term, the new remuneration system only resulted in a lowering and levelling of local employees' wages, with no upward movement in the pay of migrants. On the other hand, nor should the campaign be interpreted as evidence of a naïve belief that 'the market' was equitable. The workers were only too aware that property rights, credit and market opportunities were unequally distributed, and that labour market and wage systems operated as they did because of huge economic disparities between regions and because their friends and families at home still belonged to China's 'unlimited supply of labour'.

Rather, migrant workers had their own political agenda in framing their bargaining with the manager in the vocabulary of market competition and merit. Their appropriation and deployment of these discourses should be understood as a rejection of their labelling as 'primitives' and thus as a bid for a truly modern identity. In showing themselves to be even more responsive to meritocratic principles than their overseers, they laid claim to being members of that mythical rational economic community that was eulogised in the media as being progressive and, above all, profitable. More importantly, they made this claim so as to highlight workers' shared characteristics. Their request to the manager to apply identical evaluative criteria to locals and migrants was inspired by the same aim. They wanted to make clear that, as employees, all were subject to identical processes of exploitation and stood in the same position relative to the factory's owner-managers and their Japanese clients. In short, migrant workers' tactics were designed to highlight their similarities rather than differences. This ought to be seen as a significant stage in the class-formation process in this factory – a stage which may establish the grounds for future cooperation against management over the terms of their participation in transnational production.

Conclusions

This case study of events in Jinshagang factory demonstrates that we cannot assume that participation in transnational manufacturing – with its attendant problems of capital exit, meritocratic discourses and political repression – will always have negative consequences for all workers. In fact, this case study illustrates why some Chinese have reason to see globalisation as a positive trend.

In material terms, all of Jinshagang's employees are now better off than they were before their employment in transnational production. In an economy characterised by a massive labour surplus and a capital shortage, transnational manufacturing not only provides earning opportunities for people who were otherwise underemployed or unemployed, it also provides a means of local capital accumulation. In Jinshagang, profits from the factory were reinvested in other business ventures, donated to the local school and used by the village government to fund a generous pension scheme for elderly residents. Migrant workers used part of their wages to subsidise living standards, finance housing construction and establish small businesses in their villages.

The events described in this chapter did not lead to immediate material gains for the workers concerned. However, they do show why some workers in China believe economic globalisation might provide them with new *political* opportunities. Local employees at Jinshagang were for a time given an insight into ownership privileges and management strategies in transnational manufacturing. They will draw on those insights in their new capacity as wage-workers. The exit option with which international capital threatened the local managers, paradoxically provided insecure unskilled female migrant workers with a chance to press for an end to discriminatory wages and conditions. Although the rhetoric of neo-liberal meritocracy and productivity-linked wage schemes is clearly designed to intensify productivity pressures on workers and reduce their motivation and capacity to organise collectively, migrants at Jinshagang actually invoked these to forge some sense of unity among workers and thereby establish a basis for future organising.

This study does not contest the general utility of independent labour organisations. On the contrary, the desirability of – necessity for – such organisations is demonstrated at a macro-level by the numerous attempts Chinese workers have made to establish autonomous trade unions and at the micro-level by the obstacles to negotiation faced by the workers at Jinshagang. Nevertheless, the study does suggest that, under circumstances where independent labour movements are prohibited, workers may still engage in (dis)organised agitation, and might still educate each other and debate the terms of their incorporation into transnational production arrangements. In China, Elizabeth Perry observes, 'among non-state workers more "traditional" place-based organizations are emerging' (Perry, 1997: 52). However, rather than these being alternatives to more class-based associations, this study shows we cannot assume that workers who are currently organising according to place-of-origin will be incapable of organising differently in the future. Indeed, workers' organisation along 'traditional' lines and their use of *ad hoc* diffuse tactics may actually be intended to bridge, not entrench, divisions created by place. For this reason, they can be viewed as forging a foundation for more effective, concerted action by all workers.

Events at Jinshagang factory demonstrate that future analyses of the changing position of workers in the global economy must be prepared to examine whether, and with what effects, workers might creatively appropriate and deploy to their advantage those discourses, managerial practices and conditions that have been conceptualised as the means of their subjugation. The insights gleaned from this one case study point to the need to conduct more intensive empirical research into the intentions, patterns and effects of workers' activism. Only thus can we begin to lay bare some of the contradictions between the everyday politics of those actually involved in transnational production and the assumptions, predictions and conclusions scholars have made on the basis of theoretical exploration, statistical surveys, questionnaires and comparative documentary research.

Notes

1 The name I have given to the factory, 'Jinshagang', is actually the name of the suburban village in Hangzhou in which the factory is located. The surname I have given to the factory's managers, Mao, is fictitious.

2 My analysis is based on data collected between June 1992 and March 1993, when I spent hundreds of hours on the shopfloor at Jinshagang factory, and many more hours visiting workers' homes, going on outings with them and attending festivities such as housewarming and engagement parties. I conducted numerous unstructured and semi-structured interviews with all levels of management, had regular social contact with two members of the factory's office staff, and enjoyed access to administrative files and personnel regulations (see Sargeson, 1999). All unsourced quotes in this chapter are taken from these interviews.

3 Under central planning, the most important differentiating criteria were workers' status as permanent, contract or temporary worker, and enterprises' status as state-owned, urban collective or rural enterprise. For a review of the material distinctions made between these categories, see Walder (1986).

4 I arrived at this estimate simply by adding together the 120 million rural residents employed in rural industries and the approximately 80 million rural residents who have migrated illegally to cities in search of work and business opportunities.

5 For similar statements, see also *Zhongguo laodong bao* (13, 27 October 1992) and World Bank (1997: 45–6).

6 In fact, there is not a particularly strong connection or channel of communication between government and the ACFTU. According to pro-market lobbyists such as the US Bureau of International Labor Relations, the absence of communication is to ACFTU's detriment:

> The lack of liaison between the Ministry of Labour and the ACFTU is striking and severely limits the ACFTU's influence over labor policy. The Ministry has transformed itself from a central-planning to a labor-service orientation and is full of fairly eager reformers. The union seems lost in the new vocabulary of reform and unable to make effective policy suggestions …
> (US Bureau of International Labor Affairs, 1993: 8)

7 For reports on the suppression of autonomous workers' organisations, see Asia Watch (1990); Hong Kong Trade Union Education Centre (1990); *China News Digest* (19 January 1999).

8 See also Rofel (1989: 235–52); *Gongren ribao* (3 June 1992); *Xinhua* (10 April 1996).

9 Legal non-union labour organisations are discussed by Li (1989) and Shankar (1991).

10 The phrase 'captive component supplier' comes from the typology of subcontracting relations developed by Gary Gereffi (1993).

11 I use the term 'semi-private' because I take control over the disposition of income to be an important component of ownership. Several recent articles debate the extent to which collective assets are being privatised in China: see, for example, Walder (1995) and Sargeson and Zhang (1999).

12 No new capital was invested in the enterprise as a result of this change. Instead, the Maos simply provided the finance and arranged for an old Hong Kong business acquaintance to become a 'foreign investor' with a limited interest in the company.

13 The only local who remained a production worker for longer than four months was under medication and regularly hospitalised for a mental illness.

14 The office manager and recruitment officer had been employed on the personal recommendation of a local government official who had assisted the Maos in their business dealings. Two small group leaders had married villagers who were related to the Maos, and been employed in the factory since its beginnings.

15 The possibility of earning money was not the only thing luring these young women to Hangzhou. Workers told me they also wanted to 'see the world', learn skills that would allow them to establish a business after they returned home, escape from their parents' old-fashioned ways, avoid arranged marriages, have fun and meet interesting people.

16 At that time, the official exchange rate was approximately 6 yuan to US$1 and the black-market exchange rate was approximately 10 yuan to US$1.

17 Zhuji is in central Zhejiang. Gu mentioned this particular county because it is the source of much chain migration to Hangzhou.

Bibliography

AMRC (Asia Monitor Resource Centre) (1995) *Asian Labour Update* no.18.

Anonymous (1992) 'Suan, tian, ku, la "da gong" ' (The joys and sorrows of life as a 'hireling'), *Dadi* (Earth) 10: 48–52.

Asia Watch (1990) *Repression in China since June 4, 1989: Cumulative data*, Human Rights Watch.

Balibar, Etienne and Wallerstein, Immanuel (1991) *Race, Nation, Class: Ambiguous Identities*, London: Verso.

Broad, Dave (1995) 'Globalization versus labor', *Monthly Review* 47, 7: 20–31.

Bryan, Dick (1995) *The Chase Across the Globe: International Accumulation and the Contradictions of Nation States*, Boulder: Westview.

Casati, Christine (1991) 'Satisfying labor laws – and needs', *The China Business Review* 18, 4: 16–22.

Castells, Manuel (1979) 'Immigrant workers and class struggles in advanced capitalism: The Western European experience', in Robin Cohen, Peter C.W. Gutkind and Phyllis Brazier (eds) *Peasants and Proletarians: The Struggles of Third World Workers*, London: Hutchinson, pp. 353–80.

Chan, Anita (1993) 'Revolution or corporatism? Workers and trade unions in post-Mao China', *The Australian Journal of Chinese Affairs* 29: 31–61.

—— (1995) 'The emerging patterns of industrial relations in China and the rise of two new labor movements', *China Information* 9, 4: 36–60.

Chinese Economic System Reform Research Institute (1987) 'Summary report', in Bruce L. Reynolds (ed.) *Reform in China: Challenges and Choices*, New York: M.E. Sharpe, pp. 3–28.

Cohen, Robin (1991) *Contested Domains: Debates in International Labour Studies*, London: Zed Books.

De Certeau, Michel (1984) *The Practice of Everyday Life*, Berkeley: University of California Press.

Deyo, Frederic (1984) 'Export manufacturing and labor: The case of Asia', in Charles Bergquist (ed.) *Labor in the Capitalist World Economy*, Beverly Hills: Sage, pp. 267–89.

Gao Shengquan (1996) *China's Economic Reform*, London: Macmillan.

Geng Shuhai and Li Hua (1989) 'Reform and social mentality of workers', *Chinese Economic Studies* 22, 4: 8–17.

Gereffi, Gary (1993) 'International subcontracting and global capitalism: Reshaping the Pacific Rim', in Ravi Arvind Palat (ed.) *Pacific-Asia and the Future of the World System*, Westport: Greenwood, pp. 67–82.

Giddens, Anthony (1991) 'Four theses on ideology', *Canadian Journal of Political and Social Theory* 15, 1–2 and 3: 21–4.

Gough, J. (1992) 'Workers' competition, class relations and space', *Environment and Planning D* 10, 3: 265–86.

Gramsci, Antonio (1971) *Selections from the Prison Notebooks*, New York: International Publishers.

Haiven, Larry, Edwards, P.K. and Bélanger, Jacques (1994) 'Globalization, national systems and the future of workplace industrial relations', in Jacques Bélanger, P.K. Edwards and Larry Haiven (eds) *Workplace Industrial Relations and Global Challenge*, Ithaca: ILR Press, pp. 275–84.

Hong Kong Trade Union Education Centre (1990) *A Moment of Truth: Workers' Participation in China's 1989 Democracy Movement and the Emergence of Independent Trade Unions*, Hong Kong: Asia Monitor Resource Centre.

Jiang Wandi (1995) 'A new problem – labor relations in foreign enterprises', *Beijing Review* 38, 20 (15–21 May): 17–20.

Jones, Andrew F. (1992) *Like a Knife: Ideology and Genre in Contemporary Chinese Popular Music*, Ithaca: Cornell University.

Kueh, Y.Y. (1992) 'Foreign investment and economic change in China', *China Quarterly* 131: 637–91.

Lardy, Nicholas R. (1995) 'The role of foreign trade and investment in China's economic transformation', *China Quarterly* 144: 1,065–82.

Larochelle, Gilbert (1992) 'Interdependence, globalization and fragmentation', in Zdravko Mlinar (ed.) *Globalization and Territorial Identities*, Aldershot: Avebury, pp. 150–65.

Lau Kin Chi (1995) 'Women pay for economic miracle in China and Hong Kong', *Asian Exchange* 11, 1: 35–8.

Lee, Ching Kwan (1995) 'Engendering the worlds of labor: Women workers, labor markets and production politics in the South China economic miracle', *American Sociological Review* 60, 3: 378–97.

Leong Liew (1997) *The Chinese Economy in Transition: from Plan to Market*, Cheltenham: Edward Elgar.

Leung Wing-yue (1988) *Smashing the Iron Rice Pot: Workers and Trade Unions in China's Market Socialism*, Hong Kong: Asia Monitor Resource Centre.

Li Hua (1989) 'The democratic management of enterprises and workers' awareness of democracy', *Chinese Economic Studies* 22, 4: 69–80.

Liemt, Gijsbert van (1992) 'Economic globalization: Labour options and business strategies in high labour cost countries', *International Labour Review* 131, 4–5: 453–71.

Murray, Geoffrey (1994) *Doing Business in China: The Last Great Market*, Sydney: Allen and Unwin.

Nash, June (1989) 'Cultural resistance and class consciousness in Bolivian tin-mining communities', in Susan Eckstein (ed.) *Power and Popular Protest: Latin American Social Movements*, Berkeley: University of California Press, pp. 182–202.

Ong, Aihwa (1987) *Spirits of Resistance and Capitalist Discipline: Factory Women in Malaysia*, Albany: State University of New York.

Perry, Elizabeth J. (1993) *Shanghai on Strike: The Politics of Chinese Labor*, Stanford: Stanford University Press.

—— (1995) 'Labor's battle for political space: The role of worker associations in contemporary China', in Deborah S. Davis, Richard Kraus, Barry Naughton and Elizabeth J. Perry (eds) *Urban Spaces in Contemporary China*, Cambridge: Cambridge University Press, pp. 302–25.

—— (1996) 'Putting class in its place: Bases of worker identities in East Asia', in Elizabeth J. Perry (ed.) *Putting Class in its Place: Worker Identities in East Asia*, Berkeley: University of California Institute of East Asian Studies, pp. 1–10.

—— (1997) 'From native place to workplace: Labor origins and outcomes of China's *Danwei* System', in Xiaobo Lu and Elizabeth J. Perry (eds) *Danwei: The Changing Chinese Workplace in Historical and Comparative Perspective*, New York: M.E. Sharpe, pp. 42–60.

Piven, Frances Fox (1995) 'Is it global economics or neo-laissez-faire?', *New Left Review* 213: 107–14.

PRC State Statistical Bureau (1995, 1996, 1997) *Zhongguo tongji nianjian (China Statistical Yearbook) 1995, 1996, 1997*, Beijing: State Statistical Bureau.

Reynolds, Bruce L. (ed.) (1987) *Reform in China: Challenges and Choices – A Summary and Analysis of the CESRRI (Chinese Economic Reform Research Institute) Survey*, Armonk: M.E. Sharpe.

Rofel, Lisa (1989) 'Hegemony and productivity: Workers in post-Mao China', in Arif Dirlik and Maurice Meisner (eds) *Marxism and the Chinese Experience: Issues in Contemporary Chinese Socialism*, New York: M.E. Sharpe, pp. 235–52.

Sargeson, Sally (1999) *Reworking China's Proletariat*, Houndmills: Macmillan.

Sargeson, Sally and Zhang Jian (1999) 'Reassessing the role of the local state: A case study of local government intervention in property rights reform in a Hangzhou district', *The China Journal* 42: 77–99.

Scott, James C. (1990) *Domination and the Arts of Resistance: Hidden Transcripts*, New Haven: Yale University Press.

Shankar, Oded (1991) *Organization and Management in China 1979–1990*, New York: M.E. Sharpe.

Strinati, Dominic (1990) 'A ghost in the machine?: The state and labour process in theory and practice', in David Knights and Hugh Willmott (eds) *Labour Process Theory*, Houndmills: Macmillan, pp. 209–43.

Taussig, Michael T. (1980) *The Devil and Commodity Fetishism in South America*, Chapel Hill: University of North Carolina.

Thomas, Henk (1995) 'The erosion of trade unions', in Henk Thomas (ed.) *Globalization and Third World Trade Unions: The Challenge of Rapid Economic Change*, London: Zed Books, pp. 3–28.

Thompson, John B. (1990) *Ideology and Modern Culture: Critical Social Theory in the Era of Mass Communication*, Cambridge: Polity Press.

Turner, Christina (1991) 'The spirit of productivity: Workplace discourse on culture and economics in Japan', *Boundary* 18, 3: 90–105.

US Bureau of International Labor Affairs (1993) *Foreign Labor Trends Report: China 1992*, Washington, D.C.: US Government Printing Office.

Walder, Andrew G. (1986) *Communist Neo-Traditionalism: Work and Authority in Chinese Industry*, Berkeley: University of California Press.

—— (1995) 'Local governments as industrial firms: An organizational analysis of China's transitional economy', *American Journal of Sociology* 101, 2: 263–302.

Warner, Malcolm (1993) 'Chinese trade unions: Structure and function in an era of economic reform 1979–1989', in Stephen Frenkel (ed.) *Organized Labor in the Asia-Pacific Region*, Ithaca: ILR Press, pp. 59–81.

Western, Bruce (1995) 'A comparative study of working class disorganization: Union decline in eighteen advanced capitalist countries', *American Sociological Review* 60, 2: 179–202.

Wood, Ellen Meiksins (1995) *Democracy Against Capitalism: Renewing Historical Materialism*, Cambridge: Cambridge University Press.

World Bank (1997) *China 2020: Development Challenges in the New Century*, Washington, D.C.: World Bank.

Wu Shouhui and Guo Jinhua (1989) 'Workers' evaluation of and hopes for trade unions', *Chinese Economic Studies* 22, 4: 56–68.

Zhu Naixiao (1995) 'China's position and role in the Pacific economic rim', *Social Sciences in China* 4: 37–47.

Newspapers and news services

Agence France Presse 14 March 1996.

Baokan wenzhai (News Digest) 24 November 1992.

Beijing Review 18–24 September 1995; 30 October–5 November 1995; 23–9 November 1998; 14–20 December 1998.

China News Digest 19 January 1999.

EIU Business China 29 May 1995.

Fazhi ribao (Legal Daily) 8 October 1992.

Gongren ribao (Workers' Daily) 3, 8, 11 June 1992; 1, 7, 9 July 1992; 17, 18, 25, 28 February 1993; 5 March 1993.

Hangzhou ribao (Hangzhou Daily) 21 May 1992.

Survey of World Broadcasts 17 December 1994; 3 April 1996.

Xinhua (New China News Agency) 10 April 1996.

Zhejiang ribao (Zhejiang Daily), 26 October 1992.

Zhongguo laodong bao (China Labour News) 7, 12, 16 May 1992; 18 June 1992; 13, 27 October 1992; 20 November 1992; 1 December 1992; 26 January 1993.

4 Export opportunities

Unions in the Philippine garments industry

Jane Hutchison

Unionisation rates in the Philippine garments industry are very low. Poor official record keeping makes it difficult to establish reliable figures on this, but the distribution of enterprise-based unions in the industry is more easily described and explained. In common with the picture for manufacturing in general, unions in this industry are overwhelmingly concentrated in factories with large in-house workforces – that is, in factories with workforces numbering in the high hundreds and even thousands. As these large factories are mainly in the export sector (Tecson, Valcarcel and Nunez, 1991), unions are also more likely to be found therein. Women workers in the Philippine garments industry thus have a better chance of belonging to a union if they sew for an overseas market than if they are employed in the domestic-oriented sector. What is more, this is not secondary occurrence: production for an export market is itself a causal factor behind improvements in the women workers' organising capacities.

This observation is clearly at odds with the existing literature on women workers in export or 'global factories', which considers low wages and poor levels of union protection to be an inevitable outcome of transnational production arrangements designed to access cheap, unprotected workers (Snow, 1978; Elson and Pearson, 1980; Robert, 1983; Fox, 1993; also cf. Deyo, 1989). This is especially true of the literature that classifies the Philippine garments industry as an exemplar of this phenomenon (Pineda-Ofreneo, 1981; Sinay-Aguilar, 1986–7; Pineda-Ofreneo and De Rosario, 1988; Aldana, 1989). According to these scholars, transnational production arrangements are a causal factor, not in so far as they originally create poor labour standards but in the sense that they constitute a persistent obstacle to the improvements in labour standards that might otherwise be expected from capitalist industrialisation. By implication, it is outside such arrangements that workers have a better chance to improve their material and political positions.

This 'new international division of labour' (NIDL) perspective (Fröbel, Heinrichs and Kreye, 1980) does not only typify the academic literature on women workers in export factories; it is also often a cogent force in popular and activist circles, framing discourses of protest in ways that single out the activities of multinational companies for special blame (see Sherlock in this volume). In the Philippines, this viewpoint has resonated strongly with nationalist elements in the labour movement and in the wider political culture, which consider workers' struggles to be part of a larger battle against 'foreign domination' (see EILER, 1988: 40; Scipes, 1996: ix). Consequently, the NIDL perspective can be seen to have had its own effect on shaping the outlook and organising strategies of workers.

But discourses of protest ought not to be confused with academic analysis. In this chapter, I explain how production for export in the Philippine garments industry tends to lift unionisation rates by limiting the amount of local subcontracting done. Of particular interest here are the ways in which struggles over the intensification of work become more direct and acute as managers in the export sector find it necessary to respond to the demands of overseas buyers and contractors by exerting greater control over labour productivity and product quality. On these grounds, I argue that the pattern of trade-union formation within this industry is chiefly explained by developments in the labour process arising from production for foreign markets.

However, the intra-industry distribution of enterprise-based unions is also a reflection of the wider legal-political environment for worker activism in the Philippines. The first part of this chapter thus covers labour-organising capacities *vis-à-vis* the state and civil society. In this regard, the focus is on the second tier of the labour movement (the mix of regional and industry federations and national labour centres that local unions are legally able to join) because, while 'the crux' of Philippine unionism is enterprise-based, it is invariably the more 'political' activities of the larger federations and centres that capture most public, media and academic attention (Ramos, 1990: 143). Against this background, in the remainder of this chapter I return to the garments industry and the local subcontracting practices that have a direct effect on factory size and hence on the pattern of enterprise unionism in that industry.

Labour, state and civil society

The main issues pertaining to Philippine labour-organising capacities in the political arena are fourfold, relating to: the laws formally governing industrial relations; the *de facto* opportunities these laws provide for effective unionism; factors forcing workers into the political arena; and the effects of changes in the general socio-political climate on political unionism over the last decade or so. The argument I develop is that, despite the existence of a number of legal rights and protections, organising capacities are constantly undermined by the reluctance and/or inability of the state to properly enforce the laws covering collective bargaining in an environment where the social structure is characterised by great inequalities in wealth and power (Woodiwiss, 1998: 87–142). In addition to this general scenario, I will outline some of the main factors contributing to fluctuations in the political influence of organised labour in the last decade or two.

Deyo (1997: 219–20) describes the laws that formally govern industrial relations in the Philippines as 'more liberal than corporatist' in that workers are able to organise independently from the state and to bargain collectively with employers at the enterprise level. As already mentioned, local enterprise unions are then also able to affiliate with a larger federation and/or labour centre. One of these centres – the Trade Union Congress of the Philippines (TUCP) – has a history of links to government (it was first founded as an arm of the authoritarian Marcos regime in the mid-1970s), but it has other rivals of various ideological persuasions – most prominently, since 1980, the militant Kilusang Mayo Uno (KMU or May First Movement) and its offshoots (see Dejillas, 1994; Scipes, 1996). In all, there is more political 'space' for organising in the Philippines than in, for example, Indonesia or Malaysia. However, organising capacities are never simply decided by legislation: there are a host of structural and historical factors which combine to explain the low levels of effective unionism in the Philippines (Ofreneo, 1994).

Deyo (1997: 218–20), for one, maintains that labour-organising capacities in Asia are profoundly influenced by 'the domestic developmental sequencing of political and industrial change'. In the Philippine case, self-organising at the enterprise level was first officially encouraged with the passing of the Industrial Peace Act of 1953. This legislation was itself a legacy of colonial ties with the United States as, in part, it reproduced the recommendations of a 1950 American report into social unrest in the Philippines that sought to remove communist influences from the labour movement. This was to be achieved by breaking the movement's links with militant peasant organisations in Central Luzon and by furthering 'economic unionism' through collective bargaining (Villegas, 1988: 44). Wurfel (1959: 593–7) argues that the 1953 Act was responsible for a marked jump in the number of local unions being granted official recognition, principally due to the fall-off in deregistrations by the then Department of Labor. Importantly, the new legislation coincided with an extended period of import-substitution industrialisation (ISI) that saw the size of the manufacturing workforce swell to levels that were unprecedented at that time or since. Deyo argues that these developments led to 'the emergence of strong local unions which, under subsequent years of martial law and state repression [under President Marcos] (1972–86), sustained a latent, community-based opposition movement' that eventually saw the return to electoral democracy in the late 1980s (Deyo, 1997: 219–20).

Otherwise, the environment for organising in the Philippines has been made difficult by repeated national economic crises, manufacturing decline and chronically high levels of unemployment and underemployment – all factors that are 'powerful impediments to strong labour movements' (ibid.: 218). Under these circumstances, the *de jure* space for enterprise unionism has actually proved a *de facto* limitation on organising capacities, in so far as most workers are thereby forced into bargaining units that are too small and isolated to be effective and sustained. The significance of this point is driven home by the fact that only some 10 per cent of the manufacturing workforce is located within the so-called 'formal sector' (Hutchison, 1997: 76). For workers outside this sector in very small enterprises, the options for organising are limited to massed protests that target the state (Ramos, 1990).

Even for those workers in enterprises where collective bargaining is a possibility, Ramos maintains that 'the reluctance, if not outright refusal, of many employers to deal voluntarily with unions for bargaining purposes' is a significant obstacle to self-organising at the enterprise level (ibid., 1990: 155). This is evidenced by issues of union recognition and the harassment of union members being regularly recorded as major causes of industrial disputation in the Philippines. On this matter, it is worth also noting that local political officials – provincial governors, mayors and industrial zone administrators – have had greater influence over the conduct of industrial relations in the last decade, principally through their roles in promoting the establishment and running of new industrial estates in formerly rural areas (Sidel, 1998). For example, before he lost office in the late 1990s, the provincial governor of Cavite province (to the south of Manila) was well known 'as the author, engineer and enforcer of a "no-strike" industrial relations policy' for the province (ibid.: 5). Cavite is home to a good number of large export garment firms.

Despite laws and policies encouraging collective bargaining in the workplace, labour organising often spills into the political arena, for reasons in addition to those mentioned above. First, the existence of a second tier to the labour movement – in the form of the larger federations and centres – provides an organisational base for government lobbying and public protest over industrial issues, as well as other matters that are not simply of concern to workers. Further to this, some of the more radical federations and centres have a particular ideological proclivity towards taking both industrial and political issues 'into the streets'. Third, there is the continued involvement of the state in setting minimum wages and conditions that act as benchmarks for organising at the enterprise level. Fourth, and finally, labour's common resort to political activism is due to 'the persisting mendicancy of Philippine patriarchalism', wherein those legal rights and protections that workers do possess are little enforced by the state (Woodiwiss, 1998: 88). In the following discussion, I expand on the last two of these points.

Since the early 1950s, various arms of the Philippine state have set minimum wages on a national, sectoral and/or regional basis. Given difficulties in organising at the enterprise level, unions in this country have long been forced to pursue improvements in wages through public campaigns for increases in the legislated minimum wage. In industries – like the garments industry – where collective-bargaining agreements rarely deliver more than the official minimum wage, the actions of the larger federations and centres in pushing for general wage increases are clearly important. As mentioned earlier, it is often the very visible campaigns of this nature that attract most attention, invariably to the second tier of the labour movement.

Woodiwiss observes that state involvement in setting minimum wages and other measures to protect the welfare of workers is a reflection of the patriarchalism of Philippine politics. However, he also argues that this patriarchalism is an especially weak variety, as the benevolence entailed in protective legislation is merely 'rhetorical' because the legislation is generally unenforced by the state (ibid.: 103, 256). Under circumstances like these, 'the invocation of the law' becomes little more than 'a variety of begging or mendicancy': workers and their movements are made 'supplicants to the state' in that much of their organising is directed at trying to get the promised protection realised in fact (ibid.: 117, 133).

Industrial conflicts in the Philippines spill into the political arena more often than a legal regime centred on collective bargaining in the workplace would imply. Thus, since the authoritarian corporatist labour regime of President Marcos (1972–86), successive administrations have attempted to limit the public face of workers' dissent. The Aquino government (1986–92) re-introduced collective bargaining and attempted to sideline the executive and legislature as targets of campaigns to increase the legislated minimum wage by passing on this responsibility to regional wage boards. The Ramos administration (1992–8) made further efforts to bring industrial laws in line with labour market flexibility and liberalisation objectives through amendments to the Labor Code to ease existing restrictions on the local subcontracting out of work. In early 1999, President Estrada established a Presidential Task Force on Labor Policy to investigate revisions to the Labor Code to further limit the right to strike, to abolish the legislated minimum wage and to introduce various profit-sharing schemes (Guevarra, 1999: 4). But, with levels of industrial disputation down, it has not been a simple matter for the regime to pin investment shortfalls on labour.

State–labour relations in the Philippines in the post-Marcos era have been characterised by various legal and administrative efforts to depoliticise industrial bargaining through the enforcement of enterprise bargaining and the promotion of various labour market flexibility programmes. All this has been in line with broader efforts to liberalise the economy after years of extensive protectionism and cronyism (Hutchison, 1997). However the efforts of government in this regard cannot entirely explain the relative decline in labour's political influence in the Philippines in the 1990s. Rather, an important factor has been the change in the societal climate for labour militancy which occurred with the restoration of formal, constitutional democracy and the concomitant aspiration for greater society-level participation and democratisation. This is well illustrated in the case of the KMU labour centre and its breakaway organisations.

Since its establishment in 1980, the KMU has been considered as constituting a distinctive, new form of unionism: 'social movement unionism' (Lambert, 1990; Scipes, 1996; West, 1997). Social movement unions are defined by their commitment to an agenda of social change beyond the workplace and by their extensive links and alliances with other social and political movements. In the

Philippine context, it is further assumed that social movement unionism is firmly nationalist in its outlook as *the* issues facing workers are claimed to be colonisation, imperialism and economic globalisation (see Scipes, 1996: ix). As evidence of its designation, the KMU is credited with initiating the *welgang bayan* (or 'people's strike') which is more than a general strike because other sectoral organisations and members of the community are also participants in the associated rallies and blockades (ibid.: 17). In addition to pressing for improvements in the legislated minimum wage, these strikes have targeted cross-sectional issues like fuel price rises, militarisation, International Monetary Fund (IMF) directives and economic liberalisation. The *welgang bayan* was also used to generate mass mobilisations against the authoritarian regime of President Marcos in the late 1980s (Lane, 1990). But in the decade that followed, the KMU's fortunes have declined, for reasons indicated below.

West (1997: 122–3) observes that the KMU's capacity as a political force was greatest when the legitimacy of the state was most in question: that is, when the opposition to President Marcos was at its height after the 1983 assassination of his political opponent, Benigno Aquino, and the subsequent debt crisis and collapse of the economy. Of special note is the fact that business support for the regime fell away sharply during this period due to chronic cronyism and obvious economic mismanagement. It would seem from this that the political space for labour as a social force is increased during times of deep national crisis, when cross-sectional alliances are more readily formed to oppose the incumbent regime (see Deyo, 1997: 208). This observation is supported by subsequent events.

The restoration of state legitimacy that accompanied the return of constitutional democracy saw a contraction in popular support for the KMU's concerted opposition to the state. The organisation's own leadership contributed to this by failing to adjust to the 'transformed landscape of coalition politics' that came with the restoration of formal democracy and associated conflicts within the left, where the KMU is positioned (Rocamora, 1994: 211–12). Rocamora describes this changed landscape as a shift away from the programme of persistent opposition leading to the 'seizure of state power', towards a preparedness to participate in the policy-making process to achieve 'more immediate and tangible' reforms instead. In 1993, divisions in the left were played out within the KMU and the organisation split into two acrimonious groups (Scipes, 1996: 219–47). The KMU found it difficult to adjust to the altered socio-political climate for societal level activism in the post-Marcos Philippines – a climate in which there has been a great expansion in non-governmental organisation (NGO) activity and a related rejection of many of the tactics of the old left (Clarke, 1998: 40). In recent years, the KMU has participated in mass mobilisations against privatisation, oil price rises and threats to alter the Constitution to extend the presidency (Ranald, 1999: 316–18). However, levels of industrial activity are well down on those that were generated by the economic crisis of the mid-1980s.

In part, this is because the financial crisis of the late 1990s has not been as severe as the one more than a decade earlier (World Bank, 1999). More significantly, the economic crisis of 1997–8 did not become a *political* crisis, as occurred in the 1980s. In contrast to the Marcos regime, the Ramos and Estrada administrations have not had to shoulder primary responsibility for the economic downturn. In a climate in which the regional crisis has been widely blamed on excessive state intervention, both presidents have gained some kudos through the economic situation not being as bad in the Philippines as elsewhere. Where once the country's poor economic performance was argued to result from the massive corruption and cronyism, its current status is seen to vindicate the 1990s programme of concerted economic liberalisation (Sicat, 1998). Whether this is the truth of the matter or not, the crucial point is that the political outcomes from the economic crises in the 1980s and 1990s have been very different. In that the legitimacy of the state has not been undermined to the same extent, the climate for labour militancy has changed.

This discussion has focused on facets of labour organising in the Philippines that are not particular to women workers in the garments industry, but which nevertheless are important in explaining their capacity to effectively unionise at the enterprise level. First, there are the legal openings – and requirements – to separate bargaining units at the enterprise level and the difficulties this presents, especially for workers in small and very small establishments. Second, there is the role of the state in setting minimum wages and conditions through legislation, while at the same time failing to provide adequate enforcement measures – a situation that means more weight is placed on the capacity of the larger federations and labour centres to apply pressure for higher wages in the political arena. Finally, this discussion has covered the question of labour's political influence beyond industrial matters, as it is in this that labour's broader potential as an opposition force can be evaluated.

Before returning to the impact of exporting on patterns of unionisation in the garments industry itself, it is useful to make some general observations about the influence different federations and labour centres can have on organising capacity at the enterprise level. As previously stated, much public, media and academic attention is focused on the second tier of the labour movement, but it is not always clear what effects rival organisations have on the ground. In the case of the KMU, it is important to establish that, although this centre's innovative tactics[1] and commitment to grassroots organising through educational and other campaigns has helped to lift union activity in the garments industry at certain times, invariably a good deal of its militancy has been directed at demarcation disputes with other centres, especially with the TUCP and its member federations. Precisely because the most easily organised workers are those in the largest factories, the KMU's interventions have often been focused on efforts to revitalise and/or affiliate *existing* enterprise unions. While competition among the different federations and centres can lead to better support for local affiliates, the conditions of existence of enterprise unionism remain much the same. It is these structural issues that my study of the garments industry particularly addresses.

The garments industry

The Philippine export garments industry is often discussed in terms of transnational production arrangements designed to provide access to cheap, unprotected labour (see Pineda-Ofreneo, 1981; Sinay-Aguilar, 1986–7; Pineda-Ofreneo and De Rosario, 1988; Aldana, 1989). But this account of the industry's origins overlooks the impact of the international regime for trade in garments between developed and developing countries – the Multi-Fibre Arrangement (MFA). As I will outline below, the MFA has been a significant factor behind the expanded production of garments for an overseas market in the Philippines in recent decades.

The current structure of this industry can be traced to the 1961 passing of legislation allowing the duty-free importation of fabrics for labour-only processing, then re-shipment to the United States. As producers making garments for the local market were prevented by law from accessing imported fabrics, the export- and domestic-oriented sectors of the industry developed quite separately. This bifurcation of the industry enables fairly simple comparisons to be made between the two sectors with regards to patterns of union formation at the enterprise level. Significantly, the domestic and export sectors shared very similar modes of work organisation before 1961 (CRC, 1974: 32). Thereafter, however, the export sector modernised more rapidly with the fragmentation of work tasks and associated flow systems, specialised machinery and mechanised cutting being introduced into the larger factories, often under the direct supervision of the foreign parent firm (Garfinkel, 1972; Abad, 1975). These changes to the labour process are consistent with those that nowadays set limits on the local subcontracting out of production.

Since 1974, exports of garments from developing countries (including the Philippines) to most of the developed world (Canada, Europe and the United States) have been governed by volume-based quotas applied under the MFA. Scholars who hold to a link between free trade and economic development often argue that the MFA works against labour-abundant developing countries by curtailing their opportunities to pursue comparative advantages in labour-intensive manufactures. But in so far as the quotas also provide these countries with a guaranteed market for stipulated volumes of garments, other researchers have demonstrated that exports from some developing countries would have been *less* without the MFA, because these countries are otherwise uncompetitive in an open market. The Philippines is one of those countries for whom MFA quotas have helped to secure overseas markets (Gotto, 1990; Trela and Whalley, 1990: 17–21). This is amply demonstrated by the Philippines' heavy reliance on markets covered by the MFA and its very poor performance in exporting to non-quota countries like Australia and Japan (Tootals Textiles International Ltd, 1987: 38–9; World Bank, 1999: 56–7).

More to the point, with the exception of a few 'critical categories', the Philippines has long been unable to even fill the quotas allocated to it under the MFA. Paradoxically, it is for this very reason that the country's export industry expanded significantly in the 1970s and 1980s – principally because, in an effort to circumvent MFA-quota restrictions on their own countries' trade, various East Asian firms (mainly from Taiwan and Hong Kong) relocated to the Philippines to avail themselves of the market openings arising from unmet quotas (Trela and Whalley, 1990: 22–3; Mytelka, 1991: 132). In the early 1990s, the industry again expanded; however, this time the key factors were different: new domestic procedures for administering the internal allocation of MFA quotas increased quota-utilisation rates, thereby lifting the volume of output overall.

In sum, the export garments industry in the Philippines owes much of its existence to MFA protectionism. In a strictly price-competitive situation, the industry would probably not have expanded as it has in the last twenty years. With the World Trade Organisation (WTO) planning to phase out the MFA by 2005, industry representatives and government officials are warning that the Philippines will most likely lose some of its current share of the international market through stiffer price competition (Luib, 1998; World Bank, 1999: 56–7). With this in mind, the future of the industry is touted as lying at the less price-sensitive 'higher end' of the market (*Asia Pulse*, 1998). Any movement in this direction will only reinforce the limitations on local subcontracting that I outline in the next section of this chapter.

Local subcontracting

For workers to establish an enterprise union, they must be gathered in the one workplace in sufficient numbers to exercise some collective strength. There is no fixed point at which the size of the workforce makes it possible to unionise; yet it is clear the process is greatly facilitated by workers being employed in the one establishment in their hundreds and even thousands. In the Philippine garments industry, factories of this size are highly concentrated in the sector that produces for an overseas market (Tecson, Valcarcel and Nunez, 1991). Here I explain why this is the case.

In a labour-intensive industry like garments, the size of an in-house workforce is partly determined by the volume of production that is engaged in by the firm. Firms in the export sector generally receive higher volume orders than those in the domestic-oriented sector, so this is a factor that contributes to the occurrence of larger factories in exporting. However, industrial garment-making is often characterised by a dense network of subcontracting arrangements, which can mean that a significant proportion of total production is not conducted in-house, but is put out to the employees of other, smaller enterprises and/or to home-workers (Pineda-Ofreneo and De Rosario, 1988). More than volume *per se*, the number of workers in one factory is thus largely determined by the level of local subcontracting that the firm undertakes. As I argue below, the largest factories in the Philippine garments industry are to be found in the export sector principally because production for an overseas market places limits on the amount of local subcontracting done. To account for this, it is important to understand why local subcontracting is practised in the first place.

Local subcontracting is widespread in the Philippine garments industry for a number of reasons. First, as elsewhere in the world, there are simply few technological barriers to the practice. With the invention of the industrial sewing machine, only the action of the needle was mechanised. Problems with the mechanical manipulation of fabrics have meant that these operations have remained in the hands of the machine's user to this day. Without the development of a mechanically integrated production line, sewing machines are as easily installed as singles in the home as they are set up as multiples in the factory. Accordingly, the machinery of industrial garment-making is readily fragmented for dispersal to different production sites. Advances in the electronic programming of stitches and in the laser positioning of fabric have not essentially altered this situation.

With no technological obstacles to production being broken up and distributed to local subcontractors, in the Philippine garments industry the decision whether to pursue this practice (or not) rests with management's assessment of the consequences it has for labour costs, labour productivity, labour-organising capacity and product quality. Other studies of subcontracting practices in this industry have stressed an associated reduction in labour costs (Pineda-Ofreneo, 1981; Sinay-Aguilar, 1986–7; Pineda-Ofreneo and De Rosario, 1988). In my own survey[2] of sixty-four garment firms in and around Manila, managers putting out the bulk (more than three-quarters) of their production to local subcontractors certainly often cited lower labour costs as their main rationale for doing so. Workers in small subcontracting establishments – and especially homeworkers – do indeed earn less than those employed in the larger factories, who receive on or about the official minimum wage. Without institutional barriers to competition and its effects, the price of labour is notoriously driven down in an oversupplied labour market. This situation is well documented in the case of the Philippine garments industry by the aforementioned studies.

However, not all the production managers I surveyed thought that subcontracting brings significant savings overall. The managers who, on the other hand, kept all or most (over three-quarters) of their production in-house, widely reported that the higher wages they paid their workers were mostly offset by the cost savings achieved through improvements in labour productivity, less wastage of materials and reductions in delays. The differences of opinion between surveyed managers over the cost implications of local subcontracting can be explained, to a large extent, by the observation that those who engaged in most putting out of work were attached to family-owned businesses which have been run in much the same way for a decade or more. Typically, these firms give little attention to improvements in the in-house labour process, preferring instead to manage costs by maintaining high levels of putting out. From this it can be seen that the different responses of managers to the issue of cost savings in relation to local subcontracting, are contingent on the attention that is given to the organisation of production in the firm – and hence to matters such as enhanced productivity through changes to work practices and savings achieved through the better management of materials usage.

However, surveyed managers' opinions on this matter were also influenced by the prevailing level of the official minimum wage. Faced with the prospect of a significant increase in the minimum wage, the managers of a number of factories that engaged in little subcontracting made it clear that they would be forced to reconsider their position if the situation did change and the in-house wage bill increased. Still, for many of the managers the organisation of production was less an outcome of systematic economic calculation – 'rational choice' – than it was a matter of past decisions becoming settled practices. This was particularly the case in the less modern firms, where subcontracting is more regularly and extensively practised.

Second to the issue of cost savings, surveyed managers engaging in a lot of local subcontracting reported that their reasons for doing so were directly related to the effects the practice has on the organising capacities of the in-house workforce. They stated either that putting out was very effective in preventing the formation of a new enterprise union or that the tactic had been previously used against an already existing union – to break it up completely or simply to curtail its strength by keeping its membership small. Managers who acknowledged that labour productivity often suffers through local subcontracting were nevertheless prepared to maintain the practice because of the perceived advantages it provided in enabling them to avoid or reduce the 'labour problems' associated with a unionised workforce. What then are these 'labour problems'?

Managers commonly answered this question by highlighting the part that unions can play in lifting the wages and conditions of workers in their factories. However, there are several observations to make on this assessment. First, there is no simple, straightforward correlation between union coverage and higher wages in a particular firm in the garments industry. In the largest factories (with workforces in the high hundreds and even thousands), workers (both male and female) are typically on or about the official minimum wage – whether they are members of a genuine union or not. But in the smaller factories (with between 50 and 200 workers in-house), the presence or absence of a union makes more of a difference to the payment or not of the minimum wage, with the existence of a union able to negotiate a collective-bargaining agreement having a positive effect on this. The managers of these factories were thus more inclined to be concerned about the wage-cost implications of a unionised workforce than those in the largest factories, although responses on this matter were also contingent on other factors – for example, managers' own past experiences with particular unions in their establishments. (Some managers expressed a preference for the local affiliates of different federations and centres, finding some to be less disruptive than others.)

However, the second observation is that the managers of the largest, non-unionised firms normally also pay their workers the official minimum wage as a deliberate strategy to avoid (or at least limit) worker dissatisfaction and the *possibility* of an independent union being established. A few of these managers took the further step of establishing their own employer–employee consultative committee – a company-controlled 'union' – for the very same reason. In this regard, there was an implicit acknowledgement that the presence of unionised workforces in the industry had discernible effects on wage levels and working conditions more generally. In other words, the potential for independent unionism was a factor which managers in the larger factories took into account when deciding levels of remuneration for their workforce. Of course, to this extent it can be seen that it is the activities of the second tier of the labour movement, in concert with local collective bargaining, which help influence wages and conditions in the organisable sector of the industry.

But wages were not always cited as the main component of the 'labour problem'. On an everyday basis, the managers surveyed were more concerned about the effects an independent union might have on their control of the workforce. In this regard, one issue often mentioned was their ability to monitor and enforce various labour-productivity targets within the factory. As previously discussed, the industrial mechanisation of sewing has proceeded in such a way that the individual operator retains considerable control over the placement and movement of the fabrics being worked on. As a corollary of this, from moment to moment each worker has considerable control over the pace of their work, with the result that managers in the industry are forced to pay special attention to how tasks are executed on the factory floor if they are to achieve productivity gains overall. While there are gains to be made from the reorganisation of flow lines and improvements in material-handling procedures, the core problem remains one of how best to manage the output of workers themselves.

In the Philippine garments industry, managers have introduced a host of measures to increase labour productivity. In their design, these measures range from the punitive to the compensatory, from those involving threatened redundancies to those with incentive bonuses – anything from monetary payments to 'gifts' of T-shirts, hair ribbons, ice-cream and even holiday trips. Workers' expressed attitudes to the use of positive incentives were mixed in the survey. Although typically opposed to 'unreasonable' productivity targets, a number took personal pride in being able to meet achievable goals and interpreted the introduction of incentive payments and 'gifts' as just rewards for their skill and effort in contributing to company profits. Still, there was opposition to the intensification of labour.

Individuals may resist attempts to have them work harder, but in the presence of a union they are generally in a better position to respond collectively to the demands that are being placed on them all.[3] In non-unionised workplaces, the uncooperative worker can be sanctioned by management without great difficulty but, in workplaces that do have a viable union, managers are more often forced into negotiations with their workforce. Workers interviewed for this survey overwhelmingly reported that being formally organised left them less vulnerable to personal harassment over productivity matters, in large part because they believed that they would be less arbitrarily dismissed. Managers generally told a similar story. What they feared most from the presence of an independent union was its capacity to disrupt the production process on a regular and coordinated basis. Wages and conditions might be an issue in this, but the greatest headaches were typically reported to be those involving the constant 'problem of getting work from workers'. This problem was made especially acute by the need to meet shipping deadlines when to fail to do so often incurs significant penalties, such as fines or even the cancellation of contracts.

Yet not all managers surveyed took the view that an independent union is a hindrance to labour-productivity gains. A number observed that union officials can assist in this area by helping to negotiate targets which their members are more likely to regard as 'reasonable'. Otherwise, the same officials can be brought in to assist with the personal problems that a particular 'non-performing' individual may be facing.[4] More generally, the presence of a union can reduce absenteeism and labour turnover rates – both matters that can significantly undermine productivity.

To summarise the discussion thus far: local subcontracting is widespread in the garments industry – given the nature of industrial sewing technology; it is variously practised to cut labour costs and/or to avoid (or curtail) the interventions of an independent union, for reasons that have also been outlined. But *most* firms surveyed regularly put out only a small fraction of their total production. What is more, their reasons for putting out were usually different. In these cases, local subcontracting was reported to be most often done to achieve 'numerical flexibility' in the workforce to, in turn, deal with the marked fluctuations in production volumes that occur at different times of the year. Hyman (1988: 56) has argued that numerical flexibility aims 'to render workers disposable rather than adaptable' by creating a secondary workforce in addition to that which is permanently employed (as the core workforce) (see also Bray and Taylor, 1991: 7). This kind of flexibility can be achieved by employing a casual workforce in the factory and/or putting excess production out to other local firms.

Otherwise, the second reason given was that the subcontracting of a small part of production enables firms to gain access to workers with specialist skills. For example, items requiring hand embroidery are often sent to homeworkers in various semi-rural areas around Manila. While this also achieves a reduction in labour costs, managers typically reported that this is not their main motivation – as evidenced by only a particular stage in the production process being sent out. Researchers in the Philippines have documented the poor returns to female homeworkers, the eye-strain that results from long hours of fine embroidery and the participation of school-age children in this work (Pineda-Ofreneo and De Rosario, 1988). Large factories with multiple-needle embroidery machines did not engage in this form of local subcontracting.

Given the various reasons *for* subcontracting, why were most of the managers surveyed in fact keeping all – or a good part of – their production in-house? In all cases, the response was that the decision *not* to put out work was made with the consequences for control over product quality firmly in mind. It is widely accepted in the industry that the use of subcontractors sees a reduction in the level and consistency of managerial control over the production process and hence over the final quality of the products being made. Like the pace of work, product quality is very dependent on the skill and attitude of the sewing machine operator. Whereas skill is something that remains with the worker after acquisition, attitude is more often circumstantial and so requires continual attention. Given constants in the quality of raw materials used, it was again the attitudes of individual workers that most troubled managers in relation to production standards and for this very reason they expressed reluctance to engage in local subcontracting practices, especially when the work is being sent to small workshops and homeworkers. In addition to the problems associated with weak supervision, outworkers are often paid on a piece-rate basis. When this occurs, workers have a strong incentive to speed up their output to earn more money, but one of the direct consequences is shoddier work as workers invariably take less care and fail to correct their mistakes. In this situation, some controls on quality can be achieved by the subcontractor refusing to pay for below-standard items, but this system is quite expensive as materials are wasted and there is a real risk of delays in the meeting of orders, for which there can be a penalty on the main contractor. It is therefore principally for quality-control reasons that local subcontracting is not done more extensively than it is in the Philippine garments industry.

But what of workers' own response to subcontracting in their industry? Overall, their response is mixed. On the one hand, unions oppose its wholesale use because of the way in which it obviously creates a marginal workforce and undermines workers' capacity to organise. The main labour organisations have campaigned nationally against government moves to facilitate subcontracting as a part of its strategy to promote small-scale entrepreneurs and enterprises, most recently in 1997 when the Labor Code was amended. Yet, on the other hand, unionists are often also quite accepting of those kinds of subcontracting that they term 'legitimate' – the main one being subcontracting that is only conducted on a seasonal basis. In this case, the core workforce finds that it is cushioned from pressures to work harder during periods of high-volume production by the use of marginal workers. Likewise, they are protected from dismissal during times when production levels are less high. This is illustrated by the fact that 1989 changes to the Labor Code which allowed casual and temporary workers to join a union were not acted on by existing unions as it was feared such a move would enable managers to stymie a certification election by hiring and firing workers. In this sense, the organised workforce saw seasonal subcontracting as playing a role in protecting the union. Interestingly, some workers in large factories were able to sustain strike actions for months at a time because they themselves were able earn an income by turning to contract sewing, or by producing items for sale in local markets in the informal sector.

Central to my argument is the observation that product quality-control standards are highest in the exporting sector of the industry. Managers in the survey reported that such standards are a requirement that overseas contractors and retail buyers set out for them as a condition of acceptance of a consignment.

The significance of this requirement is that it establishes a causal link between exporting and constraints on local subcontracting in the Philippine garments industry. Not surprisingly, the constraints on local subcontracting are mostly at the so-called 'higher end' of the market, where quality is at a premium. Whereas the exporters of casual clothing for mass consumption were often actively putting out, the exporters of more value-added and/or brand-name items were putting out virtually nothing. This is well illustrated by the production strategy of the multinational company, Levi-Strauss. In Manila, this firm 'never' puts out its high-quality items for the Japanese market, whereas just about all of its production for the local Philippine market is put out to subcontractors on a regular basis. As previously noted, with the winding down of international quota arrangements under the MFA, the country's export garments industry is expected to rely more heavily on the 'higher end' of the market, in which local subcontracting is least performed.

It is important to note that many exporting firms also have the large volumes of output which translate into the formation of very large workforces in one place so long as local subcontracting is curtailed. In the domestic-oriented sector, product-quality requirements are commonly not as great or, when they are, they are associated with smaller, family-run enterprises in which modern production techniques are less used. The point is that quality-control measures under these circumstances are more likely to involve corrections rather than prevention – hence, there is an increased preparedness to engage in local subcontracting. By contrast, in the largest exporting firms, production for an overseas market has directly encouraged the intensification of management's supervision of labour as the task of better directing workers' physical movements and mental processes becomes more acutely a problem.

Transnational production arrangements have been widely associated with a distorted form of proletarianisation in which workers are exploited through their rapid exhaustion and replacement, especially in labour-intensive manufacturing. However, in this study, I have found that the international subcontracting of production for labour-only processing in a lower-wage country can actually see a deepening of capitalist class processes in factories where product-quality issues are at a premium. What is more, these same circumstances can increase labour-organising capacity at the enterprise level, with the result that managers are forced into closer negotiations with their in-house workers.

Conclusion

This chapter has shown that the organising capacity of women workers in the Philippine garments industry is greater if they are employed in a factory with a large or very large workforce. In turn, I have sought to explain that the gathering of many workers in one workplace only occurs when certain limitations are placed on the amount of local subcontracting. Exporting has an effect on this because it is principally the quality and delivery-timing requirements of overseas contractors and buyers that curtails this practice in this industry. Managers opt to keep the bulk of the workforce in-house so that they are better able to observe and control what their workers are doing. An unintended consequence of in-house production is that workers have better opportunities to form a union and pursue collective bargaining, as the law allows.

What general conclusions can be drawn from this one-industry study? On one hand, there are clearly certain contingencies pertaining to the Philippines which make it difficult to suppose that the effects of exporting will be the same in garments industries elsewhere. Most particularly, the political space for independent organising is probably greater than in many other countries in the region – Indonesia and Malaysia, for example. Yet it is important to recall that this study reaches conclusions that are different to those associated with previous studies into just the same industry in the Philippines. Precisely because other researchers have considered this industry a 'critical case' with regards to the hypothesised effects of transnational production arrangements on women workers' welfare, it is important not to end with the impression that my findings *vis-à-vis* patterns of unionisation and exporting are only based on an exceptional empirical case. Rather, I will finish by making the point that this study draws different conclusions because of the different methodology used.

As Lim (1990) has previously observed, much of the literature on women in export factories in Asia *deduces* a causal link between exporting and poor labour standards from the original proposition that country-to-country wage differentials are the main factor driving international investment decisions. In contrast, this study has focused on the decisions made in relation to production rather than investment, the part that exporting plays in shaping this and the consequences for workers' self-organising capacity, given other factors are constant. Significantly, the observations made do resonate with those of Kabeer (1987) and Vasquez (1987), who found that female garment workers in export-processing zones in the Philippines experienced better wages and conditions than those employed outside the zones. More recently, Chant and McIlwaine (1995: 129–71) have indeed expressed the view that the female workers of exporting factories are 'relatively privileged' in relation to the employment alternatives that are there in the Philippines for them and their male counterparts. The difference between our studies is that I deal directly with the issue of labour-organising capacity.

Notes

1   One of these innovations was the formation of alliances of unions and workers in different workplaces in the same region and/or industry. Although without legal standing as a legitimate bargaining unit, these alliances have enabled additional negotiations at the enterprise level. The garments industry has a number of these alliances.

2   This survey was conducted in the early 1990s, but the observations stand as I have taken account of the economic and political context in which they were made (see Hutchison, 1992). The following discussion does not detail the *numbers* of firms in the survey engaged in subcontracting or not because, although the sixty-four firms concerned provide a cross-section of the industry, they are by no means a representative sample. I am trying here to elucidate certain processes rather than report on their

statistical occurrence. It is also worth noting at this point that only a small number of export garment firms are located in an export-processing zone, as long-standing arrangements allow the duty-free importation of raw materials for labour-only processing in other locations as well.

3   For a collective, coordinated response, it is not necessary that the workers be unionised; however, in this study I am specifically interested in patterns of unionisation and its effects.

4   In one particular case, the officials of a local union helped a female worker with child-minding arrangements that were troubling her when at work.

Bibliography

Abad, Ramon (1975) *The Garment Industry: A Study Prepared for the NEDA-PDCP-UP Special Course in Corporate Management and Industry Evaluation*, Manila.

Aldana, Cornelia H. (1989) *A Contract for Underdevelopment: Subcontracting for Multinationals in the Philippine Semiconductor and Garments Industries*, Manila: IBON Databank Phils.

Asia Pulse (Philippines) (1998) 'Philippine clothes exporters urged to move up-market', http://www.asiapulse.com (2 November).

Bray, Mark and Taylor, Vic (1991) 'Introduction: Flexibility, marginal workers and unions', in Mark Bray and Vic Taylor (eds) *The Other Side of Flexibility: Unions and Marginal Workers in Australia*, Sydney: Australian Centre for Industrial Relations Research and Teaching, pp. 1–13.

CRC (Centre for Research and Communication) (1974) *A Study of the Perceived Product and Productivity Problems of Selected Garment Firms in the Greater Manila Area*, Manila.

Chant, Sylvia and McIlwaine, Cathy (1995) *Women of a Lesser Cost: Female Labour, Foreign Exchange and Philippine Development*, London: Pluto Press.

Choudhry, Saud (1997) 'Women workers in the global factory: Impact of gender power asymmetries', in Satya Dev Gupta (ed.) *The Political Economy of Globalization*, Boston, Dordrecht and London: Kluwer Academic, pp. 215–36.

Clarke, Gerard (1998) 'Non-Governmental Organizations (NGOs) and politics in the developing world', *Political Studies* 46: 36–52.

Dejillas, Leopoldo J. (1994) *Trade Union Behavior in the Philippines, 1946–1990*, Manila: Ateneo de Manila University Press.

Deyo, Frederic C. (1989) *Beneath the Miracle: Labor Subordination in the New Asian Industrialism*, Berkeley: University of California Press.

Deyo, Frederic C. (1997) 'Labour and industrial restructuring in South-East Asia', in Garry Rodan, Kevin Hewison and Richard Robison (eds) *The Political Economy of South-East Asia: An Introduction*, Melbourne: Oxford University Press, pp. 205–24.

EILER (Ecumenical Institute for Labor Education and Research) (1988) *GTU: Course on Genuine Trade Unionism*, Manila: EILER.

Elson, Diane and Pearson, Ruth (1980) *The Latest Phase of the Internationalisation of Capital and its Implications for Women in the Third World*, Brighton: Institute of Development Studies, University of Sussex.

Fox, Julia D. (1993) 'Transformations in the labor process on a world scale: Women in the new international division of labor', in Berch Berberoglu (ed.) *The Labor Process and Control of Labor: The Changing Nature of Work Relations in the Late Twentieth Century*, Connecticut and London: Praeger, pp. 135–51.

Fröbel, Folker, Heinrichs, Jurgen and Kreye, Otto (1980) *The New International Division of Labour*, Cambridge: Cambridge University Press

Garfinkel, Abraham (1972) *Garment Industry Report (Final)*, Vienna: United Nations Industrial Development Organisation.

Gotto, Junichi (1990) *A Formal Estimation of the Effect of the MFA on Clothing Exports from LDCs*, Washington, D.C.: World Bank, WPS 455.

Guevarra, A. (1999) 'Fast forward martial law in the labor front', *Business World (Philippines)* 24 February: 4.

Hutchison, Jane (1992) 'Women in the Philippines garments export industry', *Journal of Contemporary Asia* 22, 4: 471–89.

—— (1997) 'Pressure on policy in the Philippines', in Garry Rodan, Kevin Hewison and Richard Robison (eds) *The Political Economy of South-East Asia: An Introduction*, Melbourne: Oxford University Press, pp. 64–92.

Hyman, Richard (1988) 'Flexible specialisation: Miracle or myth?', in Richard Hyman and Wolfgang Streek (eds) *New Technology and Industrial Relations*, Oxford: Blackwell.

Kabeer, Naila (1987) *Women's Employment in the Newly Industrialising Countries: A Case Study of India and the Philippines*, Brighton: Institute of Development Studies, University of Sussex.

Lambert, Rob (1990) 'Kilusang Mayo Uno and the rise of social movement unionism in the Philippines', *Labour and Industry* 3, 2–3: 258–80.

Lane, Max (1990) *The Urban Mass Movement in the Philippines, 1983–87*, Political and Social Change Monograph 10, Canberra: Research School of Pacific Studies, Australian National University.

Lim, Linda Y.C. (1990) 'Women's work in export factories: The politics of a cause', in Irene Tinker (ed.) *Persistent Inequalities: Women and World Development*, New York and London: Oxford University Press.

Luib, Romulo T. (1998) 'Philippines: Garments sector seeks survival plan with removal of quota system', *Business World (Philippines)* 15 October: 5.

Mytelka, Lynn Krieger (1991) 'Technological change and the global relocation of production in textiles and clothing', *Studies in Political Economy* 36 (Fall): 109–43.

Ofreneo, Rene E. (1994) 'The labour market, protective labour institutions and economic growth in the Philippines', in Gerry Rodgers (ed.) *Workers, Institutions and Economic Growth in Asia*, Geneva: International Institute for Labour Studies, pp. 255–301.

Pineda-Ofreneo, Rosalinda (1981) 'Domestic outwork for export-oriented industries', *Philippine Social and Humanities Review* XLV, 1–4 (January–December): 51–65.

Pineda-Ofreneo, Rosalinda and De Rosario, Rosario (1988) 'Industrial homeworking in the Philippines', *Philippine Labor Review* 12, 1: 32–45.

Ramos, Elias (1990) *Dualistic Unionism and Industrial Relations*, Quezon City: New Day Publishers.

Ranald, Patricia (1999) 'Analysing, organising, resisting: Union responses to the Asian economic crisis in East Asia, South Korea and the Philippines', *Journal of Industrial Relations* 41, 2: 295–325.

Robert, Annette (1983) 'The effects of the international division of labour on female workers in the textile and clothing industries', *Development and Change*, vol. 14, pp. 19–37.

Rocamora, Joel (1994) *Breaking Through: The Struggle Within the Communist Party of the Philippines*, Manila: Anvil Publishing.

Scipes, Kim (1996) *KMU: Building Genuine Trade Unionism in the Philippines, 1980–1994*, Quezon City: New Day Publishers.

Sicat, Gerardo (1998) 'The Philippine economy in the Asian crisis', *ASEAN Economic Bulletin* 15, 3: 290–6.

Sidel, John T. (1998) 'The underside of progress: Land, labor and violence in two Philippine growth zones, 1985–1995', *Bulletin of Concerned Asian Scholars* 30, 1: 3–12.

Sinay-Aguilar, V. (1986–7) 'ASEAN women workers in export-oriented manufacturing: Industrial relations issues and responses', *Philippine Journal of Industrial Relations* 8, 2 and 9, 1: 118–37.

Snow, Robert (1978) 'Export-oriented industrialization and its impact on women workers: The case of the Bataan Export Processing Zone', *Philippine Sociological Review* 26, 1: 189–99.

Tecson, Gwendolyn, Valcarcel, Lina and Nunez, Carol (1991) 'The role of small and medium-scale industries in the industrial development of the Philippines', *The Role of Small and Medium-Scale Industries in Industrial Development: The Experience of Selected ASEAN Countries*, Manila: Asian Development Bank, pp. 313–422.

Tootals Textiles International Ltd (1987) *A Review of the Export and Domestic Garments Industry with Proposed Strategies and Plans 1987–96*, submitted to the Garment Textile Export Board, Manila, April.

Trela, Irene and Whalley, John (1990) 'Unravelling the threads of the MFA', in Clive Hamilton (ed.) *Textile Trade and Developing Countries: Eliminating the MFA in the 1990s*, Washington, D.C.: World Bank, pp. 11–45.

Vasquez, Noel D. (1987) *Mobilising Surplus Labour through International Exchange: Philippine EPZs, Overseas Employment and Labour Subcontracting*, Quezon City: Ateneo Centre for Social Policy, Ateneo de Manila University Press.

Villegas, Edberto M. (1988) *The Political Economy of Philippine Labor Laws*, Quezon City: Foundation for Nationalist Studies.

West, Lois A. (1997) *Militant Labor in the Philippines*, Philadelphia: Temple University Press.

Woodiwiss, Anthony (1998) *Globalisation, Human Rights and Labour Law in Pacific Asia*, Cambridge and Melbourne: Cambridge University Press.

World Bank (1999) *Philippines: The Challenge of Economic Recovery*, Washington, D.C.: East Asia and Pacific Region Poverty Reduction and Economic Management Sector Unit, World Bank.

Wurfel, David (1959) 'Trade union development and labor relations policy in the Philippines', *Industrial and Labor Relations Review* 12, 4: 582–608.

5 Labour and work organisation in Malaysia's Proton

Rajah Rasiah[1]

The capacity of workers to organise in many parts of East and Southeast Asia has been generally weak. One explanation is that the exigencies of low labour costs in export-oriented manufacturing have seen strong anti-union manoeuvres on the part of both capital and the state. Capitalist development under such circumstances is said to expand the international division of labour whereby workers in host investment sites are exploited so as to facilitate transfer of surplus to home sites (Wallerstein, 1979; Fröbel, Heinrichs and Kreye, 1980). These arrangements are argued to be an institutional innovation of capital specifically designed to facilitate profit taking under changed social and technological conditions. However, rapid accumulation, industrial deepening and the significant involvement of local capital in host countries have raised serious doubts about the peripheralisation thesis. Moreover, up to the mid-1990s, there had been improvements in the material circumstances of workers in a number of economies in the region – although predictions about the marginalisation of organised labour held largely true.

Drawing particular attention to the issue of work organisation, Deyo (1989) argues that conditions of employment in labour-intensive manufacturing deny workers the capacity to influence improvements in their working conditions. Given that there have been significant shifts to more capital- and technology-intensive, flexible forms of manufacturing in various parts of East and Southeast Asia – including Malaysia (Rasiah, 1988; 1993a; Rasiah, Ishak and Jomo, 1996) – what changes have there been to the conditions of employment of workers and, hence, what new opportunities exist for them to form independent unions? Various industrial organisation theorists have predicted that shifts towards 'flexible specialisation' in manufacturing will induce more training and workplace participation of workers (Sengenberger and Pyke, 1991). In Malaysia, transformations in the organisation of work have indeed, in a number of cases, enhanced worker involvement in the labour process (especially in competitive industries such as electronic components) but these changes have not been associated with any relaxation of controls on independent unionism.

As the example of the state-controlled Proton[2] car firm in Malaysia demonstrates in this chapter, both the introduction of more flexible forms of work organisation and their implications for labour relations are strongly mediated by local political and historical circumstances. A combination of three factors – rents gained from various government interventions, policies designed to favour *Bumiputeras* (ethnic Malays) in business and strong continuities in state controls over organised labour – have seen only the partial adoption of flexible and cooperative methods of production and worker management. Prior to the 1997 financial crisis, the organising capacity of the in-house union was not advanced by changes to the labour process that had occurred; since then, a drop in demand for cars has made the union only more fragile, despite the workers' concomitant awakening to their worsened economic situation. The sharp fall in rents received by the company has cut deeply into remuneration levels once enjoyed by Proton workers, consequently forcing a rise in resignations. The recent harsh nature and scale of labour 'shedding' in Proton merely demonstrates another form of marginalisation inevitable in hostile structures.

This chapter is divided into five parts. There is a brief, initial discussion of 'flexible specialisation' in the international automobile industry. Since it is the broader political and economic context which shapes workers' experiences of capitalist work relations in the Proton car firm, the second section outlines the evolution of labour organising in Malaysia. The third and fourth sections return to the specific case study, discussing respectively Proton's business history and the evolution of its labour and work organisation. The fifth section concludes the chapter with the impact of the financial crisis on the poorly developed in-house union framework in Proton.

Flexible specialisation

The international automobile industry has been a site for important debates over contemporary changes in the technology and organisation of manufacturing, production and marketing – central issues being the nature and extent of shifts from 'neo-Taylorist' and 'Fordist mass production' to 'flexible specialisation', and the factors accounting for these changes (Palloix, 1978; Sabel, 1986; Hoffman and Kaplinsky, 1988; Landesmann and Scazzieri, 1995; Deyo, 1996). Neo-Taylorist work organisation is characterised by the use of predominantly unskilled and dextrous semi-skilled labour under intense supervisory control, whereas Fordist mass production involves 'the manufacture of standardized products in high volumes using special-purpose machinery and predominantly unskilled labour'. Flexible specialisation, on the other hand, is said to be associated with 'the manufacture of a wide and changing variety of customised products using flexible, general-purpose machinery and skilled, adaptable workers' (Hirst and Zeitlin, 1991: 2). In addition to the training and broadening of skills of workers, flexible specialisation is also claimed to demand a workplace culture in which divisions between managers and the workforce are broken down and replaced by an atmosphere of trust and cooperation (Sengenberger and Pyke, 1991: 3). This transformation in the method of getting work from workers is said to be matched by improvements in wages and conditions, so as to encourage better work performance. However, there is further debate over the impact these developments may have on workers' self-organising capacities (see Thomas, 1995: 9).

Theoretical accounts of the factors behind greater flexible specialisation vary. Some writers see its emergence as an inexorable outcome of inevitable crises of capitalism, whereas others attribute it to new technologies like microelectronics and/or to the greater competition that results from market expansion and fragmentation. In such cases, these factors are generally thought to apply universally. By contrast, writers such as Hirst and Zeitlin (1991) and Sengenberger (1992) stress the importance of local conditions and contingencies, especially the ways in which particular production systems are embedded in broader social and political frameworks, conflicts and accommodations. As will be seen, this chapter supports the view that context is important; for that reason, the next section examines the history of state–labour relations in Malaysia.

Organising labour in Malaysia

Labour activism first emerged with the opening of the then colonial Malaya to economic extraction, plantation agriculture and trade. Prolonged and often brutal struggles – particularly in the estates – eventually led in the early 1940s to legislation providing for the official recognition of unions and their rights to industrial action. However, this legislation was so restrictive that it amounted to little more than 'state-controlled unionism' (Jomo and Todd, 1994: 65–6). In the late 1940s, a period of post-war anti-colonial and labour militancy was crushed through the twofold 'suppression of persons and activities suspected of being subversive' and the 'paternalistic encouragement' of those considered amenable to the status quo (ibid.: 85). These policies were maintained after independence in 1957 (ibid.: 106–7) but, in addition, the decade saw the beginnings of official steps to include unions in the shaping of work relations. The Employment Act of 1955 still remains the governing source for employment matters in Malaysia. Under other ordinances, union and related exemptions were offered to firms classified as 'pioneering', and unionisation was limited to particular trades, occupations or industries. Capital's dominance and its alliance with the state tended to ensure draconian labour practices and the arbitrary definition of 'pioneering' opened collective bargaining to easy violation by firms. A strong male bias in the demand for labour under import-substitution industrialisation (ISI) made it possible for the state to also enforce protective conditions for women, including prohibitions on their working the night shift.

The union movement suffered another major setback when the government enacted the 1967 Industrial Relations Act, barring collective bargaining or strikes over matters involving promotions, transfers, recruitment, retrenchment, dismissal, reinstatement or the allocation of duties (Rasiah, 1997a: 125). On top of this, unions lost their right to strike once a dispute had been referred to the industrial court. With the shift to export-oriented industrialisation and associated efforts to stimulate foreign investment from 1968 – but especially from 1972 when the free trade zones were opened – the situation which had been evolving in formal labour relations deteriorated further. Amendments to the 1955 Employment Act offered pioneering export-oriented firms the option of rejecting unionisation and allowed night shifts for women workers. The government subsequently promoted its industrial strategy, aggressively referring to Malaysian women workers as 'cheap, literate and docile'.

Interpreting industrial peace as that which ensures a favourable climate for the inflow of outward-oriented transnational operations, the state prevented the slightest expression of worker dissent. Even small grey areas within the already restrictive Employment and Industrial Relations Acts were generally ruled in favour of transnationals. Carefully cultivated relations between firms' personnel officials and Ministry of Labour officials ensured quick interventions by the state in their favour (Rasiah, 1993a). *Inter alia*, such relationships helped to avert potentially disruptive labour activism in the 1970s and early 1980s when real manufacturing wages remained fairly stagnant. Yet conditions were worse in the plantation sector, where the pro-government National Union for Plantation Workers (NUPW) failed to stem a fall in the real wages of rubber tappers throughout the 1970s and 1980s (Jayakumar, 1996). In this case, a steady inflow of foreign workers – particularly from Indonesia – ensured sufficient labour reserves to limit real wage rises. Falling commodity prices and increased speculation in and sale of plantation land for industrial and housing purposes also ensured that the relative demand for labour did not rise sharply.

In export-oriented manufacturing, the widespread use of neo-Taylorist labour practices gave workers little further room to manoeuvre. As well as being footloose and based on low technology, firms were characterised by work organisations anchored to high work fragmentation and low skills. The nature of production required dexterity-intensive but non-technical work tasks, which need only short training periods. In this situation, supported by poor retrenchment benefits and a large labour reserve arising from high unemployment levels, firms were ensured quick replacements for labour turnovers and lay-offs; in addition, they were able to take on a high proportion of temporary workers. The casualisation of work – made possible by a combination of labour surplus, work organisation and draconian state legislation – fettered the development of better working conditions. Moreover, on the assembly line, labour control methods normally entailed the strict monitoring of workers by direct supervision to the point of applying injurious discipline. Under these conditions, there was obviously little cooperation along vertical lines and hierarchies of rigidly defined work tasks remained the rule.

Industrialisation for much of the 1970s was thus characterised by low levels of labour activism; export-oriented firms especially were able to shield themselves through their 'pioneering' status. Nonetheless, some unions did gradually appear in the export manufacturing sector. The Electrical Industry Workers Union (EIWU) was formed in 1974 and textile unions began organising workers from 1978. Electronics workers – primarily those in the free trade zones – were, on the other hand, denied any form of unionisation until 1989. Yet the presence of a union did not necessarily make a significant difference: the working conditions of textile workers who enjoyed the right to join a union have been no different from those of the non-unionised electronic workers.

The narrow framework for collective bargaining drove some unionists to challenge the ruling government through political channels. Notably, V. David and Ahmad Noor, leaders of the Malaysian Trades Union Congress (MTUC) – the largest national labour centre – successfully gained parliamentary seats through the opposition Democratic Action Party (DAP) in 1990. However, their terms ended in 1995 when the former did not contest and the latter lost his seat. More recently, in the wake of the political crisis, the government has begun involving the MTUC in a number of its councils, offering union leaders carrots to prevent a mass movement of workers to the opposition. MTUC's president, Zainal Rampak, switched in 1998 to the ruling United Malay National Organization (UMNO) and Mahathir appointed him a senator. However, the ramifications of this for the labour movement remain unclear, as there are otherwise no formal links between it and the dominant political parties.

Towards industrial deepening

By the early 1990s, developments emanating internally and externally had opened the gates for some changes to work relations in key manufacturing industries in Malaysia. Intense competition and miniaturisation in the electronic components industry induced changes in work organisation which necessitated training, skills broadening and participatory work relations for all levels of workers (Rasiah, 1989). The introduction of collaborative management practices and the trend towards job permanence helped to improve working conditions in the industry from the mid-1980s. In addition, buoyant growth in the domestic economy after 1987 began to exhaust labour reserves in the country. The unemployment rate fell from 8.5 per cent in 1986 to 6.0 per cent in 1989 and, eventually, to 2.5 per cent in 1995 before the financial crisis (Malaysia, 1996). For that period, resulting acute labour shortages forced the government to abandon its employment generation goal. By the 1990s, official government policy discouraged labour-intensive investment in the Western corridor; crowded industrial states such as Penang and Selangor began to assist already operating labour-intensive firms to relocate, either in East Malaysia or abroad. Enjoying a higher bargaining position *vis-à-vis* foreign firms from the late 1980s than it did until then, the government even stopped offering incentives to labour-intensive firms, turning its attention instead to the development of strategic high-technology industries (Rasiah, 1997a: 138).

Typical macro-economic arguments posit that a relative increase in demand for labour will not only reduce unemployment, but will also enhance the bargaining power of unions and, with that, bring strong benefits for workers. Coupled with this, the infusion of high technology and collaborative managerial practices in electronic-component assembly created strong internal dynamics for positive industrial relations practices. However, improved circumstances from the late 1980s failed to offer unions greater bargaining power, although real wages did begin to rise. Arguably, the state became more authoritarian during this time, partly as an after-effect of Prime Minister Mahathir's narrow victory over his challenger for the leadership, Tengku Razaleigh, in the 1987 UMNO general elections. Evidence for this comes from policies and legislation directed at depressing wages, raising labour flexibility, enhancing managerial prerogatives and controlling unions (Jomo and Todd, 1994: 152). The participation of several union leaders in politics under opposition umbrellas did not help. Union formation in electronics – the country's largest manufacturing industry, employing over 20 per cent of the manufacturing workforce in 1993 – was also prevented by continued opposition from transnational firms, especially from American firms.

Fascinated by their role in Japan, the Malaysian government from 1983 actively encouraged in-house unions over national industry unions, thereby increasing their number from 36 in 1982 to 154 in 1992. The share of unionised workers in in-house unions rose from 6.5 per cent of the total in 1982 to just under 30 per cent in 1992 (Zulkifly, 1995: Table 5). Yet the rising trend towards enterprise unions has failed to stem a gradual fall in unionisation. Union density in Malaysia has not kept pace with industrial expansion, decreasing from just under 12 per cent in 1982 to 8.5 per cent in 1996 (Rasiah and Von Hofmann, 1998: 17, 21). Where firms have been opposed to their formation – as in the electronics industry – even in-house unions have generally failed to gain much access. By 1992 there were only eight in-house unions in the electronics industry and their participation hardly reflected acceptable roles (Rasiah, 1996). On the other hand, most state-controlled industrial companies (including Proton) have in-house unions.

However, in-house unionism in Malaysia differs from the Japanese model. In post-war Japan large employers preferred in-house unions to the more militant national unions as the development of democracy and civil society coincided with the struggle for unionisation (Clark, 1978; Aoki, 1984; Florida and Kenny, 1988). Thus, in that country, enterprise unionism was met by collaborative work relations on the factory floor: developments outside the firm conditioned a complementary mode of worker organisation on the factory floor. By contrast, there has been no concomitant democratisation of labour legislation in Malaysia. The flexibility and cooperation established between management and labour in Japan has obviously not evolved in Malaysia. Not only has the political structure in the country not been conducive to greater cooperation in the workplace, but the agents establishing such relations have also done little towards creating a favourable environment for its emergence. The state has maintained repressive controls on labour to hold labour costs down and curb disruptions to production so that competitiveness can be sustained. Thus, even where the internal dynamics of technological change and re-organisation of the labour process strongly favoured collaborative work relations, managements have preferred to establish such relations without unions.

At the same time, confrontations between labour and management have been significantly reduced. Labour militancy – marginal though it is – has been confined to the national unions, mostly emerging in the mid-1980s when large numbers of workers faced retrenchments (Rasiah, 1988). In-house unions that have been accepted by management hardly have the room to engage in combative bargaining. Not only has the broader external structure set serious constraints on their role, but leaders of in-house unions have also generally been cultivated by management to act more as complementary working units. Where their creation has not been associated with sound labour-management objectives, they have operated as fairly incoherent units with no clear aims. In-house unions in state-owned firms have largely functioned in this way, including the one in the Proton car firm. Before describing work practices and the role of the union in that company, it is necessary to set out the factors behind its establishment and the subsequent pattern of development.

Proton

As with most state-led ventures in Malaysia, Proton and its operations have been coloured by national political concerns. In the early 1980s, disappointed with the pace of upward economic mobility faced by the *Bumiputeras* – particularly their level of involvement in the upper occupational rungs of the private sector and in the ownership of large manufacturing enterprises – the government set out to create a platform for their active participation in manufacturing. In 1981, Prime Minister Mahathir thus established the Heavy Industry Corporation of Malaysia (HICOM), a key objective being to promote the business interests of indigenous Malays. Proton is a subsidiary of HICOM. It was incorporated in 1983 and has been turning out cars since its initial production run in 1985 in Shah Alam. Other industries with HICOM involvement include steel, cement and clinker.

The automobile industry was first established in Malaysia in 1967 as foreign firms relocated their final-stage assembly processes so as to adapt to tariffs designed to promote ISI. By 1981, there were twenty-eight car assemblers in the country; however, government policies giving Proton privileged access to the domestic market – coupled with severe cuts to demand as a result of the mid-1980s economic downturn – saw the total number of car manufacturers halved to fourteen by 1985. This number fell further to nine in 1988, although by 1992 it had risen again to eleven. The associated decline in passenger car output was very significant – between 1983 and 1988 there was an annual average 19.6 per cent drop from 100,223 to 33,685 units. However, Proton's rapid expansion and a sustained upswing in the domestic economy from the late 1980s soon turned these figures around – total output rose by an annual average rate of 59.3 per cent to 136,184 units in 1991 (Chan, 1994: Appendix 2). At the same time, Proton's share of the domestic market increased from an initial 11 per cent to a peak of 74 per cent in 1993, thereafter falling slightly to 72 per cent in 1995 (Proton, 1995: 6). Exports began in the second year of production, first to Bangladesh. Almost ten years later, the firm's overseas market had stretched to twenty-eight countries, the main destination being Britain (ibid.: 7). During that same decade, Proton's production capacity also doubled from 80,000 to 160,000 units, making it the largest automobile plant in Southeast Asia. After some initial losses, the firm quickly began returning an operating profit from 1986.

The expansion of Proton's production capacity, alongside contractions and closures in other parts of the industry, saw the firm's share of the automobile assembly workforce in Malaysia increase from 11.5 per cent in 1985 to 44.4 per cent in 1992. Yet, despite the fact that labour in the country had gained considerable final car- and parts-assembly experience by the time Proton was established, policies designed to favour *Bumiputeras* meant workers retrenched from the closures of other car assemblers were deliberately not absorbed into Proton. Hardly any of the new employees had past working experience in the industry, so previous skills and technical capabilities did not figure in the firm's start-up. Thus, after employment had grown from 678 to 4,843 in the ten years from 1985 to 1995, *Bumiputeras* accounted for over 98 per cent of Proton's employees at all levels. Similar ethnic profiles exist at the firm's five subsidiary and eight associate firms which are engaged in component manufacture and car assembly. In addition, joint venture operations in the Philippines and Vietnam have used *Bumiputera* personnel in management.

Over the last three decades, some of the new entrants into the international automobile industry – Semco in Brazil, Hermosillo in Mexico and Hyundai in South Korea – have absorbed so-called 'best practice' work techniques from abroad (Amsden, 1989; Shaiken, 1990; Kaplinsky, 1994). Like their more established competitors, these newer companies have been able to achieve a well-integrated, firm-wide take up of flexible and collaborative methods. The more recent entrant, Proton in Malaysia, has attempted to make up for a lack of indigenous technological capability by aligning itself with the Japanese *zaibatsu*, Mitsubishi, in a joint venture arrangement involving technology transfers. In 1995 state-led capital effectively controlled 54.5 per cent of shares, with Mitsubishi controlling just over 17 per cent. However, the level of absorption of flexible modes of work organisation has been superficial in comparison with Semco, Hermosillo and Hyundai. After more than a decade in operation, Proton has not been able to demonstrate a coherent strategy for the application of lean production and collaborative work organisation.

In 1996, Proton's production capacity was limited to body and shell assembly, painting and vehicle assembly. Research and development (R&D) was generally limited to vehicle design and components development. The firm thus still lacks more sophisticated design capability – the engine and the gearbox remain import items from Mitsubishi, while that company's experts continue to visit the Malaysian plant to monitor the diffusion of assembly technology associated with new models. There has also been little participation at Proton in the development and customisation of materials and parts supplied by foreign firms – air conditioners, stereo sets, antennae, metals, safety gadgets and so on – something often done by leading firms like Toyota, Mercedes, BMW, General Motors, Honda and Ford. Proton is thus still far from the technology frontier.

One of the prime tools used to support Proton's growth has been government-imposed tariffs and excise duties. On one hand, this has meant prices facing domestic consumers have been considerably higher than world prices. On the other hand, rents arising from these tariffs and excise duties have enabled the realisation of substantial value-added from the domestic market, despite the heavy dependence on foreign technology. Tariffs and excise duties have been highest on completely built units; nevertheless, components have also come under relatively high duties to reduce the yen effect on imports and, again, to encourage *Bumiputera* suppliers. These interventions have enabled government to achieve high levels of local content in a relatively short period of time,[3] although the *Bumiputera* industrialists who are involved have been largely inexperienced. However, the importance of obtaining immediate sales and repairs support for Proton vehicles has meant the government has been more accommodating towards existing Chinese involvement in this part of the industry. Despite some initial apprehensions, Chinese operators have thus been keen to take advantage of the rents obtainable in non-production aspects of the value-added chain. Nevertheless, ethnic cleavages have continued. The resultant truncation of links between sales and repairs and production has led to poor feedback from the market and customer-service to the shopfloor. The effect of this has been that delivery times remain at between one and three months and relatively high defect rates have not been reduced.

In sum, the automobile industry in Malaysia was slow to expand during the ISI phase. The entry of Proton, coinciding as it did with an economic recession, caused a big drop in passenger car output in the mid-1980s. However, with state support and a subsequent upswing in demand, Proton rapidly expanded from 1989 and this had the knock-on effect of lifting the total output of the industry. Given the significance of ethnic politics in its establishment and localisation policies, the control, employment and development spin-offs from Proton have strongly favoured *Bumiputeras*. The consequent formation of a new business class can be viewed as a twofold process in which the *Bumiputeras* have not only had to catch up with domestic Chinese industrialists, but also achieve competitiveness in the international arena. However, ethnic divisions have contributed to relatively poor levels of coordination at an industry-wide level.

Labour and work organisation in Proton[4]

The production workforce at Proton has been entirely composed of males. The firm reports this gender bias is due to the physically strenuous nature of assembly work and to cultural practices that limit female participation in such tasks. However, management has also actively ruled out of contention the few women who have shown interest in the production department in order to avoid sexual harassment. Female employees of Proton are thus only employed in clerical and security jobs.

In keeping with other state-controlled firms, the workers at Proton belong to an in-house union. Within the production department, union members range from base-level workers to foremen. Unlike the in-house unions in the electronics industry – where few (if any) members have been aware of employment and industrial relations practices in the country – Proton's workers have been exposed to employment regulations and industrial relations practices through formal courses and statutes distributed to members. In line with national regulations, collective agreements with management have been made once every three years and, up until the financial crisis struck, there were no deadlocks in negotiations. However, the authoritarian environment in which they are situated means workers at Proton have always enjoyed little political leverage to engage proactively in collective bargaining. By avoiding affiliation with a national umbrella body – even with the conservative Malaysian Trades Union Congress (MTUC) – the in-house union managed to steer clear of potentially damaging confrontational struggles with management – that is, prior to the 1997 financial crisis. Nevertheless, committee members have been elected independent of management influence and benefits successfully generated through the union have included better bonus payments, allowances to account for inflationary pressures and safety measures at work. However, the comparatively high wages Proton workers earned before the crisis were sustained by rents, high skill requirements, growing demand and the tight Western Peninsula labour market.

Conditions before the 1997 financial crisis

Extensive use of overtime and the high levels of rents achieved by Proton enabled workers to enjoy relatively high total wages for over a decade. At RM350, the nominal basic starting wage of Proton's production workers – which has remained the same since production commenced in 1985 – is close to that of the manufacturing average. However, workers in the firm are entitled to transport, food and hardship allowances, which raise their income above that average. The average real wages of workers interviewed for this study (excluding overtime benefits) exceeded that of the average for skilled workers in the manufacturing industry from 1987 to 1995. Once overtime and bonuses are added, they were among the best-paid line workers in the country before the financial crisis hit. The nominal income – after overtime is included – of the workers (including one foreman and six assistant foremen) ranged from RM1,100 to RM3,000 in 1995.

In addition, Proton's workers enjoyed several other benefits. Once every two years, all employees were entitled to purchase a Proton car at subsidised rates. These subsidies amount to around RM8,000 per car and there was the further advantage that the vehicle could be sold straight away to anyone. Thus the workers, foreman and assistant foremen interviewed reported selling the car immediately after purchase, to either their relatives or their friends. Employees – including direct workers – have also been issued preferential shares. Special loans at subsidised interest rates ensured that even those workers without enough cash were able to access this lucrative channel to further returns. However, my interviews show that neither the cars nor the shares have generated a sense of belonging among workers, as both have largely been used instrumentally to generate immediate cash. If stock sharing in other leading international automobile firms has helped to generate stronger participation by workers in the labour process, effects along these lines have only been superficial in Proton, with no concomitant directing of the loyalty and trust gained to innovative activities.

Proton's workers faced no retrenchment threats until the financial crisis struck in 1997, but this was due to continued growth in output rather than to the union's own bargaining strength. Domestic sales increased so rapidly that production required expanded capacity and every worker was in heavy demand for overtime work. In addition to lengthening the working day through overtime, the firm took on new employees to meet demand. These developments enabled Proton's workers to produce significantly higher numbers of cars per annum than other assemblers in Malaysia. In 1985, productivity levels in Proton were similar to those in the overall industry: around eleven cars per worker per year.[5] However, by 1988 the difference between the two amounted to some seventeen cars per worker per year in favour of the state-controlled firm. In 1993, the gap was smaller – at nine cars per worker per year – but Proton remained in the lead.

However, my interviews show that increased overtime has stifled skills-deepening and subjected workers to tiring work routines. The long hours of work have also affected the family life of several workers – a finding which was acknowledged by the managers interviewed. As a result there were often high levels of absenteeism; while labour turnover was very low – 1–2 per cent a month – the rate of absenteeism in the production department in 1995–6 was around 20 per cent monthly. During festive seasons, absenteeism sometimes reached 50 per cent of the direct workers. Of course, there were other reasons for such high rates of absenteeism: namely, traffic jams, health problems and festive hangovers. Instead of enriching work and reducing work time, Proton's response to high rates of absenteeism has been to hire surplus workers – two on average for each shift at each station. Workers themselves were not motivated to cultivate a creative atmosphere at work, therefore they viewed work as merely a means to an income. They voluntarily undertake overtime to increase that income – none of the workers interviewed have ever been coerced into working longer hours – but such actions cannot be viewed as a commitment to the firm. This is the case even though labour control at Proton has not been as dehumanising as that experienced by Malaysian workers in the electronics and textile industries until the late 1980s (Rasiah, 1993a: ch. 3; 1993b).

On the other hand, three factors – Proton's infancy, its commitment to creating a *Bumiputera* managerial and technical class, and a management policy that places little emphasis on past experience – have ensured relatively easy upward mobility in job functions within the firm (Rasiah, 1997b). In the sales and repairs area, experienced employees from rival automobile firms have been attracted strongly to Proton by the huge rent potential, but this has not occurred in the manufacturing plant. Among the ten workers interviewed, all began car-assembly work at Proton between 1985 and 1990 at a Grade 1 or Grade 2 level.[6] By 1995 all had been promoted – one had become a foreman, six had become assistant foremen, one was a Grade 4 worker and the remaining two had moved up to the Grade 2 level.

In line with the general industrial relations norm in the country, Proton's union has enjoyed no jurisdiction on matters related to training and innovation. Given the absence of strong collective bargaining, skills enrichment in the firm has been dictated by the firm and the state. State governance in training in Proton took the form initially of the Double Deduction Incentive for Training (DDIT), which was in use from 1988–92, and later the Human Resource Development Fund (HRDF), which replaced it in 1993. Given its deliberate policy of employing direct workers without experience, Proton has had to participate considerably in training. In 1985, 18 managers and 239 direct and indirect staff were sent for training to Mitsubishi in Japan (Chan, 1994: 64). This decade, the local component of training increased substantially to about 80 per cent of the total; nevertheless, batches of staff are still sent to Japan to acquire assembly skills – especially when new models are introduced. In addition, a small number of Japanese experts visit Proton from time to time to advise and coach local employees.

Despite extensive emphasis – including via investment – on training, Proton still does not offer state-of-the-art support to complement technological deepening in the firm. The lack of a coherent *kaizen* culture – which emphasises constant improvements in employees' conduct so as to continuously enhance the efficiency and performance of the firm – and the relative inexperience of Proton's management meant that external training was initially confined largely to the acquisition of assembly know-how from Japan, as governed by technology-transfer agreements with Mitsubishi. Proton began to access the DDIT, which offered a tax rebate of twice the approved cost for training, from 1988. However, employees were generally only sent for work procedure and motivational courses. The emphasis has thus been confined to technical training, with little attention being paid to the development of innovative faculties. Similar developments took place following the introduction of the Human Resource Development Fund (HRDF) in 1993. Officials from the Human Resource Development Council reported that Proton has claimed around 90 per cent of the mandatory 1 per cent of their payroll contributed to the fund. Proton opened its own training centre and modular training programmes have been introduced since. However, Proton does not operate as a platform for continuous education, nor do workers have any actual control over the training process.

The labour process itself at Proton has evolved into an incoherent mixture of several different forms of work organisation – it cannot be referred to as neo-Taylorist, but neither is it exclusively mass production or flexible specialisation. On one hand, management has not treated workers as a cost that needs trimming: high rents and a management without aggressive, big-business experience allowed Proton workers job security and a somewhat benevolent remuneration package up until the financial crisis of 1997. There has not been recourse to neo-Taylorism or 'flexible casualisation' (Sabel, 1986; Hirst and Zeitlin, 1991), yet neither has labour been considered a special resource; the emphasis on innovation and productivity as the basis of competitiveness has been only moderate. Proton has been seriously lacking in the application of the kind of productive-process techniques familiar to state-of-the-art firms. This form of work organisation does not fit the notion of flexible specialisation, nor Sengenberger and Pyke's reference to 'the high road to industrial restructuring' (Sengenberger and Pyke, 1991: 10–11).

The eclectic nature of work organisation in the firm is reflected in the introduction of process techniques. Quality control circles (QCCs) have been introduced since 1985, and small groups have contributed various innovative ideas and solutions to help improve production. Workers cooperate among their own ranks through small group activities – especially in problem solving. Yet the extent of vertical cooperation within the in-firm division of labour in Proton has been relatively small – direct workers are still exposed to standardised, horizontally fragmented tasks around a conveyor belt. The organisation of work is generally oriented towards different segments in the production hierarchy having their own jurisdiction, with none clearly interlocking with others. Groupworking has evolved along mass production lines, where semi-skilled and skilled workers are still bound strongly by a supervisory chain of command under foremen. Employees at different levels within the work hierarchy only meet once a month, while foremen and assistant foremen have a large span of control – over from twenty to forty workers. The firm does not have statistical process control (SPC) – methods deployed to monitor operative processes – and quality control inspectors still occupy a separately defined job. As we have seen, workers' participation in shaping the work process has been further limited by the absence of efforts to enhance the role of skilled workers.

My interviews show that Proton managers still lack a well-defined strategy to develop, or even implement, existing process technologies effectively – including *kaizen* features. Thus the slow adoption of flexible specialisation and collaborative production techniques appears to be due to a poverty of planning, institutional support and coordination, born of rents-induced organisational fat. Under such circumstances, the extent of teamworking, multi-skilling, cross-skilling and innovative participation by workers has been limited. This lack of effective institutional coordination in Proton's launch and subsequent operations has been the prime obstacle to the effective adoption and development of technologies in the firm (Rasiah, 1996).

Conditions after the 1997 financial crisis

The potentially catastrophic consequences of working in a state-supported company that was shielded from foreign competition and lacked effective institutional coordination came to the fore when the financial crisis engulfed Malaysia in 1997: the destabilising effects of this crisis had immediate serious ramifications for Proton's workers. In 1998, passenger vehicle production levels fell by a dramatic 58.8 per cent,[7] exposing the company to serious overcapacity problems. Management has responded to this situation by employing short-term strategies to reduce costs. Resultant rationalisation and austerity measures have not only reduced training and development outlays, but also sharply decreased workers' income-earning opportunities by wiping out the overtime allowances they previously enjoyed. Workers thus report a decline in income of 40–60 per cent in 1998 – this bringing many of them down to the mere starting wage of RM350 per month.

In addition, management has begun to use various channels to trim the workforce. In particular, a sizeable number of workers have been relocated to subcontracting firms, where they either face working conditions that are far worse or ultimate retrenchment. Interviews with two such workers in October 1998 showed that most of the transferred workers have remained in employment, but primarily in casual jobs unrelated to their skills and with significantly smaller salaries. Through these and other means, my enquiries suggest that the Proton workforce declined by more than 20 per cent in 1998. Cuts in wages and the transfer of workers to menial tasks (like weeding and cleaning) that were previously contracted out, have strongly demoralised the workers who remain.

The acquiescent approach of the Proton in-house union has been found wanting by the crisis. Rocked by the developments that followed, the union leadership has now begun to recognise the dangers of confining their role to the firm. As a result, they have commenced active negotiations to merge or federate with the Transport Equipment Workers Union (TEWU). In 1998, the officials of both unions stated they were working towards the establishment of a framework that is conducive to their workers' interests. The TEWU leadership also reported that they had foreseen the repercussions now occurring at Proton.

The amalgamation of passenger car manufacturers into one national union might be easier now that the MTUC's president is an UMNO member and Senator. The MTUC has become more consolidated at the national level with the entry in 1997 of its smaller former rival, the Malaysian Labour Organization (MLO), and through its leadership achieving a resounding victory in elections conducted in 1999. The MTUC–MLO merger has seen the re-emergence of a single national labour centre. Although only a third of registered unions are affiliates of the MTUC, it does cover over 60 per cent of the unionised workforce (Rasiah and Von Hofmann, 1998: 19). While some might question the efficacy and integrity of some of MTUC's current crop of leaders, the relative independence of the TEWU may offer the dynamism required to negotiate Proton's in-house union's entry into the national body. However, much will depend on the domestic passenger vehicle demand patterns and the mood of the government. Otherwise, more broadly, the weak institutional framework prevailing in the country has reduced the potential for pickets and mass protests, thereby masking the reservoir of discontent that has been growing since the financial crisis struck.

Conclusions

The Malaysian experience obviously shows that local structures substantially influence workers' organising capacity and the material gains they achieve. The state has from the 1980s supported the formation of in-house unions. Despite their lack of organising powers (and in many cases even collective bargaining awareness), workers in a number of firms with in-house unions have enjoyed relatively better conditions of work than others in nationally organised unions. As with several non-unionised electronics component firms, the capacity of some firms with in-house unions to offer better working conditions than those with national unions has been due largely to the nature of work organisation necessitated by technological and market requirements, and to the implicit threat of workers affiliating with national unions. Several firms in high-technology electronics component industries have experienced concrete work improvements – including in remuneration – irrespective of the role of the union. Proton has offered better working conditions to its workers due to heavy domestic rents generated from protection and the state policy to promote *Bumiputera* participation in the firm. However, despite improvements on the factory floor, the political structure in the country has fettered mass organisation.

Sheltered through high monopolistic rents, a somewhat eclectic work organisation has evolved at Proton. The management has introduced some elements of teamworking, job permanence, training and retraining, relaxed labour-control methods and relatively high remuneration. Yet few features that characterise flexible specialisation are in place in the firm. Most notably, workers still do not participate extensively in innovative activities. Nevertheless, Proton's work organisation also does not demonstrate exclusively neo-Taylorist or mass production structures. A mixture of *most* work organisations has emerged within a technological structure oriented towards mass production.

However, the perceived benevolent remuneration practices at Proton have quite clearly come to an end since the financial crisis crippled domestic demand. Being part of one of the most seriously affected industries, Proton's workers have arguably suffered one of the sharpest declines in wages and job transfers. The stark reality of one possible future facing Proton's workers has now been demonstrated, even before the removal of trade barriers shielding the firm. Any efforts to reduce protection and subsidies sheltering Proton – which could come due to the imposition of the World Trade Organisation (WTO) clauses by 2003 – would further undermine wages and employment. Unless Proton manages to establish global competitiveness, the only survival alternative available would seem to be seeking shelter – through a merger – under the aegis of a foreign company that wished to use Malaysia's position within the South to access markets. Its pioneering partner, Mitsubishi, or other foreign companies might assume control, if this option proved viable. Otherwise, the future for Proton's workers is not very bright. In the absence of access to rents, wages are likely to eventually match the industry average.

The devastating effect of the financial crisis has encouraged Proton's workers and its in-house union to begin negotiations for a possible merger with the national level TEWU. The move towards a merger with the national industry-wide union should help the workers enjoy greater protection, especially during times of crisis. However, unless drastic changes take place, the restrictive industrial relations framework in the country will continue to thwart the emergence of effective unionism.

Notes

1 Helpful editorial comments from Jane Hutchison are gratefully acknowledged. The usual disclaimer applies. This chapter has benefited immensely from research undertaken in Germany in 1996, when I was a senior research fellow at the Friedrich Ebert Stiftung in Bonn.
2 The firm's full name is Perusahaan Otomobil Nasional Berhad (meaning 'National Automobile Industry Limited').
3 In 1995, Proton managed to source 3,511 components domestically – 88 per cent from domestic vendors, the bulk of the remainder in-house. Against the value of gross output minus imports, Proton in 1995 had a record of 67 per cent local content but, by the government's own local-material content policy, the figure is 80 per cent. This is a remarkable achievement over a relatively short period of time (compare with South Korea, for example – Doner, 1991: Table 1).
4 The analysis in this section is based on information gathered from company documents and fieldwork over the period 1995–6. Seven managers, one section head, one foreman, six assistant foremen and three direct workers were interviewed. Given the difficulty associated with accessing company employees, the only criterion used in their selection was long service in the firm. The foreman and assistant foremen themselves joined Proton as direct workers in 1985.
5 These figures have been computed from various issues of the Malaysian government's *Industrial Survey* and from Proton (1995).
6 Grade 1 workers joined after their Sijil Pelajaran Malaysia (SPM), which is the equivalent of a GCE 'O'-level in Britain. Grade 2 level is offered to workers with a technical certificate.
7 Computed from Bank Negara (1998: 84).

Bibliography

Amsden, A.H. (1989) *Asia's Next Giant: South Korea and Late Industrialization*, New York: Oxford University Press.
Aoki, M. (1984) *The Economic Analysis of the Japanese Firm*, Amsterdam: North-Holland.
Bank Negara (1998) *Quarterly Economic Bulletin*, Kuala Lumpur: Bank Negara Malaysia.
Chan, K.H. (1994) 'Program Lokalisasi Industri Kereta: Satu Kajian Pembuatan Kereta Proton Malaysia', unpublished undergraduate dissertation, Universiti Kebangsaan Malaysia, Bangi.
Clark, R. (1978) *The Japanese Company*, New Haven: Yale University Press.
Deyo, F. (1989) *Beneath the Miracle: Labor Subordination in the New Asian Industrialism*, Berkeley: University of California Press.
Deyo, F. (ed.) (1996) *Social Reconstructions of the World Automobile Industry*, London: Macmillan and New York: St Martin's Press.
Doner, R. (1991) 'Approaches to the politics of economic growth in Southeast Asia', *Journal of Asian Studies* 50, 4: 818–49.
Florida, R. and Kenny, M. (1988) 'Beyond mass production: Production and the labour process in Japan', *Politics and Society* 16, 1: 121–58.
Fröbel, F., Heinrichs, J. and Kreye, O. (1980) *The New International Division of Labour*, Cambridge: Cambridge University Press.

Hirst, P. and Zeitlin, J. (1991) 'Flexible specialization versus post-Fordism theory: Evidence and policy implications', *Economy and Society* 20, 1: 1–56.

Hoffman, K. and Kaplinsky, R. (1988) *Driving Force: The Global Restructuring of Technology, Labor and Investment in the Automobile and Components Industries*, Boulder: Westview.

Jayakumar, D. (1996) 'The plight of plantation workers in Malaysia', mimeo.

Jomo, K.S. and Todd, P. (1994) *Trade Unions in Peninsular Malaysia*, Kuala Lumpur: Oxford University Press.

Kaplinsky, R. (1994) *Easternization: The Spread of Japanese Management Techniques to Developing Countries*, London: Frank Cass.

Landesmann, M. and Scazzieri, R. (1995) *Forms of Production Organization*, Cambridge: Cambridge University Press.

Malaysia (1996) *The Seventh Malaysia Plan 1996–2000*, Kuala Lumpur: Government Printers.

Palloix C. (1978) 'The labour process: From Fordism to neo-Fordism', *The Labour Process and Class Strategies*, Conference of Socialist Economists Pamphlets, pp. 46–67.

Proton (1995) *Corporate Profile*, Shah Alam: Proton.

Rasiah, R. (1988) 'The semiconductor industry in Penang: Implications for the NIDL theories', *Journal of Contemporary Asia* 18, 1.

—— (1989) 'Competition and restructuring in the semiconductor industry and its implications for technology absorption in Penang', *Southeast Asian Journal of Social Sciences* 17, 1.

—— (1993a) *Pembahagian Kerja Antarabangsa*, Kuala Lumpur: Malaysian Social Science Association.

—— (1993b) 'Competition and governance: Work in Malaysia's textile and garment industries', *Journal of Contemporary Asia* 23, 1.

—— (1996) 'State intervention, rents and industrialization in Malaysia', in J. Borrego, A. Bejar and K.S. Jomo (eds) *Capital, the State and Late Industrialization*, Boulder: Westview.

—— (1997a) 'Political economy of Malaysia', in G. Rodan, K. Hewison and R. Robison (eds) *Political Economy of South-East Asia: An Introduction*, Sydney: Oxford University Press, pp. 121–47.

—— (1997b) 'Rent management in Proton', in M. Khan and K.S. Jomo (eds) *Rents and Development*, Melbourne: Cambridge University Press.

—— (1998) *Workers on the Brink: Unions, Exclusion and Crisis in Southeast Asia*, Singapore: Friedrich Ebert Stiftung.

Rasiah, R., Ishak, S. and Jomo, K.S. (1996) 'Globalization and liberalization: Implications for growth, poverty and inequality in East and Southeast Asia', in A. Woodfield, (ed.) *Globalization and Liberalization and Its Implications for Poverty and Inequality*, Geneva: UNCTAD.

Rasiah, R. and Von Hofmann, N. (eds) (1998) *Workers on the Brink: Unions, Exclusion and Crisis in Southeast Asia*, Singapore: Friedrich Ebert Stiftung.

Sabel, C. (1986) 'Changing models of economic efficiency and their implications for industrialization in the Third World', in C.F.D. Alejandro *et al.* (eds) *Development, Democracy and the Art of Trespassing*, Notre Dame, Indiana: University of Notre Dame Press.

Sengenberger, W. (1992) 'Intensified competition, industrial restructuring and industrial relations', *International Labour Review* 131, 2.

Sengenberger, W. and Pyke, F. (1991) 'Small firm industrial districts and local economic regeneration: Research and policy issues', *Labour and Society* 16, 1.

Shaiken, H. (1990) *Mexico in the World Economy: High Technology and Work Organisation in Export Industry*, San Diego: Center for US–Mexican Studies.

Thomas, H. (1995) 'The erosion of trade unions', in Thomas Henk (ed.) *Globalization and Third World Trade Unions: The Challenge of Rapid Economic Change*, London and New Jersey: Zed Books, pp. 3–27.

Wallerstein, I. (1979) *The Capitalist World Economy*, Cambridge: Cambridge University Press.

Zulkifly, O. (1995) *The Impact of Unionism on Wages in the Manufacturing Sector*, paper presented at seminar on Governance Mechanisms and Technical Change in Malaysian Industrialization, Universiti Kebangsaan Malaysia, Bangi, 15–16 August.

6　New organising vehicles in Indonesia

Origins and prospects

Vedi R. Hadiz

In the 1990s, new industrial workers in Indonesia increasingly sought to challenge existing state–society arrangements by developing semi-clandestine, community-based organisational vehicles, often in association with non-governmental organisations (NGOs). However, significant as these developments have been, labour currently remains too organisationally weak and fragmented to capitalise on some of the political openings made available by the fall of Suharto in May 1998. Labour-organising capacity at the workplace level has been severely compromised by the continuing economic crisis, while – in the political arena – it is as yet unclear how labour will be positioned in future state–society arrangements, as the *reformasi* movement is currently largely dominated by middle-class politicians and intellectuals with few organic connections to the labour movement.

This chapter begins with some of the theoretical issues raised by the emergence of new organising vehicles in Indonesia. These include matters pertaining to class analysis and, more specifically, to evaluations of the organising capacity of women workers in export-oriented manufacturing. The second section then explains how state controls over independent organising during the New Order were principally part of a broader campaign to strictly limit opposition to the Suharto regime. In spite of this climate of repression, three decades of sustained industrialisation prior to the crisis helped to create a better social base for labour to self-organise in Indonesia – particularly in export-oriented manufacturing. The third part of the chapter thus outlines how new conditions of everyday life resulting from rapid urbanisation, improved literacy rates and crowded living conditions facilitated the formation of alternative, local-based organising vehicles in the 1990s – citing the Tangerang region in West Java as a case in point. In the fourth section, the nature of these organising vehicles is discussed in more detail, including the fact that various NGOs have often played an important role in supporting, and sometimes instigating, these unofficial organisations. However, questions are also raised about the effectiveness of these bodies in the longer term, especially *vis-à-vis* the goal of establishing more conventional union structures. Finally, the chapter briefly covers developments following the 1997 financial crisis and subsequent removal of President Suharto.

Approaches to labour

This account of labour's organising efforts in the 1990s needs to be set against trends in the study of Indonesian politics and society, increasingly characterised by the liberal belief in the more or less *naturally* progressive role of the middle class and bourgeoisie. Within this liberal scheme of things, it has been often assumed that the latter will eventually achieve a loosening of authoritarian reins through democratic reforms. Conversely, when the democratic impulse in Indonesia has been at its weakest, it is postulated that this is rooted exclusively in the present immaturity of these classes. The predominance of this largely liberal problematic has resulted in analyses confined only to a particular realm of politics deemed relevant to the interests of the expanding middle and capital classes. These typically involve the workings of the parliament and political parties, the conduct of elections, the extent of press freedoms and the stature of the armed forces. Thus analysis is restricted to the role of institutions and groups that are also more or less recognised by the state to have a formal place within the 'legitimate' realm of political life. However, the 1990s struggles of new industrial workers have necessarily taken place *outside* these official channels. In that such developments are only rarely included in most liberal analyses of politics and society in Indonesia, the enforced separation of labour from politics in the New Order has been the basis for its further neglect in intellectual discourse. In analysing Indonesia's new worker movements, it is necessary to thus abandon the liberal problematic and focus attention on the processes of class formation and class struggle that take place beyond the officially legitimated realm of politics.

But in so doing, the point also needs to be made that it is highly unfruitful to frame analyses of contemporary developments in Indonesia according to preconceived ideas about how workers understand and act on their interests. Traditional ideas of revolutionary class consciousness, for example, are demonstrably inadequate, as revealed in discussions of the politics of the working class in industrialised countries. These have been closely linked to debates about workers' 'objective' interests being tied to the overthrow of capitalism and its replacement by socialism. As Burawoy (1985: 5–7) indicates, the failure to achieve this historical mission is then viewed as grounds for accusing workers of 'false consciousness' and an inability to influence their circumstances – in this way, messianic visions are used to 'conjure away' the actual activism of workers. But the inclination to write off the workers of advanced capitalist societies in this way has not dissuaded some scholars from looking for the emergence of a revolutionary proletariat in the later industrialis-ers of the Third World (Andrae and Beckman, 1998). The world-systems approach of the World Labor Research Group tries to link the decline in labour militancy in the capitalist core to its rise in the periphery (see Silver, 1995). However, I argue that framing analyses of new working classes in Indonesia in terms of the goal of finding a lost revolutionary proletariat would be equally detrimental to political and intellectual endeavours in the labour arena.

Having said this, it is also vital to acknowledge that the new industrial working class in Indonesia is emerging in an historical, political and socio-economic context far less hospitable than that which stimulated class analyses in earlier, European industrialisers. A major theme in the literature on labour in East and Southeast Asia is thus their inability to form the kind of industrial and political organisations associated with capitalist industrialisation in other places and times. In this regard, the work of Frederic Deyo (1989; 1997) has been particularly influential. Largely taking the development of working classes as a given, Deyo explains how various 'circumstances have inhibited and distorted the development of trade unions and labour movements' which 'elsewhere has enfranchised and empowered workers' (Deyo, 1989: 2). One of his main arguments is that the establishment of authoritarian controls over labour in many East and Southeast Asian countries prior to the adoption of export-led industrialisation has curtailed the possibility of effective labour movements developing in the region. These controls were established, according to Deyo, for reasons mainly having to do with pre-empting or suppressing the perceived internal or external threat of communism. As the next section of this chapter shows, the imposition of stringent state controls over labour in Indonesia indeed had much to do with the historically close links between sections of the pre-New Order labour movement and the now outlawed Indonesian Communist Party (PKI).

However, a couple of Deyo's other observations need to be treated with more caution in view of the rise of alternative organising vehicles in Indonesia. In his analysis, the absence of strong working-class movements in the region is in part also linked to the limited political role that Asian working-class *communities* have played, compared to those in Latin America that 'provide an essential foundation for labour protest' (ibid.: 8–9). But labour organising in 1990s Indonesia has often been initiated at the community level because of the immense difficulty and danger frequently involved in organising openly in the workplace. As discussed later in this chapter, the specific milieu encountered in the congested and fast-growing industrial areas in and around Jakarta has been very conducive to the initiation and development of independent organising activities that have largely escaped the long arm of the state.

Deyo also makes the claim that labour's marginalisation is due to the kind of working class engendered by the labour-intensive, export-oriented industries that initially spurred the process of industrialisation. He writes that:

> The attraction of young, low-skilled, often female workers to employment characterised by low pay, tedium, minimal job security, and lack of career mobility encourages low job commitment, high levels of turnover, and lack of attachment to work groups or firms. These circumstances impede independent unionisation efforts among workers in light export industries …
>
> (ibid.: 8)

By contrast, he argues, the more highly skilled, male workers in heavy industry tend to be more permanently employed and so more successful in creating effective labour organisations.

Indonesian labour organisers do often talk of the difficulties in sustaining bases of influence in factories because the tendency of workers to change places of employment can result in the often sudden disbanding of local worker groups.[1] If stable leadership and membership of workers' groups within particular factories cannot be guaranteed because workers enter and leave employment quickly, this has obvious ramifications for the development of an effective working-class movement. However, the mobility of workers can simultaneously be a source of organising strength – that is, when the economic situation allows for quick re-employment. Many young, female workers I interviewed before the 1997 crisis indicated that they were not particularly afraid of losing their jobs through industrial action because it was not too difficult for them to acquire another. Apparently, this was more the case for the very young, aged between 18 and 21. As discussed further below, the structural constraint to organising that Deyo suggests is inherent to low-wage, export-oriented industries has not been sufficient to eliminate altogether the possibility in Indonesia of independent organising at the level of local communities.

Alternatively, a number of feminist scholars have highlighted the impact that gender-based identities and power relations can have on labour-organising capacity. Writing about female factory workers in Tangerang, West Java, in the early 1980s, Mather (1983) – for example – identified the influence of Islamic-derived patriarchal values as the cause of local labour's docility. Her argument was that the female employees of factories in the area simply moved from one milieu of subordination to another, from their roles in the family to the male-supervised workplace. On this basis, women workers' relative passivity is claimed to be rooted in the low esteem given to women in Islam.

However, there are problems with Mather's identification of Islamic-derived patriarchal values as the primary cause of labour docility. First, neighbouring areas to the south of Jakarta (which she identified as displaying more labour militancy) also had a largely female, Muslim factory workforce. These women would have been only slightly (if at all) less devout than their Tangerang counterparts. Second, precisely because the religious belief of the majority of factory workers is different from those of often foreign or Indonesian Chinese supervisors and employers, Islamic values have arguably acted in more recent times as a mediating factor to the emergence of a sense of working-class solidarity, itself related to growing experience in engaging in confrontation with state and employers. Employers have been known to complain about the time that is lost as workers demand the right to observe the Muslim requirement of daily prayers at set times, two (out of five) of which would take place during regular work hours. It is conceivable that some workers have made this demand not exclusively for reasons of piety, but as a small gesture of resistance to the grinding routine of factory work. From this point of view, Islamic values can simultaneously act as a basis for both labour subordination and empowerment.

Nevertheless, some labour leaders do cite the effectiveness of the reprimands of local, usually male, notables – such as the head of a neighbourhood-level unit – in preventing women from participating in organising activities on the basis of some normative code of appropriate female behaviour. Certainly, many worker meetings take place in the evening and involve some travel by young women in the dark of the night, followed by huddling in cramped quarters with male counterparts. Otherwise, some labour organisers argue that young women are more likely to entertain the prospect of resolving their hardships in the workplace through marriage. Yet one of the most outstanding features of labour unrest in the 1990s – including in the now more industrialised Tangerang area – is the militancy and leadership role taken by many women workers. As the feminised workforce in export-oriented manufacturing has expanded in the last decade, not unsurprisingly it has become a key source of labour activism. Even if Mather's analysis is accepted for the time and place that she did her fieldwork, there is thus good reason to question its applicability to the contemporary situation. Before describing the conditions under which new industrial workers have been able to make some gains in organising, the next section covers the role of the state in the New Order era.

Labour politics and history

As the work of such scholars as Ingleson (1986) and Shiraishi (1990) suggests, the history of Indonesia's labour movement stretches back to the early period of the nationalist struggle in which it played a leading role. Though crippled by Dutch colonial power in the 1920s, labour organisations resurfaced to take part in the 1945–9 armed struggle phase of the independence movement. Armed labour units called *lasykar buruh*, for example, were involved in defending workplaces against enemy forces and were known to have seized foreign-owned production facilities in the nationalist cause. Because of such a history, labour organisations – usually linked to the array of political parties that existed at that time – played a legitimised, prominent part in the politics of the early independence period (Tedjasukmana, 1958; Hasibuan, 1968).

The unconsolidated nature of state power and the absence of a significant domestic bourgeoisie provided a milieu that allowed the labour movement, particularly its more militant elements, to thrive in early post-independence Indonesia. These elements also fared well because the euphoria of revolution had not subsided. Sections of the labour movement were influential enough at this time to effectively spearhead the nationalisation of Dutch and other foreign-owned companies in the late 1950s. Initially the idea was that these companies would be run by worker-led councils. Nevertheless, they eventually became military-run state enterprises, within which the more militant sections of the labour movement struggled to survive (see Hawkins, 1963; Hadiz, 1997).

This history of a fairly active (and overtly political) labour movement was interrupted in the mid-1960s, with the establishment of the New Order by a coalition of forces led by the army, which saw the destruction of the army's old nemesis: the Indonesian Communist Party (PKI). While the conflict between the two had earlier roots,[2] the army's growing political and administrative – as well as economic – role in the early 1960s was increasingly pitting it against the PKI, which by that time constituted the only other substantial social-political force in Indonesia. Significantly, the army's earlier assumption of managerial functions over state enterprises meant that it had developed a vested interest in the maintenance of industrial peace, which resulted in direct confrontation with the more radical unions associated with SOBSI (*Sentral Organisasi Buruh Seluruh Indonesia* or All-Indonesia Central Workers' Organisation), the PKI-linked labour federation. Because SOBSI was inevitably caught up in the destruction of the PKI in 1965–6, its elimination from the scene automatically meant that labour would be significantly weakened as a force at the onset of the New Order.

The consolidation of state power took place rapidly after the establishment of the New Order, although the process had already begun in the latter years of Sukarno's 'Old Order'. Stringent controls were imposed on labour during the early New Order, as mentioned earlier, especially because of labour's links with the communists via SOBSI. In 1973, as the culmination of a long and complicated process of elite-initiated manoeuvres, the remaining labour organisations – most of which had aligned themselves with the army against the dominant SOBSI – were goaded into establishing the FBSI (*Federasi Buruh Seluruh Indonesia* or All-Indonesia Labour Federation) as the sole, state-sanctioned labour entity (see Hadiz, 1997: 90–104). With the establishment of the FBSI, what links the labour movement still had with political parties were severed at the same time as it was directed to strictly confine itself to the 'social and economic' realm (Sudono, 1981: 26). Thus, in spite of the New Order's ideological aversion to the liberal/social democratic tradition of Western trade unionism – liberalism is regarded as being as much in contradiction to the harmonious, family-based principles of Pancasila[3] as is communism – it clearly adopted the idea of the separation of the 'economic' from the 'political' in its domestication of the country's previously vibrant labour movement.

In 1985 the FBSI underwent a transformation into the even more centralised, hierarchical and therefore more easily controlled SPSI (*Serikat Pekerja Seluruh Indonesia* or All-Indonesia Workers' Union), before yet again being re-christened in 1995 as the FSPSI (*Federasi Serikat Pekerja Seluruh Indonesia* or Federation of All-Indonesia Workers' Unions). Especially in the 1980s, the organisation was geared towards assisting the security apparatus in identifying and dealing with potential destabilising developments in the labour area (Tanter, 1990). Indeed, from the onset of the New Order, labour has been presented in the official discourse as a potential source of disruption to the political stability regarded as the essential precondition for economic success. Thus the main function of the FSPSI and its previous incarnations has been to prohibit the development outside the control of the state of labour-organising vehicles. Indeed, the institutional framework of state–labour relations has been geared towards the control and demobilisation of labour as a social force and, in this sense, was an integral part of the New Order's strategy of political exclusion.

However, in later years, the monopoly of the state-backed union has been challenged by the proliferation of local community-based organising vehicles which have often operated in conjunction with labour-based NGOs. The latter range from the SBM *Setiakawan* (*Serikat Buruh Merdeka Setiakawan* or Solidarity Independent Workers' Union), formed in 1990, and the SBSI (*Serikat Buruh Sejahtera Indonesia* or Indonesian Prosperity Trade Union), formed in 1992 – both of which are attempts to directly form trade unions independent of the state – to a wide range of smaller groups. All carry out activities as diverse as promoting workers' education, cooperatives, organising training programmes and discussion groups. The 1994 establishment of a third union, the PPBI (*Pusat Perjuangan Buruh Indonesia* or Centre for Indonesian Working Class Struggle), involved links between student- and worker-groups in Indonesia that suggested some parallels with those that arose in South Korea in the 1980s (Minju, 1987; Ogle, 1990). However, this smaller, more radical organisation was the object of intense state repression in 1996 and was crippled by its leaders being implicated by the government in riots that took place in Jakarta in July that year.

In spite of considerable state repression, the 1990s saw a resurgence of labour activism in Indonesia, involving large numbers of strikes and the proliferation of semi-formal labour-organising vehicles generally beyond the reach of the state. Most of these involved workers employed in the country's increasingly important manufacturing sector,[4] and have been centred in the new, vast working-class neighbourhoods and areas conjured up by capitalist industrialisation. The next section covers these developments in more detail.

Factory, community and labour organising

Sustained industrialisation during three decades of New Order rule vastly altered Indonesia's social landscape. New social classes associated with the maturation of capitalism emerged: among these, a new industrial working class. Indeed, a new generation working class – raised or perhaps even born in an urban environment – has been recently coming of age, especially in Java. For the majority of such workers, life in the city and work in the factory is not at all conceived of as being temporary, as it probably was by their predecessors. Because the factory is the main source of livelihood and the city is the major source of living experience, contemporary workers have more or less inevitably come to feel that they have a greater stake in the struggles that take place in the urban milieu. Some scholars thus argue that the point at which urban residence is perceived as being permanent by workers is crucial (see Hanagan, 1986), particularly to the development of active working-class responses to the social and political environment.

However, while the new material conditions of everyday urban life have been conducive to labour organising, it is clear that the great transformations taking place in the cities as the result of industrialisation are closely linked with those taking place simultaneously in 'rural' Indonesia, especially in Java. The development of what Young (1994) calls the 'urbanisation of the rural' has indirectly helped to foster workers' propensity to organise by socially and culturally preparing them for struggles in the cities. Young argues, for example, that areas in Java usually regarded as 'rural' have gradually taken up many of the characteristics of those considered 'urban'. These now have population densities and access to facilities, such as education, transport and communications, that would be regarded as 'urban' under current definitions. Thus, for many contemporary workers, the transition from a 'rural' lifestyle and world outlook to one that is more clearly associated with an 'urban' existence may not involve such a great cultural or physical leap as it once did. As the workforces for some industrial areas are drawn in from villages around cities, a growing labyrinth of highways envelop and slowly transform these villages like the city itself.

The higher levels of education and literacy that have accompanied industrialisation have also been supportive of greater organisational propensities, especially when combined with other demographic characteristics of the new industrial working class. Researchers have consistently found, for example, that the ages of contemporary urban industrial workers range from the mid-teens to the late twenties (Roesli, 1992: 34; White, 1993: 133) and that their education level has been higher than that of previous generations.[5] In fact, in contrast to the less sizeable urban industrial workforce of fifteen or twenty years ago, it is more common today for graduates of secondary schools to be employed in low-wage and low-skill manufacturing jobs, though primary-level education is still the norm (Roesli, 1992: 34; White, 1993: 133).[6] Thus today's urban worker is also typically more literate than those of the past. One worker argues that newspapers and news magazines have had a considerable role in raising the awareness of workers as they:

> always publish pictures of workers who are undertaking strike action. News of workers' strike action is a means of communication and education among workers. They can see that the workers' struggle has spread everywhere.[7]

Because of rising literacy levels, workers have also been more inclined to document their personal experiences, including those involving confrontation with employers or the state apparatus, for use by others. This is an important means by which valuable lessons are constantly being transmitted. In the long run, this may prove to be very important, as the legacy of current struggles is preserved (rather than lost) and bestowed on the next generation of workers.

Arguably, young and relatively more educated urban workers tend to have greater aspirations in terms of their future and are inclined to make greater demands than an older, uneducated and less urbanised workforce. For this reason, labour organising outside the state is more effective today than in former times, although up until now it has been largely confined to the level of the local community. But the greater propensity to develop alternative organising vehicles has to do with more than just urban sensibilities, age and literacy. The social setting encountered in Tangerang, located just to the west of Jakarta and one of the most important manufacturing centres of Indonesia, provides a good illustration of some of the social changes ushered in by the process of industrialisation and how they facilitate the development of these vehicles.

Tangerang

Up to the early 1970s, the regency of Tangerang was no more than a network of *kampung* (kampong) dotting an unremarkable, rather dry, expanse of 423.96 km^2 (Roesli, 1992: 32). Locals used to subsist primarily on agriculture-based activities, although many were also involved in small trading and craft-related work. In most ways, therefore, Tangerang was quite indistinct from other areas in the periphery of the largely condensed metropolitan centre that constituted Jakarta-proper at the time. However, as Jakarta spread out, Tangerang (along with Bekasi in the east and large, much greener, areas to the south, which lie in between the capital and the town of Bogor) became subsumed and integrated into its life and economy. Thus, though politically a part of the province of West Java, today's Tangerang has become an organic and integral part of Jakarta. Nothing underscores this fact as much as the network of roads and highways which now links Tangerang to Jakarta, traversed by innumerable people each day as they commute to and from the now not-so-remote Tangerang.

Industrialisation has not only altered the physical appearance of Tangerang, but also irrevocably changed the nature of life itself in the regency. As late as 1980, the population of Tangerang stood at a mere 228,000, compared to the figure of more than 1.5 million that it reached a decade later (Hancock, 1994: 54). Initially, the process of change occurred quite gradually. Nurbaiti (1986: 70), for example, noted the existence of only 115 factories of varying sizes in the regency as late as 1985. Today, however, any casual inspection of the area will no doubt register the seemingly endless rows of foreboding high factory walls and closed factory gates, through which countless workers (mostly migrants from other parts of Java, as well as other islands) routinely stream in and out in the early mornings and late afternoons.

Indeed, by the late 1980s, no less than 900 mostly export-oriented factories were in operation in Tangerang (Roesli, 1992: 32). Once an ordinary, quiet, rural setting, Tangerang is now a crowded, noisy, polluted and dusty urban formation. It has thus become in many ways no different from large parts of the increasingly inhospitable (and uninhabitable) capital of Jakarta. It was the shift to an export-led industrialisation strategy in the mid-1980s that accounted for the greater pace of change in the last decade or so. As more factories were built, further waves of (predominantly young female) migrants that have come to call Tangerang home have transformed it into a multicultural hub of Sundanese, Javanese, Sumatrans and Sulawesians.[8]

Most industrial workers live near their places of employment or occupy dormitories made available by employers nearby. Indeed, a worker typically rents a small *bedeng* (barrack) in the environs of their place of employment, together with as many as three or four co-workers at a time. Such barracks conform to the description that White has given with regard to workers' accommodation in general:

> crowded and cramped rooms, poorly lit and ventilated, often with damp earthen floors and with minimal facilities for cooking, personal hygiene, etc. Furniture is minimal (no beds or chairs) and even basic items like soap and toothpaste are likely to be shared …
>
> (White, 1993: 155)

Clearly, the intensive, regular interaction taking place among workers in densely populated communities, where the nature of everyday life necessitates the sharing of such basic amenities as sources of water, not only helps to enforce a culture of sharing, but also helps create a sense of solidarity among workers. This in turn facilitates the undertaking of collective action by workers when it is necessary. One labour organiser has pointed out that the regular morning and late-afternoon congregations at communal wells provide an opportunity to exchange gossip, experiences and information. Sometimes discussions give rise to plans for staging collective actions of protest. An alternative mode of accommodation for workers, especially in the case of young unmarried women, is to live in spartan, company-owned dormitories that effectively separate them from their immediate environment and hinder interaction and exchange of information with other groups of workers (Djajusman, 1992: 55–7).

Life and work in the city and factory also casts the rank-and-file worker in the midst of a social setting that considerably helps them to shape and form new sensibilities, aspirations and worldviews. Along with new hopes and aspirations, however, there inevitably come new pains and frustrations as workers come into greater proximity and are exposed to everyday evidence of glaring social disparities. This is not surprising, as the conditions of their own immediate living environment may contrast starkly with those which are located not too far away. Given the heavy concentration of wealth in a few major cities, especially Jakarta, such stark contrasts are not generally seen or directly experienced outside the urban centres proper. While it is difficult to say exactly how workers experience and make sense of such a situation, it is not hard to imagine the ease with which a sense of injustice could arise.[9] The deep impact of this sense of injustice on the psyche of a growing number of young, urbanised, literate men and women, forced to consider their own bleak futures in the context of a society clearly growing in affluence, should not be underestimated. Workers I talked to, for example, were often angry that minimum wage rises are a contentious issue, given the huge salaries they perceived that managers received. They claimed that these rises anyway only allowed them to keep up with the cost of living.

Large concentrations of impoverished, young and relatively educated workers have provided a good social setting for the emergence of better local and sometimes semi-clandestine efforts at organising. Indeed, the site of much of the independent organising of workers has been the new, sprawling, congested working-class communities – such as those found in Tangerang. It is within these contexts, recently conjured up by a rapid industrialisation process, that we find some of the conditions which have enabled the development, though limited, of labour's organising capacity, in spite of the severe restrictions on factory-based organising. The following section discusses the nature of new organising vehicles that emerged as a result.

New organising vehicles

In the decade before the 1997 financial crisis hit, incidences of strike action increased significantly in Indonesia. Table 6.1 only shows official figures in this regard, however, and they must be considered as very conservative in that a good many strikes go unreported. Other estimates of levels of strike activity vary widely. One labour activist has put the total number of strikes from 1989 to 1994 at an amazing 3,000 (Razif, 1994). On the other hand, sources quoting the SPSI put the number of strikes in 1992 and 1993 as 340 in both years (American Embassy, 1994: 29–30) and 1,130 in 1994 (Jordan, 1995: viii). Clearly, whatever the actual figures, a consensus exists that strikes markedly increased in the years prior to the economic crisis.

Table 6.1 Industrial action, 1988–94

Year	1988	1989	1990	1991	1992	1993	1994	1996
Number of strikes	39	19	61	114	250	180	367	350

Source: Department of Manpower Statistics, various years.

Not surprisingly, the distribution of these strikes generally followed the geographic pattern for manufacturing. As employment in manufacturing had expanded rapidly in the Jabotabek region (including Tangerang), much of the industrial unrest came to take place there. Of note is the fact that this region is also the site of the greatest concentration of export-oriented factories, as well as of the proliferation of new, more distinctly working-class neighbourhoods. However, as there has been a gradual spread of export-oriented production to new locations, there has also been a wider geographical spread of industrial unrest. Most notably, East Java and North Sumatra have witnessed a significant surge in industrial action. Labour struggles in East Java received much attention because of the widely publicised Marsinah case, which involved the brutal kidnapping, torture and murder of a female labour leader in 1993. North Sumatran labour struggles also received much attention because of the Medan riots of April 1994 (which involved mass action by an estimated 20,000–30,000 workers) and the clampdown on labour activists that followed.

Most of the cases of industrial unrest have had to do with demands for higher wages and better working conditions. Some labour unrest has also been spurred by worker demands for the establishment of workplace-level organisation units free from employer or government intervention. (F)SPSI workplace units, as a general rule, have been under the control of employers; thus many have been derided for being unaccountable to workers and an ineffective means to channel aspirations. Still other cases have involved actions of solidarity, for example, for unfairly dismissed or maltreated colleagues – often those most actively organising other workers. Importantly, an aim frequently expressed in workers' discussion groups (often organised in conjunction with NGOs) is the necessity of establishing effective independent trade unions as an alternative to the (F)SPSI.[10] While much of the industrial activism is impromptu and locally based, there does seem to be a greater level of coordination and collaboration developing between workers in different workplaces, and even in different areas. In this regard, NGOs also have often been able to play a facilitating role.

Much of the alternative organising has been community-based, rather than just at the factory level, given the intense controls over organising in the workplace. The process of organising this way, effectively bypassing the official industrial relations system, frequently involves a protracted effort which sometimes frustrates even the most eager of participants. It has been the case that labour-oriented NGOs have at times been the initiators of alternative organising. But it is equally common for already active informal groupings of workers to make contact with NGOs, usually on the basis of personal relationships, and then cooperate in undertaking various kinds of organising-oriented activities. In other cases, groupings of workers have operated without NGOs, or even shunned them altogether.

Workers who have been fired because of their involvement in organising activities or leading strikes have played a crucial role in this very grassroots type of organising. Some have acted as liaisons between other workers and NGO activists. Often branded 'troublemakers' by employers, they may find it difficult to find employment and therefore have to either shift to a different area to find work or become full-time organisers. Many leaders emerging from the rank and file – frequently young women in their twenties – have been those with experience in confrontation with employers, the state's security apparatus or both. This emergence of a young female leadership from the rank and file is important, as the NGOs have tended to be dominated by male activists – although in recent times it is also the case that women-oriented NGOs have been more active on the labour front, especially those established by middle-class feminists.

Semi-formal organising of this kind typically evolves from the establishment of a core group of workers on the basis of extended involvement in activities that are ostensibly welfare, educational, cultural or religious in nature (such as prayer meetings). Members will congregate in the home of one of the workers or (usually at a later stage) at a small, cramped house rented especially for the purpose of facilitating organising. The renting of such premises, together with the provision of information on labour laws and the encouragement of group discussions, is usually the kind of contribution offered by NGOs in assisting workers. Educational and discussion activities may incur costs for photocopying material which cash-strapped workers could find difficult to meet. Nevertheless, many groups do introduce the collection of dues among their members or the creation of a fund to develop self-help schemes or cooperatives in order to cultivate self-reliance where possible.

Members usually come together in collective activities like these because of an initial interest in gaining access to an alternative source of knowledge and education (in, for example, labour laws, methods of organising, or even general political or economic issues). Often, a good deal of the discussion centres on personal experiences in dealing with employers and the much-feared state security forces. There are also, of course, practical benefits to participation in the setting up of cooperative and self-help schemes. Otherwise, workers can be attracted to such groups initially just to socialise, to find amusement and entertainment when outside the grinding routine of factory work. Thus some workers have enthusiastically joined workers' theatre or musical groups, which are often run in conjunction with NGO activists.

In undertaking various worker education programmes, some of the more radical NGOs tackle political and social issues beyond the workplace. These particular NGOs tend to also have strong links with radical elements of the student movement. A good example is the aforementioned PPBI, founded in 1994 but since subject to state clampdowns. Ideologically, the PPBI was more committed to openly confronting the state and so did not attempt to seek official recognition as a union (Hadiz, 1997: 154). However, other NGOs have been more politically conservative. On one hand, there are a number which prefer to work through and reform existing formal channels. These have thus not participated in the setting up of alternative organising vehicles, working instead from largely within the state-sponsored SPSI (ibid.: 142). Otherwise, there are NGOs whose involvement in labour issues stems from a democratic pluralist commitment to the rights of workers to self-organise within a capitalist economy. Examples in this regard are the SBM and SBSI (again mentioned earlier). The SBSI, like the SBM before it, became an object of international attention as a symbol of the growing independent labour movement. This attention forced the Suharto regime to be initially somewhat guarded in its response to the organisation. However, after the 1994 Medan riots, the government acted more forcefully against the SBSI and its leadership, jailing its founder, Muchtar Pakpahan, and others (ibid.: 169–71).

Outside organisations like the SBSI there is an array of lower profile, smaller grassroots organisations, many of which are not affiliated with umbrella bodies. While it would be wrong to attribute the growing propensity of workers to organise informally only to the work of such NGOs, it is clear that they have had an important role in that they are able to provide the resources necessary to begin organisational work. These NGOs have not been constrained by the tight regulations which have governed the establishment of unions, especially prior to the fall of Suharto in May 1998. Because they are usually relatively small and flexible, they are well suited to evading the long arm of the state. The crucial question has always been whether the kind of locally based organisational vehicles described above will eventually develop into fully functioning, independent unions capable of properly representing workers *vis-à-vis* state and capital. It is only very recently that this question is beginning to be answered. The fall of Suharto, and the subsequent progressive unravelling of the New Order, has created the incentive to establish new unions. In the euphoria of the president's downfall up to a dozen new unions were registered at the Department of Manpower within months but, twelve months on, it is not certain that these new legal entities are more effective, especially as the economy continues to contract.

In spite of the limitations that constrain the effectiveness of labour struggles, it is clear that the escalation of labour unrest in the 1990s described above openly challenged the myth of social harmony based on Pancasila cultural values actively propagated by the state. The emphasis on such values as harmony, partnership, authority and responsibility in 'Pancasila Industrial Relations' has helped to legitimise restrictions on freedom to organise (Moertopo, 1975). But Pancasila has also been a source of expectations that the state's propaganda regarding harmony and common interests translate into policies that *protect*, not harm, the interests of workers. Thus the same patriarchal values that legitimise the authority of the state as benevolent father figure, simultaneously may contribute to the alienation of workers when the state has demonstrably used that authority to serve particular individual interests.[11]

Surprisingly, perhaps, given the general effectiveness with which the New Order was able to quell dissent over the years, an effective state response was not easily found to resolve tensions associated with mounting labour activism. In the past, any escalation of labour unrest was confidently dealt with by simply utilising the 'security approach' – involving overt repression by the state's security/military apparatus. However, in the course of the 1990s, a strictly repression-oriented response seems to have come to be regarded as inadequate and so was combined with some limited, reformist responses. To dissuade workers from becoming involved in alternative organising vehicles, the (F)SPSI was revamped to provide it with greater credibility. More significantly, the Minister of Manpower directed that there be periodic rises in the state-determined minimum wage so as to deter workers from striking over wage-related issues. Between 1990 and 1997, the minimum wage thus almost trebled in value in rupiah terms. Significantly, this was carried out in spite of protestations regarding the threat to Indonesia's export competitiveness: some business figures at the time complained that they could only tolerate increases in the minimum wage if bureaucratic levies on their business activities were reduced. Despite these gestures, the Minister of Manpower failed to make significant reforms in the area of labour's right to associate freely.

The 1997 crisis

After the financial crisis struck Indonesia in 1997, levels of industrial unrest fell sharply as workers found themselves too organisationally weak and fragmented to launch effective action against the mass retrenchments, soaring basic commodity prices and, after March 1998, government-imposed wage freeze they were experiencing. Workers' movements were also relatively slow to join street protests against the faltering Suharto regime, only finally becoming involved once the student-led movement was well under way. However, with the departure of the long-time president, the new government – eager to display reformist credentials in all areas, including industrial relations – took up policies which theoretically, though certainly not always in practice, allow greater room for independent labour organising (Hadiz, 1998). In the expanded political space, levels of industrial action quickly shot up again. At least in part in response, the government removed the freeze on wages, resulting in two increases in the minimum wage in mid-1998 and early 1999, in spite of protests from employers (see Table 6.2).

Table 6.2 Minimum wage in selected regions: 1990, 1996 and 1999

Region	1990	1996	1999
Jakarta	2,100	5,200	7,700
West Java	1,200	4,662	6,958
Central Java	780	3,400	5,100
East Java	1,409	3,724	5,699
North Sumatra	1,930	4,600	7,000

Sources: *Warta Ekonomi* (25 February 1991: 17); *Economic & Business Review Indonesia* (15 May 1996: 9); *Kompas* (19 February 1999: 2).

Note: Figures represent daily wage in rupiah.

Although the regulations pertaining to union activity remain strict, the Department of Manpower has moved to allow more unions to register as legal entities. So as to bolster its *bona fides* internationally, the Habibie government specifically invited the SBSI to seek official recognition as a union within a few days of Muchtar Pakpahan's release from prison in late May 1998. In doing this, the Department of Manpower dropped its long-held one union policy that granted the (F)SPSI a monopoly over worker representation. In the face of greater competition, the SPSI has been greatly weakened in a very short time, especially after eleven of its thirteen industry affiliates withdrew from the organisation in August 1998 (Hadiz, 1998: 122). While many labour-based organisations have sought legal recognition, most of the more militant ones have not bothered to register, viewing the process with disdain. Significantly, however, a number of these have responded to the altered political circumstances by resolving to limit the role of NGOs in their activities, in order to encourage a rank-and-file leadership to emerge in the future.

Otherwise, there have been new Islam-associated unions formed, although these generally focus on the white-collar middle class or the urban lumpenproletariat, rather than specifically on industrial workers. While religious differences have figured quite strongly in the formation of new political groupings, they do not appear to be a source of division in the labour movement – this may change in the future, as a fair number of labour-based NGOs have been led by Christians.

The aftermath of the fall of Suharto has generated a flurry of activity. But it can be characterised as proliferation rather than consolidation. While, in the past, extra-legal loose coalitions were necessary to avoid state repression, it is not generally a good basis upon which to build effective unionism in the longer term. While some developments are encouraging, those involved in the labour struggle will still need to be in it for the long haul. Significant progress will not be achieved overnight, as labour in Indonesia is currently a long way from being the social and political force that other sections of society would need to strike alliances with. At the moment, those alliances that do exist are still confined (as in the Suharto era) to a few elements of the NGO and student movements, whereas the *reformasi* movement driving changes in the formal political arena is largely controlled by middle-class politicians and intellectuals, with few, if any, associations with the labour movement (Hadiz, 1998).

Conclusion

The growth of a new industrial working class in Indonesia has seen the recent emergence of alternative, locally based organising vehicles. However, hopes for the further development of these vehicles must be tempered by the recognition of the persistence of state repression, due primarily to continuing wariness among political elites of the potentially destabilising effect of an independent workers' movement, even after the fall of Suharto. In addition, they must be tempered by a recognition of the constraints of operating in a chronically labour-surplus economy, as well as an international context that places pressure on governments of very late industrialising countries like Indonesia to compete to create the kind of social, economic and political conditions that would attract foreign investment. Moreover, the current Asian economic crisis, which in Indonesia has resulted in record levels of unemployment and underemployment, diminishes the bargaining position of workers.

Still, it is undoubtedly the case that labour organising has been much more successful today than fifteen or twenty years ago. The inroads that have been made recently in organising, as well as the rise of strike action in the face of state repression, testify to this fact. A period of political uncertainty which seems to be accompanying the political 'transition' period after Suharto's fall could still provide a 'window of opportunity' for the working class, as it is clear that the institutions of state–society relations maintained during Suharto's rule cannot survive intact.

As yet, it is unclear whether local community-based organising vehicles will serve in the future as the basis for the development of a more effective, national-level labour movement, or what role NGOs could play in such a development. There are clear indications, however, that this is what many organisationally active workers strive for. Large, often semi-clandestine meetings are taking place ever more frequently, in which delegations of workers representing different industrial areas in Java, and sometimes Sumatra and other islands, congregate to discuss common strategies for the future, while recognising the need for an effective national trade union.

Indeed, only a further growth of working-class organisational capacity will ensure the strengthening of the currently weak reformist impulse within the state in relation to labour. Only when the working class is sufficiently well organised and, thereby, gains in strength, will the state (as well as capital) be more inclined to accommodate its demands. As long as the working class remains poorly organised, the option of dealing with labour activism through coercive measures will continue to remain attractive to elites, as its political costs remain low. A poorly organised working class is repressed or, worse, ignored.

Notes

1 Interviews and discussions with groups of workers in Bogor (23 January 1994) and Cengkareng (1 February 1994).
2 Perhaps it can be traced to the so-called 'Madiun Affair' of 1948, in which the PKI was annihilated by a military force loyal to the central government of Sukarno and Hatta, whose authority was then being challenged by the party leader, Musso (see Anderson, 1994).
3 The Pancasila (Five Principles) comprise Belief in One God, Humanitarianism, Indonesian Unity, Popular Government by Consultation and Representation, and Social Justice. The fourth principle was interpreted as distinguishing the practices of the Indonesian political system from those of liberal democracies. This interpretation emphasised the consultation and deliberation process involved in decision-making to produce a government by 'consensus', and therefore recognised no opposition.
4 In 1971, 6.5 per cent of the labour force was in manufacturing, whereas in 1990 that figure was 11.6 per cent (World Bank, 1994: 197). In the mid-1990s, employment in manufacturing peaked at around 12 per cent of the labour force, although after the crisis in 1998 it dropped to just under 10 per cent.
5 This is supported by the macro-level data. See Manning (1992: 33) for figures on the rising educational level of the urban population.
6 During fieldwork I encountered cases of workers who had tertiary education experience. In an interview on 3 July 1994, one Tangerang factory worker told me of a co-worker who had a *sarjana* (Bachelor of Arts) degree in economics. Accounts given by labour organisers also suggest that some factory workers had some tertiary-level education.
7 This excerpt is taken from 'Masalah Bredel, Masalah Buruh' by Moktar, a former factory worker in West Java who has had considerable experience with labour-based NGOs. It appears in *Media Kerja Budaya* (1 November 1994). Many workers read second-hand newspapers or magazines.
8 This is somewhat different from my impression of the industrial areas that lie south of Jakarta, where West Javanese workers seem to predominate, including those who originate from villages and towns that are relatively close by.
9 See various editions of *Cerita Kami, Koeli, PHK* and other labour-activist publications.
10 I participated in numerous such discussions during the course of fieldwork in November 1993–July 1994 and in February–March and April–May 1996, as well as periods between May and November 1998.
11 For example, Saut Aritonang, a founder of the *Setiakawan* independent union, suggested in an interview on 8 December 1993 that the 'social justice' appeal of Pancasila is personally important to him. In a similar vein, Deyo notes that 'the

Confucianism among politically active South Korean students' stresses such things as morality and justice (Deyo, 1989: 88–9).

Bibliography

American Embassy (1994) 'Labour trends in Indonesia', unpublished report, Jakarta.

Anderson, Benedict (1994) 'Rewinding back to the future: The Left and constitutional democracy', in David Bourchier and John Legge (eds) *Democracy in Indonesia: 1950s and 1990s*, Clayton: Centre of Southeast Asian Studies, Monash University, pp. 128–42.

Andrae, Gunilla and Beckman, Bjorn (1998) *Union Power in the Nigerian Textile Industry: Labour Regime and Adjustment*, Uppsala: Nordiska Afrikainstitutet.

Burawoy, Michael (1985) *The Politics of Production: Factory Regimes under Capitalism and Socialism*, London: Verso.

Department of Manpower of the Republic of Indonesia (1992–3) *Laporan Akhir Penelitian Dampak Pemogokan terhadap Perusahaan dan Kesejahteraan Pekerja, Pusat Penelitian dan Pengembangan Tenaga Kerja*, Jakarta.

Deyo, Frederic C. (1989) *Beneath the Miracle: Labour Subordination in the New Asian Industrialism*, Berkeley: University of California Press.

—— (1997) 'Labour and industrial restructuring in South-East Asia', in Garry Rodan, Kevin Hewison and Richard Robison (eds) *The Political Economy of South-East Asia: An Introduction*, Melbourne: Oxford University Press, pp. 205–24.

Djajusman, D. Suziani (1992) 'Di Seberang Gerbang Pabrik: Asrama Buruh Perempuani', *Prisma* 3: 51–8.

Hadiz, Vedi R. (1997) *Workers and the State in New Order Indonesia*, London and New York: Routledge.

—— (1998) 'Reformasi Total? Labor after Suharto', *Indonesia* 66 (October): 109–24.

Hanagan, Michael (1986) 'Agriculture and industry in the nineteenth-century Stephanois: Household employment patterns and the rise of a permanent proletariat', in Michael Hanagan and Charles Stephenson (eds) *Proletarians and Protest: The Roots of Class Formation in an Industrializing World*, New York: Greenwood Press, pp. 77–106.

Hancock, Peter James (1994) 'West Java: A Demographic Anomaly', B.A. thesis, School of Social Sciences and Asian Languages, Curtin University of Technology, Perth, September.

Hasibuan, Sayuti (1968) 'Political Unionism and Economic Development in Indonesia: Case Study, North Sumatra', unpublished Ph.D. thesis, University of California, Berkeley.

Hawkins, Everett D. (1963) 'Labour in transition', in Ruth McVey (ed.) *Indonesia*, New Haven: Yale University Press, pp. 248–71.

Ingleson, John (1986) *In Search of Justice: Workers and Unions in Colonial Java, 1908–1926*, Singapore: Oxford University Press.

Jordan, Bill (1995) 'Preface', in David R. Harris (ed.) *Prisoners of Progress: A Review of the Current Indonesian Labour Situation*, Leiden: INDOC, FNV, INFID, pp. vii–ix.

Lambert, Rob (1990) 'Kilusang Mayo Uno and the rise of social movement unionism in the Philippines', *Labour and Industry* 3, 2–3: 258–80.

Manning, Chris (1992) 'Survey of recent developments', *Bulletin of Indonesian Economic Studies* 28, 1: 3–38.

—— (1993) 'Structural change and industrial relations during the Suharto period: An approaching crisis', *Bulletin of Indonesian Economic Studies* 29, 2: 59–95.

Mather, Celia (1983) 'Subordination of women and lack of industrial strife in West Java', in John G. Taylor and Andrew Turton (eds) *Sociology of Developing Societies*, New York: Monthly Review Press.

Minju No-Jo (1987) *South Korea's New Trade Unions: The Struggle for Free Trade Unions*, Hong Kong: Asia Monitor Resource Centre.

Moertopo, Ali (1975) *Buruh dan Tani dalam Pembangunan*, Jakarta: Center for Strategic and International Studies.

Nurbaiti, Ati (1986) 'Pengaturan Perburuhan dalam Penataan Struktur Politik Orde Baru: Kasus Buruh Industri Tekstil di PT ITM, Kec. Tangerang, Kabupaten Tangerang', S-1 thesis, University of Indonesia, Jakarta.

Ogle, George E. (1990) *South Korea: Dissent within the Economic Miracle*, London: Zed Books.

Razif (1994) 'Sejarah Pemikiran Serikat Buruh Indonesia', unpublished paper.

Roesli, M. Arief (1992) 'Buruh dan Kesadaran Kelas', unpublished paper.

Shiraishi, Takashi (1990) *An Age in Motion*, Ithaca: Cornell University Press.

Silver, Beverly J. (1995) 'Labor unrest and world-systems analysis: Premises, concepts and measurement', *Review* 18, 1: 7–34.

Sudono, Agus (1981) *FBSI Dahulu, Sekarang dan Yang Akan Datang*, Jakarta: FBSI.

Tanter, Richard (1990) 'The totalitarian ambition: Intelligence and security agencies in Indonesia', in Arief Budiman (ed.) *State and Civil Society in Indonesia*, Monash Papers on Southeast Asia no. 22, Clayton: Centre of Southeast Asian Studies, Monash University, pp. 213–88.

Tedjasukmana, Iskandar (1958) *The Political Character of the Indonesian Trade Union Movement*, Ithaca: Modern Indonesia Project, Cornell University.

White, Benjamin (1993) 'Industrial workers in West Java's urban fringe', in Chris Manning and Joan Hardjono (eds) *Indonesia Assessment 1993 – Labour: Sharing in the Benefits of Growth?*, Canberra: Department of Political and Social Change, Research School of Pacific Studies, Australian National University, pp. 127–38.

World Bank (1994) *Indonesia: Sustaining Development*, Report No. 11737-IND, 25 May.

Young, Kenneth R. (1994) 'A new political context: The urbanisation of the rural', in David Bourchier and John Legge (eds) *Democracy in Indonesia, 1950s and 1990s*, Monash Papers on Southeast Asia no. 31, Clayton: Centre of Southeast Asian Studies, Monash University, pp. 248–57.

7 After the Kader fire

Labour organising for health and safety standards in Thailand

Andrew Brown

This chapter reflects on some developments in labour organising in Thailand during the 1990s, via a focus on issues of workplace health and safety standards. Although job-related accidents and illnesses have posed major problems for Thai workers and their families over many decades, such problems have become more pressing during the 1990s. Indeed, the onset of the 1997 economic crisis notwithstanding, the decade for labour may well be best remembered for a series of spectacular accidents and multiple cases of occupation-related illnesses that have left a trail of dead, maimed and injured in their wake. Arguably, the incident that highlighted most dramatically the health and safety dangers confronting Thailand's industrial workforce was the fire at the Kader Industries (Thailand) factory on 10 May 1993, which left 188 workers dead and almost 500 injured.

While a great deal of criticism has been levelled at employers and the government for the failure to either conform to or enforce legislated health and safety standards, the trade union movement has also been taken to task for its inability to protect workers against occupation-related accidents and illnesses (for example, see Nidhi, 1993: 4). Such criticisms have provided further input into a growing body of critical literature, produced both within and outside the ranks of organised labour, that seeks to account for the declining industrial and political fortunes of the trade union movement in Thailand.[1] In the first part of this chapter, I note some of the factors that have been advanced to explain the current weak, fragmented and politically impotent state of organised labour. I then examine problems of workplace health and safety, describing how labour has taken up the issue and has organised around it. It will be suggested that, in the context of ongoing struggles to rebuild, reorganise and revitalise the trade-union movement, activism seeking to improve health and safety standards has seen some new alliances and networks forged between labour and non-labour actors. Although the material gains won through this activism have been limited, it is suggested that some interesting developments have occurred in terms of organising and consciousness which might prove significant in the future.

The rise and fall of organised labour

For many, the early to mid-1970s is seen to mark an important moment in the development of organised labour in Thailand (Mabry, 1977; Vichote, 1991). Import-substitution industrialisation, adopted at the beginning of the 1960s, generated not only an expansion in industrial wage-labour but was by the end of the decade also accompanied by the appearance of vigorous public forms of struggle and organisation among the newly created industrial workforce. Through their activism, workers demonstrated an intention to build organisations at workplace, industry and national levels, through which they could not only deal with employers, but also join with a coalition of social forces struggling for a range of broader social and political rights (Morell and Chai-anan, 1981: 181–204). This period of activism, which peaked around the mid-1970s, forced a general restructuring of state–labour–capital relations. The repressive controls imposed under the authoritarian, military-led regimes of the 1958–73 period gave way to the development of new modes of labour control that relied less on coercion and more on consultation and mediation within institutionalised tripartite arrangements where workers, employers and government were to cooperate in solving industrial conflict and disputation (Saowalak, 1990a). For both state and capital, this regime of control has apparently proven successful: industrial militancy declined throughout the 1980s and rates of economic growth reached unprecedented levels. Likewise, taken at face value, the data indicate that the system has also served working-class interests well, as labour organisations have grown steadily in number (see Brown, 1997: 171–2).

However, a simple focus on the expansion of institutions and the changing forms of struggle can be misleading, for it hides a reality which is quite different from the initial impression. Rather than representing growing strength within a modernising industrial relations framework, the proliferation of unions actually represents a disorganisation of organised labour and a consequent undercutting of the capacity of unions to represent the interests of workers. By the early 1990s, the trade-union scene comprised a plethora of small, financially strapped and badly managed enterprise-based organisations whose coverage extended to less than 5 per cent of the industrial workforce (Somsak, 1995: 152–3).[2] At the national level, there were eight labour councils riven by factionalism, internal competition and infiltrated by outside bureaucratic, military and business interests (see Banthit, 1996). Thus, while rapid industrialisation has furthered the growth of an industrial working class, the past two decades have actually seen the trade-union movement grow progressively weaker and ineffectual in representing working-class interests in negotiations with employers and governments. At the same time, it has also managed to alienate large sections of 'the general public' with whom it once joined forces in combating various social and political injustices. Whether Thai 'unions will rebound' or are 'instead doomed to a slow but definite extinction' (Thana, 1996a: 2) – a question which would have been unthinkable during the heady days of the 1970s – is one that has been widely asked in the 1990s, even before the financial crisis compounded labour's difficulties.

Explaining the reasons for the declining industrial and political fortunes of organised labour has occupied the energies of many, both within and outside labour ranks.[3] Broadly speaking, these explanations refer *inter alia* to the structural fragmentation and demobilisation of the workforce associated with rapid industrialisation, the adoption of lean production and neo-liberal arrangements which, combined with a host of locally specific economic, social, cultural and political conditions, have not only contributed to the undermining of unions already established but have also placed major obstacles in the path of any further endeavours to develop effective, independent labour organisations.

Within this literature, the impact of the role of the state has, however, been the subject of particular scrutiny. While, for much of modern Thai history, state control over labour organising has relied on various forms of repression, workers have over the past two decades possessed a broad range of rights and guarantees that have permitted them to legitimately negotiate the conditions under which their labour is exercised. But the formal granting of rights has represented something of a double-edged sword for workers. On one hand, they have been legally entitled to a space within which they could build their organisations and have a legitimate voice in broader industrial and political frameworks. On the other hand, the specific nature of the space and continuing struggles over this space in the face of stiff opposition from powerful elements of capital and state have placed major obstacles in the way of the development of meaningful, independent unions.[4]

For example, from the late 1970s onwards, some private-sector employers, aided by a ready supply of labour power, have systematically sought to combat and inhibit labour organisation. The strategies used to this end include the widespread use of short term contracts; closing militant sections of factories; sacking the promoters of unions (made possible by legal loopholes); drawing out bargaining negotiations and encouraging splits within union leadership, and closing factories to reopen them with newly recruited workforces. These and other measures have been reinforced with threats, beatings and the strategic murder of a few union officials and activists (Hewison and Brown, 1994).

For its part, the state has also made a major contribution in restricting the space available to organised labour. Here reference can be made to the failure to close the many loopholes in the labour law, not enforcing employer compliance and a continuing refusal to ratify International Labour Organisation (ILO) conventions that cover workers' basic rights.[5] More particularly, however, specific elements within the state have sought to restrict worker autonomy. In the late 1970s, for example, the military (which has a long history of involvement in labour affairs) established its own organisation – the National Free Labour Congress – to compete with and promote divisions within organised labour at the peak council level. The military has also consistently fostered competition within labour councils. A good example of this was sponsorship by the Internal Security Operation Command (ISOC) of its own faction within the Labor Congress of Thailand, which led to the ousting of the president, Paisan

Thawatchaianan, and the break-up of what was then the strongest and most progressive body of organised labour (Brown and Frenkel, 1993: 92–4).

Other sections of the state have also played a significant part in the weakening and fragmenting of organised labour. As noted above, the number of unions and other labour organisations grew rapidly during the 1980s and early 1990s. Rather than representing growing union strength within a maturing industrial relations framework, these developments are directly related to competition between union leaders to establish their own congresses and compete for prestigious seats on various tripartite bodies, such as the National Advisory Council for Labour Development and the Labour Court. This competition has been facilitated both by the law itself, which grants each union one vote regardless of the size of membership, and by elements within what was the Department of Labour (now part of the Ministry of Labour and Social Welfare). A review of Department records conducted in May 1993 revealed that officials have been in breach of the law by granting registration to unions without first receiving detailed information concerning the names of union officials, by not including details of annual general meetings and by generally failing to ensure that registration cards had been completed appropriately. Preferred unions and their candidates have thus been able to monopolise positions on tripartite bodies, contributing further to labour disunity.

Though the fortunes of organised labour were partially revived during the period of the Chartichai administration (1988–91) (see Brown, 1997: 173–4), they once again nose-dived following the military coup in February 1991, which brought the National Peacekeeping Council (NPKC) to power. The coming to power of conservative forces led by the military saw workers and the union movement placed under considerable pressure. The NPKC leadership launched a sustained offensive against organised labour, with some claiming that the policies implemented by the new regime represented 'the greatest success the state has ever had in splitting and controlling the power of labour' (Poronmet, 1991: 23). Through a variety of legislative measures and adjustments to the 1975 Labour Relations Act, the NPKC removed state-enterprise workers – who in the past had formed the organisational heart of the trade-union movement – from coverage under the 1975 law, thus forcing a radical restructuring of peak labour councils. These legislative amendments also placed further impediments in the path of union formation in the private sector. The combined effect of these changes was to alter industrial relations regulations in ways fundamentally detrimental to labour and favourable to capital and the state. Justifications for these changes were couched in terms of meeting the demands of the economy, as well as maintaining national peace and security (*Khao Phiset*, 1991; Sungsidh, 1992: 2).

Although the NPKC's grip on power was to be relatively short-lived, the inability of the officially sanctioned trade-union movement to mount an offensive *as a movement* and join with popular demonstrations to oust the regime, created an increasing sense of crisis among workers and their unions, stimulating the development of a process of internal debate, self-reflection and reorganisation which has yet to run its course. In part, this process of reorganising is occurring as a result of the rise of a new, younger and more progressive generation of leaders (cf. Thana, 1996b). It is entailing a process of critical reflection on the past objectives and strategies of existing organisations and the institutional structures in which they operate (Banthit, 1993; Nikhom, 1994; Sakool, 1994). Against the recent background of a weak and divided trade-union movement undergoing an ongoing process of revaluation, problems associated with workplace health and safety standards have arisen as a major issue.

Rapid industrialisation and health and safety problems

As mentioned briefly above, health and safety problems have long posed challenges to those incorporated into the wage–labour relation in Thailand. As far back as the late nineteenth century, for example, thousands of workers engaged in the construction of Thailand's railways were reported to have died from malaria and other jungle fevers (Skinner, 1957: 115). A similar fate also befell many wage-labourers who worked in the mining areas, where it was claimed even 'bars and bolts' could not prevent workers from fleeing as the death-rate among new arrivals exceeded 60 per cent (ibid.: 110–11). Although job-related accidents and illnesses have continued to be a major source of concern for workers and their families over the decades, rapid industrialisation over the past thirty years has seen accident- and injury-rates escalate alarmingly. The mobilisation of cheap unskilled wage-labour in the production of goods for sale on local, regional and world markets has demanded not only low wages, but also that little consideration be given by either employers or government to protecting the health and safety of the workforce in an increasingly competitive market. Although available figures need to be treated with care, both the incidence and rates of workplace accidents and related illnesses have increased alarmingly over recent years, alongside industrial expansion. For example, rates of accidents increased nearly fourfold between 1974 and 1984 from 1,173 per 100,000 to 4,003 per 100,000. Across all industries, death-rates by the mid-1980s stood at 31.7 per 100,000 compared with 2.1 per 100,000 for Britain and 4.6 per 100,000 for the Netherlands (Symonds, 1997: 23–4).[6]

Despite the long history of worker concern, however, it has only been during the 1990s that problems of workplace health and safety have attracted increasing attention outside the workplace. This has followed in the wake of the occurrence of a number of terrible industrial accidents that have cost the lives and health of not only workers, but also members of the general public.[7] However, the one incident which served to draw most attention to what has been an appalling history of neglect of health and safety standards was the Kader fire.

The Kader fire

Kader Industries (Thailand) was a joint venture involving Hong Kong, Taiwanese and Thai interests producing dolls and children's toys for export to European and US markets (Symonds, 1997). The toy industry has benefited considerably from government support through the provision of a range of tax holidays and other incentives. The total value of exported toys grew from roughly US$2.5 million in the early 1980s to US$380 million by the early 1990s. By the mid-1990s there were some 115 firms involved in the industry, with some of the largest factories employing 10,000 workers (CLIST, 1995: 130).

The toy industry in Thailand has become well known for its low wages, long working hours, despotic forms of managerial control, poor working conditions, feminisation and casualisation of its workforce, vigorous opposition to the formation of trade unions and, in particular, its disregard for legislated health and safety standards. The temperature in toy factories is high and there are often inadequate fresh water and toilet facilities. Work spaces are often cramped and cluttered. The labour process requires workers to handle various chemicals, often without recourse to the use of protective equipment. Because of poor ventilation and the lack of air filters, the shopfloor is filled with dust and lint particles; as a result, many in the industry suffer from lung diseases, sinus problems and debilitating allergies. Workers are also often exposed to fire risks due to the presence of highly flammable materials in buildings that are constructed cheaply without provision of adequate fire escapes. Emergency fire-training is virtually non-existent (ibid.: 128–30; Nophaphon, 1993b: 51–7). Conditions within the factory operated by Kader Industries (Thailand) generally conformed to these 'industry standards'.

The majority of workers employed by Kader Industries (Thailand) were unskilled and low-paid women who were engaged on short-term contracts, renewed every four months, that precluded the right to receive welfare benefits and form trade unions (ICFTU, 1994). Supervision of the labour process was highly authoritarian in nature; the sole emphasis was on meeting production targets, with little regard shown for worker fatigue or basic needs such as adequate toilet and drinking facilities. Failure to reach set production quotas was accompanied by harassment, intimidation and occasional violence. Though a statement from Kader Industries claimed that the factory in Thailand was 'one of the most modern air-conditioned industrial complexes in Thailand' (*Bangkok Post*, 1993), the four main buildings in the factory complex contained a number of major structural flaws, including the use of non-insulated steel pillars; stairwells, entrances and exits that were too narrow, and the absence of a functioning fire-alarm system. Ventilation systems were inadequate and inflammable materials were stored in various passageways. Subsequent investigation revealed that collectively these factors contributed to the very high death toll among workers.[8] The nature of the materials stored in the building generated intense heat that the supporting steel structures – not coated with fire-insulating materials – were unable to withstand. Within twenty minutes of the fire breaking out, the first floor of the building in which the fire started collapsed;

this caused the three floors above to cave in on top of workers who had found their escape routes blocked because exit doors had been locked, supposedly to prevent the petty thieving of raw materials by staff. The fire raged for some six hours before being brought under control. Of the 188 killed, 159 were women, with many dying as a result of being overcome with poisonous fumes before they had a chance to escape.

Though the Kader fire attracted enormous national and international media attention, it was (as noted above) only one of a series of accidents to have occurred during the 1990s. In the following section, I examine the nature of the responses by workers and their organisations to the dangers associated with the workplace.

Organising for improved health and safety

Incidents such as the Kader fire have placed workplace health and safety issues under broader public scrutiny and debate in Thailand. A notable feature of the debate has been the range of social interests and actors who have become involved. Nationally, individual workers, trade unionists, academics, various non-governmental organisations (NGOs), health-care workers, lawyers, monks, civil liberty groups, bureaucrats and child-welfare agencies, as well as police and politicians, have all been drawn into the debate, as have international media, labour federations, unions and other welfare, development and labour agencies. This plethora of actors, interests and agencies have proffered widely different explanations for incidents like the Kader fire in particular and the problem of health and safety in general. These explanations range from the supposed carelessness of individual workers, the lack of adequate health and safety training at the workplace, the avarice of employers, the nature of national development goals, the corruption of local officials, the character of the relationship between business and government, the lack of popular participation in Thai social and political institutions, and the extremely detrimental impact of globalisation on workers in the South. Importantly, the health and safety crisis has also been seen to be partly the result of the ineffectiveness and weakness of existing labour organisations (Nidhi, 1993: 4; Nophaphon, 1993b). The Kader fire has been seen as a case which exemplifies this weakness.

The fire occurred in an industrial area which has a long history of industrial conflict and labour activism. During the 1970s, the district had been known for the preparedness of its workers to struggle and organise against employers. Labour organising in the area also formed an important industrial basis for the leftist Labour Coordination Centre of Thailand (LCCT). However, as a result of structural changes and hostile opposition by employers with the tacit consent and sometimes direct involvement of state officials, labour organisations in the region had been almost totally destroyed by the 1990s. By the early part of the decade, Nakhon Pathom province contained some 7,583 large- and small-scale firms, employing about 53,000 workers; yet only seven unions operated in the region, one of which was located in the Kader factory. The union at Kader was established in March 1991 and at the time of the fire it had 413 members out of a workforce of some 3,000. It had links to the National Free Labour Congress (established by the military in the late 1970s) and seems to have basically been established as part of wider struggles within the trade-union movement over competition for seats on various tripartite bodies (Nophaphon, 1993b: 53; Voravidh, 1998: 78).

It is clear that the health and safety record at Kader Industries (Thailand) was poor. Not only did Kader employees experience problems with allergies and lung-related illnesses, but they had also previously experienced the dangers posed by fire. Fires had occurred at the site on two prior occasions – in 1989 and early 1993.[9] As a result of these incidents, the company had been ordered by local building inspectors to make significant changes to health and safety practices. Despite this history, the Kader union had been unable to force any improvement in safety conditions within the factory by ensuring that official directives were indeed implemented. Immediately after the fire, the local union simply disintegrated (ibid.: 78). In the words of one union member:

> We were affiliated with the National Free Labour Union Congress. Two days after the fire, officials from the Congress came [to the factory], but I don't see that they have done anything. They came for a while, went away and then they did not do anything. Workers have to help themselves. They cannot rely on trade unions very much. The members of the trade union complain that the union has not helped them.
>
> (cited in Symonds, 1997: 34)

The inability of the Kader union to protect the working conditions of its members seems to epitomise some of the problems within organised labour more generally. The inability to protect the rank and file, its precarious existence in a region known for its anti-unionism, as well as its linkages with a military-sponsored peak labour body, reflected some of the persistent difficulties that have beset labour organisations nation-wide. However, at the same time, the incident furthered the resolve of some and convinced them of the utmost importance of regrouping and rebuilding organisations that would have a greater capacity to not only improve health and safety standards, but advance workers' class interests across a range of economic, social and political issues as well. Below I demonstrate the existence of such a resolve by looking at attempts to organise to improve health and safety standards, noting in particular the links that have been forged between labour and non-labour actors. In doing so, it is worth drawing a distinction between activism that has been conducted to cater for the needs of those immediately affected by specific accidents and campaigns that have been initiated to bring about longer-term improvements in health and safety standards.

Committee for Assisting Kader Employees (CAKE)

One type of activism to have emerged has been aimed at providing immediate assistance to those workers and family members who have been directly affected by accidents or occupation-related illness. For example, the suspected heavy-metal poisoning of electronic workers at Lamphun Industrial Estate located in the north of Thailand has been accompanied by 'a new alliance of women workers, specialist medical staff, media and activists groups' which has sought not only to assist those affected, but 'also has helped bring attention to the neglect of environmental health issues in government policy' (Forsyth, 1998: 210). Similar kinds of alliances were formed after the Kader fire.

Chaos reigned in the immediate aftermath of the Kader fire. The company was unable or unwilling to post lists of those who were actually in the building at the time of the accident, the local union was unable to provide any information to family members who came to the site looking for their relatives, while government officials arriving from different state agencies only added to the confusion. As the dead were laid out in rows and the injured carted off to different hospitals, panic, confusion and shock set in amid wailing sirens, the smell of burnt flesh and the ever-present traffic congestion. It was in this situation that a new, loosely linked network began to form, drawn from relatively independent elements within labour councils, labour federations, district labour collectives who, together with representatives of NGOs, academics and members of the legal profession, began operating as the Committee for Assisting Kader Employees (CAKE).[10] Apart from providing immediate material assistance to the families of injured workers, CAKE became involved in lobbying politicians to have the government provide longer-term support for victims, ensure that Kader workers received adequate compensation and make certain that those found to have breached safety standards be brought to trial.

One of the main aims of CAKE was to ensure that Kader workers received adequate compensation. Initially compensation levels were calculated on the wage individual workers received at the time of the fire. As most of those employed were receiving the minimum wage, these compensation levels were deemed to be totally inadequate. The families of deceased workers were originally to receive a mere 10,000 baht (US$500). CAKE argued that the fire was no accident, but arose as a result of the company's disregard for labour laws, and that compensation payments should be increased. When the company began dragging its feet on the issue of increasing payments, CAKE stepped up its campaign. Representatives from CAKE and two Kader workers travelled to Hong Kong where they joined with local activists in a two-week campaign that involved holding demonstrations outside Kader Headquarters and calling for an international trade boycott against Kader products – to which consumer groups in Australia, Hong Kong and the United States responded (*Asian Labour Update*, 1993: 4). Demonstrations were also held outside the Bangkok offices of the giant Thai multinational, Charoen Phokpand, which held interests in the Kader (Thailand) operations. As an International Confederation of Free Trade Unions report later stated: 'These actions attracted media attention and served to mount sufficient pressure on the company to properly recognise negotiations with [CAKE]' (ICFTU, 1994: 12).

In July 1993, the company agreed to negotiate with workers and raise compensation levels. Agreement was reached and compensation levels were raised to 300,000 baht (US$15,000) (*Asian Labour Update*, 1993: 1; Voravidh, 1998: 79). Kader also agreed to meet medical costs not covered by the government and to provide funds for the education of children of deceased workers. Payments were further made to those who were previously excluded from receiving compensation as a result of their having been employed on short-term contracts. Kader in addition offered jobs to injured workers, to relatives of victims and to other workers who had been in its employ for more than three years. Finally, the company also agreed to pay all outstanding wages and holiday payments (ICFTU, 1994: 12).

Significantly, these cooperative efforts between Thai- and Hong Kong-based labour groups spawned a more permanent campaign through which working-conditions in toy factories in China, Indonesia, the Philippines, Thailand and Vietnam are being monitored by local activists in cooperation with the Hong Kong-based Asia Monitor Resource Centre (AMRC). Another development to have occurred through this activism was the formation of a regional network that links together groups of injured workers. Finally, the linkages between Hong Kong-based activists and Thai labour organisations have continued through various exchanges (see Apo, 1998). As Voravidh (one of the academics involved in CAKE) has recently stated, the activities of the group underscored the importance of forging solidarity between both labour and non-labour groups, as well as developing domestic and international networks (Voravidh, 1998: 79).

Health and Safety Campaign Committee

In the latter part of 1993, CAKE organised a public seminar, the aim of which was to invite suggestions as to how the group might continue to be active on health and safety issues so as to ensure that incidents such as the Kader fire were never repeated. From these public discussions, a new group was formed – *khana kammakan kanranarong phua sukaphap lae khwam phlot phai khong khon ngan* or the Health and Safety Campaign Committee (HSCC). Like CAKE, the HSCC was formed through a coalition of labour and non-labour actors.[11] Working out of the offices of the Arom Phongphangan Foundation, a labour-affiliated NGO, the members of the HSCC met regularly through 1993 and in February 1994 the HSCC declared itself openly for the first time, making a number of recommendations for the improvement of health and safety standards to the Ministry of Labour and Social Welfare, Ministry of Health, Board of Investment and the Parliamentary Commission on Labour and Social Welfare (Banthit, 1997b: 10). Since 1994, the HSCC has continued to be active on health and safety issues, becoming involved in organising a range of activities, such as public seminars, street marches, demonstrations, lobbying politicians to have new legislation passed and improve enforcement procedures, and establishing a Health and

Safety Hotline through which workers could inform authorities of health and safety breaches in factories, as well as seeking to have an independent occupational health and safety institute established (Voravidh, 1998: 79). At the same time, activists involved have developed sophisticated analyses of problems of health and safety, and through contacts in the media have ensured that the issue remains the subject of public debate (see Banthit, 1997b).

A theme running throughout these campaigns has been to challenge the centralised bureaucratic control over decision-making on issues of health and safety. This is itself a rejection of the limitations of existing labour laws that restrict union activity to economic issues only. However, members of the HSCC assert that labour participation in the development of workplace health and safety, as well as in the formation of public policy which deals with health and safety matters, is absolutely essential. As Aruni Srito (a long-term activist and the chair of the HSCC) has stated, we can

> no longer allow the mechanisms for protecting and overseeing workers'
> health and safety to be located within the bureaucratic system, both workers
> and employers have to have a role in overseeing safety issues.
>
> (cited in Cadet and Nakul, 1997: 10)

This aim of forcing the state to cede a greater space for worker participation in the process of developing improved health and safety can be documented through a brief account of the HSCC campaign to establish 10 May as National Health and Safety Day and to have an independent health and safety institute established.

In late 1994, the HSCC began a campaign to have May 10, the date of the Kader fire, designated as National Health and Safety Day. The HSCC argued that the day would serve to commemorate the victims of the Kader fire, encourage all interested parties to appreciate the importance of health and safety issues and ensure that they work hard never to allow a repeat of the Kader tragedy. The occasion would also provide a day on which the activities of government departments charged with responsibility for health and safety could be assessed, and finally it would give a sense of hope and encouragement to those workers injured as a result of workplace accidents (Banthit, 1997b: 10). Activism to have May 10 designated as National Health and Safety Day has led the HSCC to become involved in numerous discussions with bureaucrats and politicians working within a range of state ministries, departments and divisions. As Banthit (1997b: 12) has noted, the aim has been to challenge the bureaucratic state which, in the past, had exercised a monopoly over the designation of nationally significant days. Through its commitment to having May 10 set aside as National Health and Safety Day, the HSCC has argued that new sets of criteria be used in determining what is and is not of national significance.

This quest for greater participation has been especially evident in the campaign for the establishment of an independent occupational health and safety institute (see Cadet, 1998). The basic thrust of the argument for the establishment of an independent institute begins by stressing that, in the past, the administration of health and safety has been the sole responsibility of a number of state agencies working under the jurisdiction of a range of different ministries. This, it is said, has led to considerable confusion, lack of coordination and inefficiency (ibid.: 84). More especially, control over the development and administration of legislation as the sole prerogative of state officials – with a singular lack of participation by workers – is seen as a root cause of health and safety problems. It is for these reasons that the HSCC adopted as one of its aims to press for the establishment of an institute which would bring various relevant state agencies together into a single autonomous body that would be responsible for workplace health and safety. A basic thrust of this campaign is thus to empower workers by institutionalising their participation in decision-making processes on occupational, health and safety issues (Voravidh, 1998: 80).

In summary, activism for improved health and safety has revolved around providing immediate material assistance and support for workers and their families, as well as mounting campaigns that aim to bring about a longer-term improvement in health and safety standards. This activism has seen the creation of new networks and alliances among a range of actors drawn from those elements that have managed to retain some autonomy within officially sanctioned trade-union structures, as well as non-labour actors. Notably these alliances and newly established organisational vehicles exist in a somewhat ambiguous legal state, standing outside the officially sanctioned parameters of labour organisation. These developments are quite significant, as they are realising in practice some of the strategies that have been established to further the process of building a more viable and effective organised-labour movement. Among the most important of these has been the view that organised labour must seek to rehabilitate its public profile by joining with other social groups and interests over issues of shared concern.[12] The activities and social composition of both CAKE and the HSCC are examples of the practical realisation of such a strategy.

Government responses

Since the overthrow of the military regime in May 1992, Thailand has had four elected governments, each of which has been confronted with the task of tackling workplace health and safety. Health and safety problems have been the subject of widespread media reporting and, as noted above, there has been considerable activism by an alliance of labour and non-labour actors. Internationally, incidents such as Kader have been seen as tarnishing Thailand's international image (*Economist*, 1993), throwing an uncomfortable and unwelcome spotlight on the country's labour standards. Politicians have been acutely aware that a failure to raise standards to internationally acceptable levels might result in embargoes placed on the sale of Thai products to European and US markets (*Bangkok Post*, 1997a). It is also being realised that improving health and safety levels are necessary if Thailand is to move away from its past reliance on cheap unskilled wage-labour to high-value-added production. If this is to occur, so the argument goes, increased investment must be made to produce a better educated and higher-skilled labour force (*Bangkok Post*, 1998c). The investment in human resources would, in turn, require improved health and safety standards.

Combined, these internal and external political and structural pressures have produced some changes. Successive governments have launched numerous inquiries into health and safety problems, adjusted and modified state agencies to ensure greater efficiency and coordination, introduced new legislation which provides for the establishment of health and safety committees in the workplace, as well as promulgating a new Labour Protection Act which, despite considerable employer opposition, contains some new health and safety provisions. Occupational health and safety training and education programmes have been extended to workers, alterations have also been made to investment promotion policies to incorporate a health and safety component, and plans have been established to train more occupational health specialists. Workers have been provided with free health and safety checks, commitments have been made to train more factory inspectors, while rates of factory inspections have also increased. May 10 has also, despite considerable opposition from elements within the bureaucracy, been officially designated National Health and Safety Day. Finally, there has been some undertaking to increase rates of prosecution of employers found to be in breach of legislated health and safety standards.

Given past governments' general neglect of health and safety issues, these developments are not insignificant. There is no doubt there has at least been some greater official recognition that a major problem exists. However, it should be recognised that it required a series of terrible accidents, considerable domestic and international criticism, as well as economic structural pressures, to force government into action. Moreover, though these measures do indicate some resolve on the part of successive governments to address some of the health, safety and environmental problems associated with rapid industrialisation, few of those involved display much optimism that lasting improvements will be achieved in the short to medium term.[13]

Notably, there have also been few government concessions towards granting workers and their organisations any greater capacity to participate in developing improved standards. Some concessions to greater worker participation in the workplace appear to have been made through legislation that provides for the establishment of health and safety committees. Some progress towards this aim has also been evident in labour participation in the drafting of legislation for the establishment of an independent health and safety institute. Nikom Cantharawithun has noted that both workers and employers participated in drafting the legislation, pointing out that this compares favourably with the past where 'labour has never had a participatory role' (Cadet and Nakul, 1997: 11). Yet many contend that these apparent concessions remain largely symbolic.

It seems clear, however, that in responding to activism over health and safety standards, the actions of various governments demonstrate that some degree of worker participation is allowable – the question being the extent and degree of participation. This is particularly clear with respect to the campaign for the establishment of an independent institute. While successive governments initiated some steps towards the establishment of such a body, the whole process has stalled.[14] A major sticking point has been the nature of the powers to be exercised by the proposed institute, especially with regard to the conduct of workplace inspections and the imposition of fines and penalties (Cadet, 1998: 88–9). For example, would the institute inspect and then leave it up to other government agencies to impose penalties? For labour activists, the proposed institute should have two main roles: administration and law enforcement. But the Ministry of Labour and Social Welfare has argued that the proposed institute should perform an administrative role first (ibid.: 91). Allowing workers a participatory role in the process of actually enforcing legislation and imposing penalties and fines has been seen as taking things too far. So, while there might be agreement on the need for an institute which would better coordinate the development and implementation of policy, there is continuing dispute over the degree of independence that the institute should have from the state and bureaucracy in the actual exercise of power.

At the level of public policy, the outcome of labour activism on health and safety thus tends to highlight the continuing difficulty of forcing governments to accommodate working-class interests. Despite the occurrence of numerous accidents that have cost hundreds of lives, and despite the national and international pressure on government to initiate effective measures to deal with the problem, it could be argued that gains have been more symbolic than real. This is not to say that new legislation may not prove significant in the future, nor that the notion of labour participation embedded in celebrating a National Health and Safety Day is totally devoid of meaning. However, given the past history of failure to enforce legislated standards and the continuing reluctance to actually implement a philosophy of labour participation, such developments must be approached with some pessimism.

Nonetheless, the campaigning and activism that have been built around the struggle to protect workers from health and safety risks has produced some interesting and not insignificant outcomes. Organisationally, this activism has seen the birth of alliances – some new, some of older origin; some labour-based and others involving non-labour actors – that are operating outside the officially sanctioned industrial relations system. Moreover, this activism has contributed more generally to the broader process through which workers are attempting to rebuild an effective and viable trade-union movement.

Conclusion

It has been argued that, despite the democratic openings which have appeared in Thailand since May 1992, the labour movement has 'remained divided and stagnant' (Deyo, 1997: 209). While 'divided' it may well be, the term 'stagnant' certainly does not adequately describe the continuing activism which has been occurring at the grassroots level, nor does it adequately account for the broader ongoing process of rebuilding of organisation that has been occurring throughout the 1990s.[15]

Focusing on activism which has arisen over the issue of workplace health and safety standards, this chapter suggests that some significant developments have indeed occurred. In the context of a weak, fragmented trade-union movement, this activism has fruitfully contributed to an ongoing process of self-conscious assessment and debate within the ranks of the trade unions. More specifically, it has seen links forged between international- and domestic-based organisations, and led to the birth of new alliances and organisational vehicles that stand outside officially sanctioned institutional structures. In terms of consciousness, it has also seen a hardening in attitude of many towards the absolute necessity of continuing the process of struggle and taking the fight into the political arena. As Somsak Kosaisuk (a member of the HSCC) asserted in a piece that commemorates the fifth anniversary of the Kader fire:

> it is clear that the government represents the interests of the capitalist class. Bureaucrats support the interests of the powerful. They cooperate with capitalists to the detriment of the interests of workers and the people more generally ... [this is yet another demonstration of the fact that] the working class ... gains nothing except through struggle ... an independent health and safety institute, social insurance, child welfare, old age pensions and unemployment benefits, rights to vote, rights for protection to form unions and other guarantees that make for a stable and secure existence are things which workers must join together to fight for ...
>
> (Somsak, 1998: 14)

These outcomes in terms of consciousness and organisation notwithstanding, there is no denying that problems of industrial health and safety will continue. Real improvements, if they are to come at all, will be slow and unevenly distributed – and for many of those who have already been maimed or incapacitated, they will come much too late. Yet there is room for some optimism that the activism that has occurred and the consciousness that has developed alongside this activism may still prove significant for the longer-term process of rebuilding an effective and viable trade-union movement.

Notes

1 See, for example, Prakanphruk (1988); Saowalak (1990b); Somsak (1991); Sungsidh (1992); Sakool and Voravidh (n.d.).
2 Somsak (1991) estimates that, by the early 1990s, only a few hundred unions out of the almost 1,000 officially registered unions were actually functioning and that the vast majority of registered unions were 'paper unions', existing in name only. The existence of these paper unions is, as explained later in this chapter, the result of factional in-fighting and competition between peak council officials for seats on various tripartite bodies.
3 See, for example, some of the analyses cited in Note 1.

4 The following three paragraphs draw on Brown (1997: 171–3).
5 Although a founding member of the ILO, the Thai state has still only ratified eleven ILO conventions, none of which are concerned with the protection of basic rights. See Nikhom (1988).
6 These figures are based on an ILO report that, in turn, draws on official figures compiled by Thai authorities. However, such figures seriously underestimate the real situation. For the most part, official figures are compiled from data collected by the Workmen's Compensation Fund (WCF). The fund, however, only covers factories which employ more than twenty workers. Such factories comprise only 10 per cent of the total number of factories registered. Suntaree notes: 'This raises a question of how many industrial accidents occur in the other 90 % of factories not covered by the WCF' (Suntaree, 1994: 21).
7 For example: In March 1991, a fire occurred in a chemical store in Klong Toey Port. Five years later some 33 people had died and 170 fallen ill as a result of inhaling the toxic fumes released by the fire (*Bangkok Post*, 1996a). In November 1996, an oil storage explosion in Rayong killed 17 people (*Bangkok Post*, 1996b). In August 1993, shortly after the Kader fire, 137 people were killed as the result of the collapse of the Royal Plaza Hotel in Korat (Suvichai, 1994). In 1997, another building collapse at the Royal Jomtien Resort killed 97 hotel workers and tourists. Another case that has attracted a great deal of attention is the suspected heavy-metal poisoning of electronic workers employed at the Northern Industrial Estate (Lamphun). On this latter case, see Forsyth (1998).
8 See comments by Nikhom Chandrawithun, who chaired the committee appointed to officially investigate the causes of the fire (McDonnel, 1994; see also ICFTU, 1994).
9 See Gold (1993), who states that fires at the factory had occurred on 16 August 1989 and on 13 February 1993.
10 For further information on CAKE and its activities, see khana thamgnan tit tam khwam chuay lua khon ngan Kader (1993). See also Nophaphon (1998) and Voravidh (1998).
11 Labour actors involved with the HSCC include the Buranakan Women Workers Group; Metals Federation of Thailand; Petroleum and Chemical Workers Federation of Thailand; Bank and Finance Federation; Textile, Clothing and Leather Federation of Thailand; Paper and Printing Federation; State Enterprise Relations Group; Thai Trade Union Congress, and Labour Council of Thailand. Also involved have been labour-affiliated NGOs, the Union of Civil Liberties and the Ramkhamhaeng University Labour Welfare Group (see *raengngan porithat*, 1994). Another group that has joined in with the HSCC is the Thai Council of Work and Environment Related Patients Network (TCWERPN), a group that has been established by victims of workplace accidents and occupation-related illnesses. On this latter group, see Sombun (1998). The HSCC has also on occasions been supported by artists, painters and sculptors, whose involvement has been sparked off by realisation that industrialisation 'has had devastating effects on the environment, whether [this involves] the safety of workers, or the poisoning of communities' (Siwaporn, 1994: 1).
12 See, for example, the concluding comment in Somsak (1993: 133).
13 See, for example, opinions expressed in the special issue of *raengngan porithat* that was published to commemorate the fifth anniversary of the Kader fire (see Somsak, 1998, for bibliographic details).
14 Currently there are attempts to use Article 170 of the new constitution, which allows 'the people' to submit a bill to parliament if 50,000 signatures are attached to the proposal (*Bangkok Post*, 1998a).
15 As a reaction to the literature, which has concentrated on explaining the weakness of existing Thai labour organisation, and to the underlying pessimistic outlook often embedded in this literature, Ji (1999) has sought to redirect attention to the continued growth of a working class in Thai society and the numerous, often bitter and volatile,

struggles that have been occurring at grassroots level, often without (and indeed in some cases in opposition to) the dictates of union leadership. The history of this activism, especially that which has occurred since the onset of the economic crisis, is yet to be adequately recorded; but see *Bangkok Post* (1997b), for example, which reports that a total of 10,881 cases were brought to the Central Labour Court between mid-1996 and mid-1997, the highest total in seventeen years. Most cases brought before the court involved workers demanding compensation from employers following the closure of businesses.

Bibliography

Apo Leong (1998) 'May the dead rest in peace!', in *raengngan porithat* (Labour Review) 12, 5: 30.

Asian Labour Update (1993) No. 12, July.

Bangkok Post (1993) 'Kader hires top sleuths to look into factory fire', 14 May: 3.

—— (1996a) 'Victim dies after five years of suffering', 13 September: 8.

—— (1996b) 'Take action to stop carnage', 14 November: 13.

—— (1997a) 'Plan to boost work safety: World standards at factories nationwide', 1 February: 6.

—— (1997b) 'Sharp rise in dispute cases', 9 September.

—— (internet edn) (1998a) 'Labour/safety at workplaces highlighted', http://www.bangkokpost.net/today/110598_News11.html (downloaded 12 May 1998).

—— (internet edn) (1998b) 'Factories must raise standards', http://www.bangkokpost.net/today/191198_Business01.html (downloaded 21 March 1999).

—— (internet edn) (1998c) 'Shift to the high-end is vital, says Chuan', http://www.bangkokpost.net/today/091298_News04.html (downloaded 12 December 1998).

Banthit Thamatrirat (1991) 'Chiwit khabuankan sahaphap raengngan thai phaitai rabop ro. so. cho.' (Life of the Thai trade union movement under the National Peacekeeping Council), in Arom Phongphangan Foundation (ed.) *Chomna raengngan thai* (The Face of Thai Labour), Bangkok: Arom Phongphangan Foundation, pp. 231–96.

Banthit Thonchaisetawut (ed.) (1993) *raengngan thai 2536: soknatakam lae wikritkan* (Thai Labour 1993: Tragedy and Crisis), Bangkok: Arom Phongphangan Foundation and Friedrich Ebert Stiftung.

—— (1996) *khrongsang sahaphap raengngan lae ongkon triphakkhi nai prathet thai* (The Structure of Trade Unions and Tripartite Organisation in Thailand), Bangkok: Friedrich Ebert Stiftung.

—— (1997a) 'bot wikhro khwamrunraeng khong sathanakan khwam phlotphai nai sathan prakopkan: botrian cak phloengnarok Kader thung royal Jomtian' (An analysis of safety at the enterprise level: Lessons from the Kader fire to the Jomtian Hotel collapse), in Arom Phongphangan Foundation (ed.) *khon phlot phai tong ma kon* (Safety Must Come First), Bangkok: Arom Phongphangan Foundation and Friedrich Ebert Stiftung , pp. 1–30.

—— (1997b) 'kan riak rong hai rataban prakat wan thi 10 phrutsaphakhom pen wan suchaphap lae khwam phlot phai haeng chat' (Demanding May 10 as Health and Safety Day), in *raengngan porithat* (Labour Review) 11, 5: 10–12.

Brown, A. (1997) 'Locating working class power', in K. Hewison (ed.) *Locating Power: Democracy, Opposition and Participation in Thailand*, London and New York: Routledge, pp. 163–78.

Brown, A. and Frenkel, S. (1993) 'Union unevenness and insecurity in Thailand', in S. Frenkel (ed.) *Organized Labor in the Asia-Pacific Region: A Comparative Study of Trade Unionism in Nine Countries*, Ithaca: ILR Press, pp. 82–106.

Cadet Chaowilai (1994) 'khwam khluanwaui phua sukaphap lae khwam phlotphai khong khon ngan 2537' (The labour movement on workers' health and safety 1994), in Banthit Thongchaisetawut (ed.) *sit raengngan thai nai yuk lokanuwat* (Thai Labour Rights in the Era of Globalisation), Bangkok: Arom Phongphangan Foundation and Asian-American Free Labor Institute, pp. 119–38.

—— (1998) 'kan khluan wai cattang sathanban khumkhrong sukhaphap, khwam phlotphai lae sing wetlom nai kan tham ngan' (Movement for the establishment of the Institute for Protection of Health, Safety and Environment in the Workplace), in *raengngan porithat* (Labour Review) 12, 5: 84–95.

Cadet Chaoawilai and Nakul Kokit (1997) 'sathaban khong rat thi pen isara: kawmai phua khum khrong sukhaphap lae khwam phlot phai khong khon ngan' (Results of a seminar on the establishment of an independent institute: A new step in protecting workers' health and safety), in *raengngan porithat* (Labour Review) 11, 9: 9–14.

CLIST (Centre for Labour Information Service and Training) (1995) 'Bad working conditions for Thai women workers in toy factories revealed', *Thai Development Newsletter*, 27–8: 128–30.

Deyo, F. (1997) 'Labour and industrial restructuring in South-East Asia', in G. Rodan, K. Hewison and R. Robison (eds) *The Political Economy of South-East Asia*, Melbourne: Oxford University Press, pp. 205–24.

Economist, The (1993) 'Industrial fire hurts image'; repr. *Bangkok Post* 24 May: 3.

Forsyth, T. (1998) 'The politics of environmental health: Industrialization and suspected poisoning in Thailand', in P. Hirsch and C. Warren (eds) *The Politics of Environment in Southeast Asia*, London: Routledge, pp. 210–26.

Gold, D. (1993) *The ILO Report on the Kader Fire*, http://www.ilo-mirror.who.or.jp/public/english/90travai/sechyg/fir01.htm (downloaded 5 March 1999).

Hewison, K. and Brown, A. (1994) 'Labour and unions in an industrialising Thailand', *Journal of Contemporary Asia* 24, 4: 483–514.

ICFTU (International Confederation of Free Trade Unions) (1994) *From the Ashes: A Toy Fire in Thailand*, Belgium: International Confederation of Trade Unions.

Ji Giles Ungpakorn (1999) *Thailand: Class Struggle in an Era of Economic Crisis*, Hong Kong and Bangkok: Asia Monitor Resources Centre and Workers' Democracy Book Club.

khana thamgnan tit tam khwam chuay lua khon ngan Kader (Ad Hoc Committee for Assisting Employers of Kader, Thailand) (1993) 'khabuan kan raenggnan kap sokna-kam ronggnan Kader' (The labour movement and the Kader tragedy), in *raengngan porithat* (Labour Review) 7, 6: 6–12.

Khao Phiset (1991) 'yaek ratwisahakit: gnanchang ro so cho' (Splitting state enterprises: The national peace-keeping council's major work), 25–31 March: 20–1.

Mabry, B. (1977) 'The Thai labour movement', *Asian Survey* 17, 10: 931–51.

McDonnel, Etain (1994) 'Kader tragedy: Has anything been done on safety standards?', *Sunday Post* 15 May: 20.

Morell, D. and Chai-anan Samudavanija (1981) *Political Conflict in Thailand: Reform, Reaction and Revolution*, Cambridge: Oelgeschlager, Gunn & Hain.

Nidhi Iawsriwong (1993) 'khrongsang khong rongngan ru khong sangkhom' (Factory structure or social structure?), in *raengngan porithat* (Labour Review) 7, 6: 3–5.

Nikhom Chandravitoon (1988) *Prathet Thai kap pramuan kotmai raengngan rawang prathet* (Thailand and international labour standards), Bangkok: Chulalongkorn University.

Nikhom Tengyai (1994) 'raengngan thai pi 2537: pi haeng kanprapplian lae kan to su' (Thai labour in 1994: A year of change and struggle), in *raengngan porithat* (Labour Review) 8, 1: 7.

Nophaphon Atiwanitchaiaphong (1993a) 'wichro botbat khabuan kan raengngnan nai kan phrutsapha thamin' (An analysis of the role of the labour movement in the May Events), in Suphachai Yimprasoet (ed.) *60 Pi Prachathipatai Thai* (Sixty Years of Thai Democracy), Bangkok: Creative Publishing, pp. 114–45.

—— (1993b) 'sup botrian soknatakam rongngan Kader' (Lessons from the Kader tragedy), in Banthit Thonchaisetawut (ed.) *raengngan thai 2536: soknatakam lae wichrokan* (Thai Labour in 1993: Tragedy and Crisis), Bangkok: Arom Phongphangan Foundation, pp. 51–67.

—— (1998) 'chiwit and khropkhrua khonngan lang soknatakamm Kader' (Livelihood and workers' families after the Kader tragedy), in *raengngan porithat* (Labour Review) 12, 5: 46–56.

Poronmet Phuto (1991) 'khu chuat phu namratwisahakit' (Threatening state enterprise leaders), *Khao Phiset* 26 August–1 September: 23–4.

Prakanphruk Chaiyaphong (1988) 'Khabuankan Kammakon Thai: 1 Thotsawat Haeng Khwam Taek Yaek' (The Thai labour movement: A decade of disunity), in *Warasan Setasatkanmuang* 6, 3: 38–68.

raengngan porithat (Labour Review) (1994) 'khongnan tong mi suanruamnai kankamnot matrathan sukhaphap lae khwam phlot phai' (Workers must have a participatory role in setting health and safety standards) 8, 3: 4.

Sakool Susongtham (1994) 'sanpi mai prathan sahaphan raengngan thanakan lae kanngoen haeng phratet thai' (New Year message from the President of the Bank and Financial Workers Union of Thailand), in *raengngan porithat* (Labour Review) 8, 1: 3–4.

Sakool Zuesongtham and Voravidh Charoenloet (n.d.) *Fragmentation of Trade Unions: Inevitable or Not?*, unpublished manuscript.

Saowalak Chaithawip (1990a) *Bot bat khong rat kap kanphatana konayut khuapkhuam raengnan thai pho. so. 2515–2525* (The Role of the State and the Development of Labour Control, 1972–1982), M.A. thesis, Thammasat University, Bangkok.

—— (1990b) 'kan khluanwai khong khabuankan raengngan thai pho. so. 2520–2525' (The Thai labour movement, 1977–1985), in Arom Phongphangan Foundation (ed.) *prawatsat khabuankan raengngan thai* (History of the Thai Labour Movement), Bangkok: Arom Phongphangan Foundation, pp. 101–13.

Siwaporn Ponsuwan (1994) 'The world faxes in their art', *Thailand Times* 16 May: 1–2.

Skinner, G. W. (1957) *Chinese Society in Thailand: An Analytical History*, Ithaca: Cornell University Press.

Sombun Srikamdokkhe (1998) 'thi ma banha lae upasak kan damnoen kan cattang sathanban khum khrong khwam phlot phai lae singwetlom nai kantham ngan' (Background and problems in establishing the Institute for Health, Safety and Environment in the Workplace), in *raengngan porithat* (Labour Review) 12, 5: 96–8.

Somsak Kosaisuk (1993) *Khabuankan raengngan thai yuk ro. so. cho. kap hetkan phrutaspha mahahot*, Bangkok: Friedrich Ebert Stiftung. (English title listed as *Labour Against Dictatorship*.)

—— (1998) 'ramluk hetsao salot 5 pi khongnan Kader phlichip' (Remembering the sadness: Five years since Kader workers left this life), in *raengngan porithat* (Labour Review)12, 5: 14.

Somsak Plaiyuwong (1994) 'bot bat khong khabuan raengngan kap sangkhom thai nai yuk loakanuwat' (The role of the labour movement in Thai society in the age of globalisation), in *raengngan porithat* (Labour Review) 7, 11: 5–6.

Somsak Samakhitham (1991) 'Kan plianplaeng lae khwam khatyaeng khong khabuankan raengngan ekachon, 2515–2534' (Changes and conflict in the labour movement in the private sector, 1972–1991), in Arom Phongphangan Foundation (ed.) *Chomna raengngan thai*, Bangkok: Arom Phongphangan Foundation, pp. 103–230.

—— (1995) *Banha raengngan* (Labour Problems), Bangkok: Khlet Thai.

Sungsidh Phiriyarangsan (1992) 'kan phatthana utsahakam phua kansongok kap raengngan samphan nai phratet thai' (The development of export-oriented industrialisation and labour relations in Thailand), in Phasuk Phonphaichit and Sungsidh Phiriyarangsan (eds) *rat thun caw pho thong thin kap sangkhom thai* (State, Capital, Local Godfathers and Thai Society), Bangkok: Political Economy Group, Faculty of Economics, Chulalongkorn University.

Suntaree Komin (1994) 'Conditions of labour in industry: A case of accelerated industrialization in Thailand', paper presented at the *International Conference on Social and Political Impact of Accelerated Industrialization in Southeast Asia*, University of Wollongong, Australia, 19–21 January.

Suthi Prasatsoet (1993) 'phrutsapha mahahot lae korani Kader: hayana cak kan pathana' (Bloody May and the Kader inferno: Development disaster), in *raengngan porithat* (Labour Review) 7, 6: 16–18.

Suvichai Pouaree (1994) 'Architects seek more clout to prevent disasters', *Bangkok Post* 14 August: 6.

Thana Poopat (1996a) 'Can unions rebound from the Doldrums?', *The Nation* 21 January: 2–3.

—— (1996b) 'Labour movement down but not out', *The Nation* 28 January: 2–3.

US Department of Labor (1996) *Foreign Labour Trends: Thailand*, Washington, D.C.: Bureau of International Labor Affairs.

Vichote, Vanno (1991) 'The role of trade unions in political development in Thailand: 1958–1986', Ph.D. thesis, City University of New York.

Voravidh Charoenloet (1998) 'The situation of health and safety in Thailand', in *raengngan porithat* (Labour Review) 12, 5: 77–82.

8 Labour and the remaking of Bombay

Stephen Sherlock

Trade unions in Bombay[1] constitute probably the oldest and most well-established wing of the labour movement in India. With a tradition of activism extending back to the time of World War I, organised labour has had a profound impact on the history and character of the city. Conditions for organising have never been ideal for the Bombay working class overall, but whole segments of workers in major industries have had a long history of involvement in unions. Today, however, the city's labour movement is in crisis with existing unions weakened, few new entrants into the workforce being organised and the number of lockouts exceeding the number of strikes.

The material circumstances which account for this crisis can be found in the remaking of the Bombay economy over the last twenty years. An old city, which combined industrial and commercial activities in its physical heartland, has been reconstituted into a commercial and service centre surrounded by restructured industrial production dispersed to ever more remote locations. In the process, the city's labour market has been transformed, with economic and spatial change reducing the bargaining capacity of organised and unorganised labour. But the following discussion also argues that the very nature of past efforts at unionisation by labour organisations in Bombay has contributed to the erosion of union strength and inability of unions to adapt to change. The labour movement in Bombay as a whole – notwithstanding its greatly varied character in terms of political connections, style of leadership and organisation – has depended on the Indian state's protectionist economic policies, a structure of labour and industrial legislation at the state and federal level, and the efforts of the Maharashtra state government to mask the effects of structural crisis and change in Bombay industry by administrative fiat. The increasing inability of the Indian state at its various levels to control the processes of capital accumulation since the 1970s, and its lessening interest in doing so since the economic reforms begun in 1991, have set the background against which the problems for unions in Bombay have developed.

The crisis in the Bombay labour movement has, of course, for some time occupied the minds of labour leaders and those commentators and scholars who study labour affairs. Especially since 1991, when the Indian economy began to liberalise, there has been growing discussion about the future of organised labour in the face of the changing structure of Indian industry, 'globalisation' and reforms to industry and labour policy. However, the key terms of this discussion continue to be dominated by economic nationalist paradigms and, hence, by the assumption that the root cause of current difficulties is India's increasing integration into the world economy (Kurien, 1993; Iyer, 1995). The problems facing the Bombay labour movement are invariably analysed in terms of the threat to Indian national interests by foreign capital and international financial institutions such as the World Bank and International Monetary Fund (IMF). As one labour publication puts it, policies to extend private enterprise and market forces have been pursued 'with great gusto so as to expand the foreign predators to come in and expand their empires [*sic*]' (*The Working Class*, December 1994: 1).

The economic nationalists in the Indian labour movement do not always articulate a coherent theoretical position, but many of their claims seem to be influenced (at least implicitly) by dependency theory, in that international capitalism is seen as a force that 'underdevelops' the Third World by holding back the formation of an independent industrial base. Hence, policies that open India to the world economy are thought to bring about 'deindustrialisation' – the destruction of domestic production capacity – as a result of competition from overseas producers. This claim resonates with earlier debates about the impact of British colonialism on India's indigenous textile industry.

At a more scholarly level, most economic nationalists refer explicitly to the thesis of a 'new international division of labour' (NIDL) (Fröbel, Heinrichs and Kreye, 1980; Iyer, 1995; Banerjee-Guha, 1996; Noronha, 1996). The NIDL thesis emerged during the late 1970s as an attempt to overcome the obvious incapacity of dependency theory to account for the then rapid industrialisation of various East Asian countries. NIDL analyses argue that, although there has been industrialisation in some parts of the Third World, it is 'dependent' in nature – that is, it is part of a strategy by transnational corporations (TNCs) to exploit reserves of cheap labour in peripheral countries. In other words, this is an externally imposed mode of economic development which perpetuates, albeit in a new form, the exploitation of Third World countries and the repression of organised labour.

There is insufficient space here to go into a full critique of the NIDL thesis, but it should be said that at a number of points NIDL does not adequately conceptualise the range of changes in the world economy since the late 1960s. Most importantly, the NIDL theoretical construction of the global economy in terms of core and periphery reduces those territories outside the advanced capitalist world to objects which are acted upon by the agents of capital, principally TNCs. NIDL overemphasises the agency of the global and reduces the role of local interests and agents to players who respond and react, rather than initiate (Kiely, 1994: 146).

In political terms, the real danger of the NIDL thesis is that it gives plausibility to essentially nationalistic responses to the crisis which lay blame on foreigners, TNCs and the ever-maligned IMF and World Bank. Such responses from Indian union leaders have been of little benefit to labour and are ultimately captive to the interests of certain sections of capital (the private and state interests in control of protected industries) and are readily co-opted by the state. The supposedly sweeping power of this new thing called 'globalisation' provides governments with ready-made justifications for any number of policies likely to be detrimental to the position of labour (Piven, 1995: 108–10). Conditions 'imposed by the IMF and World Bank' become an easy way to shift responsibility to forces beyond the government's control. Employers are also increasingly using the spectre of competition from TNCs as the rationale for job cuts, refusals to negotiate on wages and so on. Even some international corporations – like Philips in Bombay – claim their restructuring is necessitated by competition from 'foreign giants'.

When labour leaders echo these arguments, albeit with different intentions, it should hardly be surprising if workers come to believe that they have no power in the face of global capitalism. In these circumstances, it is more likely that workers will accept the employers' than the unions' formulae for adapting to such competition, solutions which of course involve labour bearing most of the cost.

Equally, organising demonstrations against the General Agreement on Tariffs and Trade (GATT), World Trade Organisation (WTO) and IMF, which has occupied so much of the time of Indian labour leaders in recent years, is far easier than (for example) taking on the task of unionising workers in restructured industries. A huge rally gives the 'big men' of the national union federations an opportunity to pose as the defenders of labour, but it is the slow and often unrewarding work of organising in the small-scale sector – where the working class is actually growing – which has the potential to enable these workers to use their strength as suppliers of labour-power to make real, if only small, improvements in their day-to-day conditions. Calling on the government, as the supposed defender of 'the nation', to change its policies is part of the tradition of a labour leadership – captured by the mainstream of nationalist politics – that has become used to the patronage of the nation-state and accepts an enfeebled condition as long as its political and personal fiefdoms are protected.

Thus, this chapter argues that preoccupation with the role of foreign capital and international financial institutions in bringing about the difficulties facing organised labour in Bombay today is, wittingly or unwittingly, a diversion from discussion of fundamental issues about weaknesses in the way unions have organised in the past and their inability to come to terms with long-term changes in the structure of the city's economy. It argues that the expansion in unionisation during the 1950s and 1960s was facilitated by protectionist economic policies and by the role of the public sector as a major employer in the city. A combination of developments, including the decline of the textile industry, general economic crisis in the late 1960s and early 1970s, and the increasing prominence of the services sector, led to pressure for the restructuring of Bombay industry. Hence there were job losses in existing industries and fundamental changes in the nature of employment in new industries. In order to defend their membership, many union leaders came to rely on attempts by the state, at both the state and federal level, to mask the effects of restructuring by administratively preventing closures of unprofitable industries, the reinvestment of devalorised capital and reallocation of land-use. The inherent weakness of this strategy was revealed in the textile strike of 1982–3, when the workers' withdrawal of labour was used by the employers as a way of restructuring the industry by other means. Meanwhile, in sectors where employment has been growing (such as services and the small-scale industries dispersed to the fringes of the city), the workforce has generally been neglected by existing unions because of the difficulties of organising in the face of opposition from small private-sector employers.

The chapter begins with a history of the labour movement in Bombay. The second section looks at recent decades of restructuring and spatial relocation in the textile industry, before and after the federal government's 1991 liberalisation programme. In the third part, discussion turns to the impact of this restructuring on workers and their organising capacity in Bombay, while the final section analyses the state of the city's labour movement today.

The emergence and containment of organised labour

The backbone of the organised labour movement in Bombay has always been the workers in the textile mills. Employment in the industry reached a pre-war peak of 148,000 in 1925 and, from the beginning of the century until after the Depression, roughly one in every ten of the city's residents was employed in textiles (Chandavarkar, 1994: 250). After the 1920s the industry stagnated, but textiles remained the city's largest single employer. There were some occasional episodes of resistance by workers in the textile mills before World War I, but the arrival of organised labour on the Bombay scene can be dated to 1917 and 1918, when there was a wave of large-scale strikes in textiles and other industries in response to the erosion of incomes caused by wartime inflation. The upsurge continued into 1920, culminating in widespread strikes throughout India and a month-long strike by 200,000 workers in Bombay, including 125,000 textile workers (Sen, 1977: 119–42). The collapse of post-war prosperity in the textile industry provoked at least four major strikes from 1924 until 1934, the defeat of the last of which was the key event in crushing workers' resistance for the rest of the decade.

The unions leading the waves of struggle in the inter-war period were fairly ephemeral organisations led by middle-class leaders connected with the nationalist movement or with the fledgling Communist Party of India (CPI). The unions existed in name for many years, but mass allegiance among most workers was restricted to periods of struggle. Workers joined the campaigns during strikes, but drifted away after they were over – either out of fear of victimisation or because they lacked a culture of belonging to permanent organisations. The strategy of the colonial state in response to the emergence of organised labour was, however, not entirely repressive, but combined paternalism and co-option. Kooiman (1989: 84–109) argues that all unions, whether left-wing, reformist or 'non-political', were undermined by the passing of the Trade Disputes Conciliation Act in 1934 and the subsequent appointment of Labour Officers to investigate workers' grievances and mediate in disputes. At a time when the Depression made conditions clearly unfavourable to labour, such intervention by the state could often achieve more obvious benefits for workers than was apparently possible through unions, which employers now felt safe to ignore. As we shall see, this close state involvement in labour relations, established in the final years of British colonial rule, was to set the pattern for post-independence Bombay. The response of the trade unions to the embrace of their functions by the state was to have major implications for their future development.

The 'progressive' phase of labour relations

After independence in 1947, government policies on industrial development and labour relations (at both the state and federal level) continued to have a profound impact on the nature of unionism in Bombay. Industry policy generally provided a conducive economic environment for the development of unions, while labour policies had contradictory effects: on one hand, protecting unions but, on the other, keeping them in a divided and weak condition. The result was a plethora of competing unions, some with close political affiliations to parties such as the ruling Congress Party, the Communists, the Socialists and, in later years, to the right-wing Shiv Sena. A current of politically independent unions also emerged, some consistently eschewing political connections and others developing links from time to time with political parties or with the charismatic individual leaders (such as Datta Samant or George Fernandes) who have been a particular feature of the Bombay labour movement.

British government policies after World War I had encouraged the development of Indian secondary industry, facilitating the diversification of Bombay manufacturing into consumer goods as well as heavy industry. World War II also had a dramatic impact on the city's manufacturing in basic metals and engineering – where employment grew by nearly 150 per cent between 1940 and 1943 – and in the chemicals and oil industry. Under post-independence autarkic protection policies, a new range of import-substitution manufacturing industries grew up in Bombay. Thus manufacturing continued to account for over 40 per cent of employment in Bombay into the 1970s, although textiles still accounted for almost half of this (Harris, 1978: Table 2.3). Bombay's origins as a port and commercial centre also continued to shape the city's economy. The Reserve Bank of India and the Stock Exchange were located in Bombay. Trade and commerce accounted for around one-tenth and transport and communication one-fifth of the labour force during the 1950s and 1960s (ibid.: Table 2.1).

The first fifteen to twenty years after independence – described by Banerji and Hensman as 'a "progressive" phase in Bombay industrial relations' (Banerji and Hensman, 1995: 5) – was a period of growth for unions in Bombay, but also a time of consolidation of the labour movement's co-option and control by the state, at both the federal and state levels. The social-democratic/state-socialist consensus in Indian political discourse, typified by Nehru's Fabianism, created an ideological environment that was conducive to unionisation – even if the Congress Party's commitment to 'industrial harmony' made it less than friendly to strikes or any action outside the official system, especially from the beginning of the 1960s (Sherlock, 1990).[2] Economic growth in India as a whole was relatively strong during much of the 1950s and employment growth in Bombay was particularly good as the city's manufacturing sector diversified behind high protective barriers.

Bombay was thus one of the few industrial centres in India where collective bargaining made some progress and a range of relatively strong unions grew up, particularly company- or enterprise-based unions – often in foreign-owned firms. Moreover, when economic conditions began to deteriorate from the mid-1960s, there was the protection afforded by the 1947 Industrial Disputes Act, which banned the closure without government permission of plants employing more than a hundred workers. This defended the constituency of many union leaders and obviated any necessity for them to reorganise the same workers if and when they were employed in restructured industries.

However, a lasting impediment to the free development of independent unionism in Bombay was the Congress Party's determination to ensure a strong political base in a key part of the city's working class: that part that was employed in the textile industry. In 1947, Congress activists established the Rashtriya Mazdoor Mill Sangh (RMMS), with a claimed membership of 32,000 textile workers. But close links between Congress and the mill owners meant that the RMMS soon gained the reputation for being what Van Wersch aptly described as 'the type of union employers call "responsible" ' (Van Wersch, 1992: 68). Unable to garner lasting support because of this reputation, and faced with the competition of active and more popular unions such as those led by the socialists and communists, the influence of the RMMS came to depend almost entirely on the support of the Congress state government. Legislation was passed that allowed the RMMS to become the sole representative union in the textile industry, a status which obstructed effective organisation by the textile workers but gave the RMMS a key role in labour negotiations in the industry. The RMMS often signed agreements with the mill owners following strikes it had done its best to undermine. Denying the RMMS what Morris (1965: 194) has called the 'legal fiction' of its representative status has been a central demand in most textile industry disputes ever since, including the historic strike of 1982–3.

The legal and political support given to Congress unions did not extend outside the textile industry and the party gave only fitful attention to building an industrial base once it had secured a place in textiles. Part of the reason for this was that it faced vigorous competition from a range of other labour organisations of varying or no political affiliation. This is in contrast to the labour movement in Calcutta, which has been dominated by union federations controlled by parties from the left (Sherlock, 1994). As well as the range of

Bombay labour organisations, it was (as mentioned above) unions associated with charismatic individual leaders that became a special feature of the city (Ramaswamy, 1988).

The first of these figures was George Fernandes, who emerged as a key leader in the Bombay labour movement in the early 1950s, when he was still in his early twenties. Fernandes was a member of the Socialist Party, but his tactical flair and brilliant style of public speaking gave him a personal profile far beyond the appeal of his political affiliations (Ovid, 1991: 209). Fernandes was a central figure in the unionisation of sections of Bombay labour in the 1950s and in the upsurge of strike action during the second half of the 1960s but, by the beginning of the 1970s, the impetus of his leadership was largely spent. Fernandes' unions certainly did not depend on state patronage in the manner of the RMMS, but he was unable to extend a reliable organisational base outside the government sector. Unionisation among workers in the Bombay Municipal Corporation and in the state-run transport and electricity services was facilitated because employment was relatively protected and because wage increases could be accommodated in the government budget. Fernandes' early successes among some workers in small-scale service industries such as hotels and restaurants should not be forgotten, but he failed to make major in-roads in Bombay's growing private-sector industries after the 1970s. After being inducted into the national leadership of the major railway union in 1973 (another state-owned utility) and leading the all-India railway strike in 1974, Fernandes' political ambitions took over and he became a member of federal parliament and, on two occasions, a minister. His departure from Bombay coincided with the onset of major problems for organised labour and his unions have long ceased to play a leading role in expanding unionisation.

Crisis and restructuring: 1960s–90s

The wave of sustained economic growth in the post-independence period came to an end in the mid-1960s. Industrial growth on an all-India basis averaged 7.7 per cent per annum from 1951 to 1965, but slumped to an average of 3.6 per cent per annum from 1965 to 1975 (Bhattacherjee, 1988: 212). The generalised crisis forced a period of restructuring for Bombay's textile industry, which had been stagnant since the 1930s. This process became part of a wider economic and spatial remaking of Bombay, brought about by a combination of economic circumstances and government policies on industry and urban planning.

The Bombay textile industry until the 1950s was largely homogeneous, dominated by a relatively small number of large industrial mills producing goods of similar quality. From the late 1950s, however, the state introduced policies to curb the expansion of mills and to encourage increased production from the handloom and powerloom sectors, because of their putative employment-generating capacities. The Controlled Cloth Scheme obliged all mills to sell a percentage of their output at controlled (that is, reduced) prices. This had the effect of exacerbating technological backwardness and poor capacity utilisation and, indeed, of greatly increasing the proportion of production accounted for by handlooms and small-scale powerlooms (Bhattacherjee, 1988: 218; Van Wersch, 1992: 27). Such trends led to the commercial non-viability of many mills but, because of state policy preventing closure, they were declared 'sick' and taken over by the state-run National Textile Corporation. From 1978, these mills took over much of the remaining private mills' Controlled Cloth Scheme production, a change that enabled the more viable units to upgrade. The mill sector thus became differentiated into old private and state-run units of variable degrees of (non-)viability and newer, more modern units, producing higher-quality output (including synthetic, silk and mixed fibres) for export and domestic markets. Many larger mills had also subcontracted part of their production to power-looms, often in arrangements of dubious legality, taking advantage of lax labour laws and of state support to the non-mill sector (Bhattacherjee, 1988: 216–21; Van Wersch, 1992: 43–56). The New Textile Policy of 1985 allowed for the closure of 'sick' mills, but other legal and administrative impediments have continued to impede many shutdowns.

The differentiation of the textile industry into a backward non-viable sector kept in existence by state policy, a modern profitable sector with expanding investment and production, and a growing small-scale sector (often producing under subcontract to larger units), became characteristic of the entire spectrum of Bombay industry. During the 1970s and 1980s, there was an overall decline in manufacturing in the city (especially in the textile mills, where employment fell from 200,000 to 70,000), but at the same time there were trends towards greater specialisation in the type of production. While the output of textiles, machinery and chemicals shrank, there was an increase in petrochemical production (Harris, 1995: 49–50).

Much of the shift from formal sector production to the informal and small-scale sector is part of a process of specialisation. To take an example, the loss-making Carona footwear factory in suburban Bombay was closed in early 1995 because the majority of its output was in cheap canvas and rubber products. In the words of the company's chairman, it was 'difficult to compete in this segment with the unorganised sector'. Of the 1,200 workers in the factory, 800 accepted government-funded redundancy and Carona was reported to be looking to establish a modern plant in Bombay 'to cater to the higher end of the shoes market', with the remainder of production to be taken up by its existing plant in Aurangabad (*Business Standard*, 8 April 1996). The company appears to have surrendered part of its production to the informal sector and to have reorganised its own output without necessarily relocating all of it outside Bombay. Similarly, Hindustan Lever moved production of its high-volume low-value goods to plants outside Bombay, much of it carried out by subcontractors, while at the same time retaining high-value production in the city because of the superior resources of skilled labour.[3]

The essence of the process we are witnessing is not the deindustrialisation of Bombay, but a spatial relocation and reorganisation, combined with an ever-increasing territorial expansion of the effective economic boundaries of the city.

Thus the central (southern) areas of the city have become less important as manufacturing centres, but production has relocated to northern suburban areas and to satellite centres such as Thane, Kalyan and New Bombay. Other production is moving still further to nearby cities such as Pune and Nasik. The older precincts have instead become increasingly devoted to Bombay's burgeoning service industries, including finance, tourism, retailing and entertainment. The service sector itself is showing signs of greater locational specialisation, with the creation of a new commercial centre at Bandra-Kurla in the north-eastern suburbs. Banking employment in Thane grew by 360 per cent during the 1980s, compared to an increase of 22 per cent in Greater Bombay (Harris, 1995: 55).

The role of the state

The state has played a contradictory and fitful, but crucial role in the remaking of Bombay. We have already seen that textile-industry policy encouraged small-scale production: this strengthened the trend towards decentralisation and dispersal into the suburbs and beyond. Policies designed to indigenise sources of raw materials also encouraged dispersal. Hindustan Lever, for instance, used to use imported materials in its soap and chemical production, but post-independence restrictions on their imports made it logical to shift production away from Bombay and its port towards areas closer to in-country sources. Such decisions on relocation were also influenced by subsidies offered by both the Maharashtra and central governments for the establishment of manufacturing in 'backward' areas.

On the other hand, impediments to the closure of non-viable textile mills, even since the New Textile Policy of 1985, have hindered the utilisation of mill land for replacement manufacture or service industries. Similarly, attempts to plan the urban development of Bombay have urged decentralisation as a means of overcoming social and environmental problems perceived to be caused by overcrowding and 'saturation' (Kosambi, 1986). At the same time, however, other policies have encumbered the processes that could allow for the reorganisation of manufacturing, service and residential land-use. Although Maharashtra government regulations since 1975 have banned new manufacturing industries in the city out of concern for Bombay's social and physical ecology (with inconsistent exceptions such as the state-owned chemical plant in suburban Chembur in the 1970s), other industry policies prevent closure of old plants (Harris, 1978: 39–46; Chowdhury, 1995). Rent ceilings and legislative controls on the sale and use of land, and on building construction, restrict the redevelopment of land and buildings, sustaining commercially inappropriate patterns of land-use, including the continuance of manufacturing plants in the heart of the city which would otherwise relocate farther afield.

The reforms of 1991

The economic reforms introduced by the federal government from 1991 are widely credited, by their enthusiastic supporters and opponents alike, with having opened India to the 'free market'. Changes to the Monopolies and Restrictive Trade Practices Act (MRTP) to allow company mergers and restructuring, and the introduction of the Voluntary Retirement Scheme (VRS) to compensate redundant workers, will facilitate industrial restructuring and hasten the relocation of some manufacturing outside Greater Bombay and beyond. But these tendencies were already well established in the post-independence period and, in the case of Hindustan Lever mentioned above, were encouraged by the very autarkic, protectionist policies apparently overturned by today's policies of 'globalisation'. For Hindustan Lever, liberalisation has merely permitted the company to increase production levels in its existing plants (and those of their subcontractors) already outside Bombay. The centrepiece of the reforms – namely, changes to the financial sector – has brought a huge increase (from a very low base) in foreign direct investment and portfolio investment in India since 1991. This has given a considerable boost to Bombay in its capacity as a financial centre. Tariff reductions and the floating of the rupee have increased both exports and imports of merchandise and services, increasing traffic in Bombay's sea- and airports.

Increased international competition will force restructuring in import-substituting industries, including relocation, but (as we have seen) the roots of such changes go back to the 1960s and 1970s. The reforms have thus reinforced and accelerated underlying trends, not changed them in any fundamental way. They strengthen Bombay's direct links into the world economy, but by international standards these remain limited. In common with those of most Third World metropolises, the Bombay economy is still relatively unspecialised and involved in a wide range of economic activities that reflect the fragmented nature of India's domestic market and the paucity of connections to the international market (Harris, 1995: 48). The remaking of Bombay is the beginning of the change of the city's economy into one, like most large cities in the developed world, based on services and the flow of information, with dispersed manufacturing located in specialised areas (Castells, 1989).

Workers and the labour market in a changing city

The restructuring of production in Bombay has naturally had profound effects on the labour market and on the organising capacity of workers in the city. The relatively uniform labour market of the past is being replaced by one with diverse characteristics. The rise of the small-scale and informal sectors, and the increased importance of service industries has significantly lowered the ability of most workers to improve their living and working conditions, or even to defend existing conditions. On the other hand, smaller numbers of workers have benefited from the growth of specialised services and manufacturing. At the heart of these changes has been the relocation of large sections of the manufacturing working class to the outer reaches of the city and out of the city altogether, as a natural accompaniment to the relocation of industry.

Greater Bombay is becoming the service centre, but still with specialised manufacturing, and the rest of the Bombay Metropolitan Region and nearby areas are being turned into centres of dispersed manufacturing. The diversification of the labour market had its roots in the post-independence growth of manufacturing, but did not become obvious until the crises and restructuring beginning in the late 1960s. The extent to which these changes were consciously undertaken by employers with the specific intention of undermining the power of organised labour is a moot point. Jairus Banerji of the Union Research Group[4] interprets the process as one in which businesses relocate to escape unionised labour and to take advantage of 'first generation' workers without previous experience of wage labour or collective action for as many years as possible before, presumably, moving on to reserves of unexploited labour in regions still farther afield (see Banerji and Hensman, 1995; Shrouti and Nandkumar, 1995).

These considerations understandably loom large in the perceptions of labour activists, but the breadth of economic forces and state policies contributing to restructuring should caution against reductionist analyses. The level of unionisation, even within well-established industries in the central City area, is not so great as to make unions the prime cause for relocating – there are sufficient weapons at employers' disposal to keep unions at bay in most industries – and it is not only unionised industries that are shifting. Rather than being specifically aimed at unionised labour, relocation is part of capital's efforts to maximise profits by reducing the overall costs of production including (but not confined to) labour costs. Remote areas are attractive because they provide access to a labour market with cheaper and more quiescent labour, but also because of cheaper real estate, government subsidies, less congested services and so on. As far as labour is concerned, the net result is not only to provide new sources of cheap labour but, by the effective extension of the geographical limits of the Bombay labour-market, to create downward pressures on the price of labour throughout the entire city. By expanding into new labour markets, capital reshapes conditions in existing ones.

There are now fewer jobs in the formal sector of manufacturing and services, and an increasing proportion of new jobs are being created in the informal sector. Even the new jobs that are in the formal sector are usually in plants that are smaller than would have been the case in the past, and they are not likely to be clustered together with like industries in the manner which characterised the old textile mills. In the days when textiles dominated Bombay's industrial scene, the concentration of large numbers of workers in a single plant facilitated union organisation. Union leaders could contact large numbers of workers at the same time and messages about meetings, rallies or strikes could be passed quickly through a plant by union activists. Similar conditions prevailed in large-scale services such as the ports, transport, government utilities and departments, and in the majority of engineering, chemical and other manufacturing plants that grew up in the 1950s and 1960s. Organising in many other service industries and the informal sector was always a difficult task, but the manufacturing workforce provided a core of organised strength to the whole labour movement.

The dispersal of manufacturing in recent decades, however, has made conditions for labour organisation much more akin to the informal sector. Workers are scattered in many small sites, under the close supervision of managers hostile to unions for reasons, at best, of paternalism and, at worst, of sheer rapaciousness. It is a commonplace of industrial relations that smaller workplaces facilitate easier labour control and that smaller employers are more likely to resist unionisation. This has always been an issue for many service-sector workers, such as those in the commercial sector, hotels and the film industry, and the growing predominance of services in Greater Bombay makes this a reality for increasing numbers of workers in the City and suburbs. In the case of workers employed by subcontractors, it is not only difficult to merely locate the myriad obscure backyard sites, but the complex and often illegal chains of production frequently also make it nearly impossible to determine who is really the employer. Production in such sites can quickly move at the first sign of a union organiser or government official.

Once again, however, it is important to stress that the dynamic is not all in one direction. Just as restructuring has not meant the deindustrialisation of Bombay, but its increased spatial specialisation, so the labour market is becoming much more diverse and desegregated. While many workers operate in a labour market paying barely subsistence wages and in appalling working conditions, the other end of the market pays wages and provides conditions that are the best in the country and that sometimes approach international standards. Workers in the higher end of the labour market include those in the modern export-oriented textile mills, in plants devoted to the production of high-value goods, in high-skilled technical positions and in certain parts of growing sectors such as finance. Many such workers are employed by international corporations or industries tied into the international market. Of course, greater numbers are likely to be found towards the lower end of the spectrum, but the days when labour was synonymous with the textile workers are long gone. A critical feature of the remaking of Bombay is that many of the commonalities of working-class experience have been eroded. Conditions of employment and standards of living now vary so much that there is less to foster the mass solidarity of thousands of workers sharing a common workplace, residence, lifestyle and employer.

The Bombay labour movement today

The turning point for organised labour in Bombay came with the textile strike of 1982–3. This massive one-and-a-half-year struggle by nearly 200,000 workers was noticed around the world and brought its flamboyant leader, Datta Samant, to international attention. Samant's militancy and his famous contempt for company balance-sheets inspired many workers to win major gains during the

1970s, and his efforts were very important in blunting the offensive against organised labour from the right-wing extremists of the Shiv Sena. Samant's reputation led the mass of textile workers to flock to Samant's banner when he was persuaded by deputations of millworkers to form a union and to begin a campaign in defence of textile jobs and wages, and to supplant the stranglehold position of the Congress-controlled RMMS as the only officially recognised textile union.

The strike was, however, ultimately defeated and its defeat revealed the limits of Samant's methods and, more importantly, the weakness of labour organisations that depend on the state to impose constraints on the capital-accumulation process. As we have seen, the textile industry had been in crisis at least since the early 1960s, but laws against closures and political pressure from the state government kept tens of thousands of workers employed in mills which would otherwise have been closed or restructured. As a result there were large reserves of unsold output and many unprofitable mills whose owners were only too keen to shut their gates. In these circumstances, Samant's single line of attack – indefinite strike – provided an opportunity for employers to restructure the industry by other means. The strike allowed accumulated stocks to be used up; run-down mills were 'temporarily' closed, never to reopen; production was farmed out to the small-scale sector. A tragic irony was that, in order to survive, many workers had to seek work in the same small-scale powerloom sector whose continued production was undermining their own struggle (Van Wersch, 1992: 64–85).

While the tenacity of the textile workers during the strike was incredible, the dispute was effectively lost in the first six months, and many workers' sacrifice brought them only unemployment or jobs under worse conditions in the small-scale sector. Like Fernandes, much of Samant's organisational muscle ultimately depended on bargaining power underpinned by conditions created by the state – in this case, attempts to freeze the process of industry rationalisation by administrative fiat. During the 1982–3 strike, Samant tried to push the possibilities of these conditions beyond their limits, undermining his own position and – more significantly – the position of the textile workers. From that time, Samant's unions in other industries were also being weakened by splits and the desertion of many of his more prominent supporters. With Samant's assassination in January 1997 (the motivation for which is still unclear at the time of writing), the future of his unions remained quite uncertain.

The textile industry had been the backbone of the Bombay economy for so long that its workers were seen as the big battalions of the labour movement. Following the strike, however, textile employment shrank by over a half. The defeat of the textile workers was a massive setback for organised labour as a whole and marked the beginning of a new period in which, for the first time since the 1950s, unionisation no longer covered the key sectors of the Bombay economy. The strike revealed the extent to which the previous levels of unionisation were dependent on a supportive (even if constricting) legal environment to protect members' interests and the conditions of existence of their capacity to organise.

Ever since the defeat of the textile strike, the labour movement in Bombay has been on the defensive. A new aggressiveness on the part of employers can be measured in the balance between the number of workdays lost in industrial disputes due to strikes and those due to lockouts – with the former decreasing and the latter increasing. It has also been marked by the appearance of employers' charters of demands, where bosses have reversed the former culture of industrial bargaining and made continuance of production conditional on the workers agreeing to demands on productivity and staffing levels. The post-1991 round of liberalisation has contributed to this environment (in particular by making closure of plants somewhat easier) but, to repeat the point made earlier, the reforms have only strengthened these trends, not created them. The introduction of the VRS has been particularly important in inducing workers in many plants to accept closures or workforce reductions (Gupte, 1994). Datta Samant's unions, in particular, were weakened when (against Samant's advice) workers in his former strongholds – such as Premier Automobiles – agreed to accept redundancy packages as part of restructuring plans.

The unions that have best survived the crisis of the last decade have been some of the other politically independent unions in the advanced sector of the Bombay economy. These unions continue in the particularly Bombay tradition of pragmatic company-based organisations using the relatively strong bargaining power of skilled labour. They have been willing to enter into productivity bargains to achieve good results in wages, allowances and conditions, but (according to critics) often at the cost of jobs. It is interesting to note, however, that the left-wing unions that for a long time refused to enter into productivity deals have changed their position in recent years.

Activists from such unions tend to be assertive (if not militant) in their approach to unionism, but with an instrumentalist rather than an ideological outlook – although some do have a background in leftist student politics. Many have, from time to time, allied themselves to party-controlled trade union centres or called in individual leaders, such as Datta Samant, but they dispense with them when they consider themselves hindered by such connections. Independent unions have sometimes enlisted Samant as nominal president of their union, in the hope that the mere association of the name would induce management to negotiate. The workers at Voltas Switchgear in Thane have reportedly joined and left Samant's union on three separate occasions since 1973 (*Business India*, 29 March 1993: 105).

The greatest weakness common to most of the independent company unions is their extreme sectionalism – the lack of a sense of solidarity with or obligation to a wider movement. As skilled workers, members of such unions are often in a position to make gains through their own independent efforts and thus tend to be impatient with calls for solidarity with workers in a weaker bargaining position. Sectionalism can extend so far that employees of some companies in Bombay have a different union from those in the same company in, say,

Calcutta. Of course, large firms such as Hindustan Lever and Philips have been extremely hostile to attempts even to form federations of their company's unions, but it is possible that the workers' own insularity has played a role in perpetuating divisions. The Secretary of the Hindustan Lever Employees' Union, Bennett D'Costa, freely admits that his union has made no efforts to organise workers in the small plants to which their company has subcontracted production.[5] Such major omissions are also a characteristic of the union federations. Vivek Monteiro of the Centre of Indian Trade Unions (CITU) is of the opinion that the tasks involved in organising in the dispersed small-scale sector is in principle the same as in large plants, yet there is little evidence that the CITU has made any major efforts to unionise these workers.[6] The situation is certainly not improved when a figure such as Datta Samant consistently opposes efforts to promote cross-union solidarity during strikes (even during the 1982–3 strike) or united campaigns over general labour issues.

The most disturbing aspect of the crisis facing the Bombay labour movement has been its subversion by clientelism, corruption and even organised crime. There has long been a current of patron–clientism in the Indian union movement, in which union leaders act as 'big men' who use their political or other connections to broker deals with employers and take money from workers seeking favours or resolution of individual grievances. This has been facilitated by legal structures of conciliation and adjudication that provide openings for the arbitrary intervention of politicians in favour of the unions they sponsor. The Congress Party-controlled RMMS is the most extreme example of this phenomenon in Bombay.[7] The power of the RMMS was first created by recognition under the Bombay Industrial Relations Act, but was boosted by legislation restricting the closure of mills that effectively gave the RMMS the power to authorise their shutdown. The RMMS has allegedly signed hundreds of secret agreements with mill-owners since the end of the textile strike, allowing the retrenchment of thousands of workers, all presumably with some form of payoff for the union leaders (*Business India*, 19 March 1990).

These forms of deal-making and corruption also invite the involvement of organised crime. One textile industrialist, Sunit Khatau, hired gangsters from Bombay's festering underworld to intimidate workers in his old mill into agreeing to its closure – agreement that was necessary under the Industrial Relations Act. The scheme worked, but also managed to embroil him so deeply in gangster rivalry that he was shot dead in his car in May 1995. Khatau's eagerness to sell the plant was motivated by Bombay's absurd, world-record breaking real estate prices, which made selling the site of the mill far more lucrative than continuing production, a situation largely created by the legal restrictions on land-use. Purportedly pro-labour laws have not prevented the loss of thousands of jobs (although they may have slowed them), but have rather strengthened the grip of corrupt union leaders. Whatever the immediate motivation for the killing of Datta Samant, it can only be understood in the context of these developments. They are probably the most pernicious results of the long-standing tendency of

Indian unions to rely first on the supportive structures of the state rather than on the collective power of their members.

Many workplaces have also suffered from the efforts of the extreme right-wing party, the Shiv Sena, to take control of labour relations. The Shiv Sena came to prominence during the 1960s as a reaction among elements of the Marathi-speaking lower middle class to competition for small business and employment opportunities from 'outsiders' from south India (Gupta, 1982). Despite some electoral success, its attempts to create a labour wing had little result. Such influence as it achieved was mainly through strong-arm tactics which, as mentioned above, were largely contained by Datta Samant's unions. The Shiv Sena enjoyed a resurgence after it became more of a Hindu fundamentalist rather than a regional chauvinist organisation. This growth has enhanced the Sena's ability to force its way into workplaces, as it attempted to do during the anti-Muslim pogrom of December 1992 to January 1993 (Lele, 1995). In sites where the Sena has succeeded, the nexus between union boss, politician and criminal seems complete. These developments have recently been taken one step further with the emergence of Arun Gawli (the son-turned-gangster of a locked-out mill worker, who has eight murder-cases registered against him), who has established a number of unions that numbers of workers have reportedly begun to support. Gawli was originally connected with the Shiv Sena but has now struck out on his own: he has begun to openly challenge the position of the Sena in workplaces and in the wider political arena, using methods perfected by the Sena itself (*Business India*, 9–22 September 1996: 175; *Indian Express*, 31 July 1997).

Promises by the Shiv Sena–BJP state government, elected in 1995, to reform the Bombay Industrial Relations Act probably have the intention of assisting the Sena's unions to carve out further influence in the labour movement, in particular by supplanting the RMMS (although the restructuring of the textile industry has made it less of a glittering prize than it once was). The only encouraging side to these developments is that the Shiv Sena apparently still cannot win a following among Bombay workers through open campaigning. Although many workers are undoubtedly affected by the rising tide of communalism, they have still been able to recognise and fight for their class interests – often alongside members of different communities.[8] The Sena has made little headway in communalising the workplace.

Conclusion

The possibilities for the working class in Bombay to sustain organised resistance to the imperatives of capital have generally deteriorated in the last two decades. From a situation in which the bulk of workers in the city were concentrated in a relatively small number of industries in a highly regulated economy protected from international competition, the remaking of Bombay is giving rise to an economy with a wide range of dispersed service and manufacturing industries, where state regulations have decreasing direct effect on the process of production. While organisation in earlier years was hardly easy, an initial period of economic growth, together with government economic, industrial and labour relations policies, generally worked in favour of a certain level of organisation among workers. Developments since the late 1960s and early 1970s have not been uniform in their effect, but the overall trend is towards the restructuring and decline in the relative importance of old industries, where unionisation was possible, and the rise of new forms of production, where any collective action is extremely difficult.

This chapter has sought to identify the principal strands of the complex web of processes that have created this new environment. One of the key problems confronting the labour movement and scholars of labour is that new and expanding forms of accumulation can present as many challenges as crisis and declining profitability. Jobs are lost and wages forced down when new industries are established in new environments as well as when old industries are shut down. These processes can proceed simultaneously and distinguishing the effects of one from the other is often a difficult task. Thus Bombay is still going through a period of restructuring that dates from the crisis of the 1960s and 1970s (partly postponed by the Indian state's attempts to mask its effects), while also adapting to the post-1991 acceleration of the city's integration into the world economy. At the same time, Bombay is losing much of its old character as an unspecialised Third World city and is being remade into a service centre specialising in flows of information as much as in the production and movement of commodities. The implication for organised labour that is common to all these processes, however, is the trend away from large-scale manufacturing employment towards smaller workplaces and to services.

Unfortunately, the great majority of union leaders in Bombay, from the communists to Datta Samant and even the Congress and the Shiv Sena, have focused their explanations on recent government policies that are said to be allowing international corporations and financial institutions to deindustrialise the Indian economy. Such arguments fail to come to grips with the fact that the forces restructuring the Bombay economy date from well before the liberalisation of recent years. But nationalist explanations are not only inadequate, they are politically dangerous because they provide a smokescreen obscuring sensitive issues about the weaknesses inherent in the structure of existing unions. A critical assessment of the history of Bombay unions shows that many owed their strength as much to the actions of the state as to their own efforts to organise workers. With the removal of these buttresses, the unions' response has been to try to persuade government to restore the regime of the past, rather than turning to the tasks of organising workers in the new industries.

The danger for Indian labour would be for it to be seduced by the illusion that the changes of the last two decades could be halted if only the state would protect India from predatory TNCs and the IMF. The post-independence economic nationalist consensus in India has collapsed to such an extent that no Indian government is ever likely to return to the industrial policies of the past. Even if this were to occur, its only effect would be to stunt the process of class formation in India, consigning the rural masses to continued underemployment and the labour movement to a rump defending the decrepit 'rotten boroughs' of a declining industrial sector.

The remaking of Bombay is the expression of intertwined domestic and global processes of capital accumulation that the Indian state and Indian capital neither direct nor control, but in which they are participants rather than 'victims'. Ideas about the existence of a distinct Indian national economy, defended by the Indian national state, which have previously been advocated by the proponents of Indian private and state capital, also penetrated into the ranks of organised labour and had the effect of tying the labour movement into a stultifying ideological and organisational dependence on the state. Now that these ideas are being replaced with the rhetoric of international competition and globalisation, we can predict that the Indian state will increasingly reformulate the ideology of nationalism as a supposed common effort by workers and employers to advance the interests of a globally competitive Indian capital. As Bryan expresses it:

> The impossibility for labor of national policy solutions goes to the heart of the nature of capitalism as a relation between capital and labor. 'Recent internationalisation' has made the global nature of class relations an explicit and systematic process ... The ideology of international competitiveness presents international class dominance as a national economic necessity, and an alternative class politics requires that this necessity be exposed as ideology.
>
> (Bryan, 1995: 190)

Seen in these terms, the principal political task for the Indian labour movement is to recreate itself around the politics of class and movement, rather than the politics of the nation-state. The practical effect would be to turn the movement's attention away from efforts to reverse the irreversible policies of the state and towards efforts to organise workers to use their own strength as sellers of labour-power (supported, where possible, with links to labour internationally) to defend and improve the conditions in which they are increasingly finding themselves.

None of this should be seen as a blanket denigration of the efforts and achievements of many unions, nor in particular should it be interpreted as minimising the past sacrifice, militancy and commitment to struggle on the part of many thousands of workers in Bombay. But, from the luxury of an outside viewpoint, it seems that the labour movement in Bombay (and India as a whole) faces a new set of challenges and that to respond to the new conditions requires, in part at least, seeing that many of the problems have been created by the very conditions that appeared to deliver success in the past.

Notes

1 Bombay is the premier centre of finance, industry and services in India and the capital of the western Indian state of Maharashtra. Based on 1991 census figures, the population of the Bombay Metropolitan Region (BMR) is around 12.5 million, making it India's largest city and the sixth largest on earth (United Nations, 1995). Reference to the 'Bombay' labour-market in this chapter includes the entire BMR and extensions into neighbouring regions such as Pune, Nasik and even Aurangabad.

2 The Congress Party, bearing the immense prestige of having been the principal leader of the independence movement, dominated post-independence politics in India at the federal level and in Maharashtra state. Congress has, however, been in gradual decline since the 1970s and lost power in Maharashtra in 1995 and in the federal election of 1996. Recent years have seen the rise of right-wing Hindu politics, articulated in northern India by the Bharatiya Janata Party (BJP) and by the Shiv Sena in Maharashtra. A Shiv Sena–BJP coalition won power in Maharashtra in 1995.

3 Interviews in Bombay (January 1996) with Bennett D'Costa, secretary of the Hindustan Lever Employees' Union, and Irfan Khan, communications manager at Hindustan Lever.

4 Interview in Bombay with Jairus Banerji of the Union Research Group (January 1996).

5 Interview with D'Costa.

6 Interview with Vivek Monteiro of the Centre of Indian Trade Unions (January 1996).

7 For a discussion of patron–client unionism in the railways, see Sherlock (1989).

8 According to D'Costa, attempts by the Shiv Sena to organise in Hindustan Lever sites were met with an almost total lack of response from the workers. Similar evidence of the failure of the Shiv Sena was related by Monteiro and Vasant Gupte of the Hind Mazdoor Sabha.

Bibliography

Banerjee-Guha, S. (1996) 'Dividing space and labour: Spatial dynamics of multinational corporations', *Economic and Political Weekly* XXXI, 8 (24 February): L21–L31.

Banerji, J. and Hensman, R. (1995) 'India: Multinationals and the resistance to unionised labour', *International Union Rights* 2, 2: 5–6.

Bhattacherjee, D. (1988) 'Unions, state and capital in Western India: Structural determinants of the 1982 Bombay textile strike', in R. Southall (ed.) *Labour and Unions in Asia and Africa*, London: Macmillan.

Bryan, D. (1995) *The Chase Across the Globe*, Boulder: Westview Press.

Castells, M. (1989) *The Informational City: Information Technology, Economic Restructuring and the Urban–Regional Process*, Oxford: Basil Blackwell.

Chandavarkar, R. (1994) *The Origins of Industrial Capitalism in India: Business Strategies and the Working Classes in Bombay, 1900–1940*, New Delhi: Cambridge University Press.

Chowdhury, R.S. (1995) 'Political economy of India's textile industry: The case of Maharashtra, 1984–89', *Pacific Affairs* 68, 2: 231–50.

Dutta, D.K. (1992) 'Planning and the regulatory role of the Indian state', *Journal of Contemporary Asia* 22, 1: 82–93.

Fröbel, Folker, Heinrichs, Jürgen and Kreye, Otto (1980) *The New International Division of Labour: Structural Unemployment in Industrialised Countries and Industrialisation in Developing Countries*, Cambridge: Cambridge University Press.

Gupta, D. (1982) *Nativism in a Metropolis: Shiv Sena in Bombay*, New Delhi: Manohar.

Gupte, V. (1994) *Voluntary Retirement Scheme and Workers' Response*, New Delhi: Friedrich Ebert Stiftung.

Harris, N. (1978) *Economic Development, Cities and Planning: The Case of Bombay*, Bombay: Oxford University Press.

—— (1995) 'Bombay in the global economy', in S. Patel and A. Thorner (eds) *Bombay: Metaphor for Modern India*, Bombay: Oxford University Press.

Hindustan Lever (1992) *Commemorative Publication*, Bombay: Hindustan Lever.

Iyer, R. (1995) 'The NEP: The dangers ahead', *Economic and Political Weekly* 29 July: 1,913–15.

Kiely, R. (1994) 'Development theory and industrialisation: Beyond the impasse', *Journal of Contemporary Asia* 24, 2: 133–59.

Kooiman, D. (1989) *Bombay Textile Labour: Managers, Trade Unionists and Officials 1918–1939*, New Delhi: Manohar.

Kosambi, M. (1986) *Bombay in Transition: The Growth and Social Ecology of a Colonial City, 1880–1980*, Stockholm: Almquist & Wiksell.

Kurien, C.T. (1993) 'Indian economic reforms in the context of emerging global economy', *Economic and Political Weekly* 28, 15 (10 April): 655–65.

Lele, J. (1995) 'Saffronization of the Shiv Sena: The political economy of city, state and nation', in S. Patel and A. Thorner (eds) *Bombay: Metaphor for Modern India*, Bombay: Oxford University Press.

Morris, M.D. (1965) *The Emergence of an Industrial Labour Force in India: A Study of the Bombay Cotton Mills, 1854–1947*, Bombay: Oxford University Press.

Noronha, E. (1996) 'Liberalisation and industrial relations', *Economic and Political Weekly* XXXI, 8 (24 February): L14–L20.

Ovid, P.J. (1991) 'Bombay trade union movement: A harbinger of dignity to Indian labour', in G. Mathew (ed.) *Dignity for All: Essays in Socialism and Democracy*, Delhi: Ajanta.

Piven, F.F. (1995) 'Is it global economics or neo-laissez-faire?', *New Left Review* 213: 107–14.

Ramaswamy, E.A. (1988) *Worker Consciousness and Trade Union Response*, Delhi: Oxford University Press.

Sen, S. (1977) *Working Class of India: History of Emergence and Movement 1830–1970*, Calcutta: K.P. Bagchi.

Sherlock, S. (1989) 'Railway workers and their unions: Origins of the 1974 Indian Railways strike', *Economic and Political Weekly* XXIV, 41 (16 October): 2,311–22.

—— (1990) 'The national commission on labour and its quest for industrial harmony', in J. Masselos (ed.) *India: Creating a Modern Nation*, New Delhi: Sterling, pp. 175–98.

—— (1994) 'Conflict and competition: Organised communalism and the labour movement', *South Asia* December: 169–82.

Shrouti, A. and Nandkumar (1995) *New Economic Policy, Changing Management Strategies – Impact on Workers and Trade Unions*, New Delhi: Friedrich Ebert Stiftung.

United Nations (1995) *The Challenge of Urbanization: The World's Largest Cities*, New York: United Nations Department for Economic and Social Information and Policy Analysis.

Van Wersch, H. (1992) *The Bombay Textile Strike 1982–83*, Bombay: Oxford University Press.

This chapter also made use of files at the Centre for Education and Documentation, Bombay, containing clippings from *Business India, Business Standard, Business World, Economic Times, The Hindu, Hindustan Times, Independent, Indian Express, Standard, Times of India* and *The Working Class*.

Interviews

The following interviews were all recorded in January 1996.

Jairus Banerji of the Union Research Group.
Bennett D'Costa, secretary of the Hindustan Lever Employees' Union.
Vasant Gupte of Hind Mazdoor Sabha.
Irfan Khan, communications manager at Hindustan Lever.
Vivek Monteiro of the Centre of Indian Trade Unions.

9   *Sangharsh*[1]

Workers' interventions in the privatisation of Indian telecommunications

Patricia Cahill[2]

Economic globalisation is widely thought to place particular obstacles in the way of effective trade unionism. In India, where the modern labour movement has been shaped by the political economy of state-directed import-substitution industrialisation, recent efforts to liberalise the economy are presenting new challenges to currently unionised workforces. In the telecommunications sector, workers and their unions have specifically been facing the recent first-time entry of private capital into their industry. Their organised opposition to this development is the subject of this chapter.

When, in 1994, the government of India first announced the opening of the telecommunications sector to private investment – outlining a strategy of private competition in the mobile telephone and paging markets and a supplementary role in the basic telephone network – unions covering telecom workers raised no initial objections. But over the next twelve months, as the policy was modified to allow private investors to build a duplicate basic telephone network, their opposition grew until, in mid-1995, some 400,000 telecom workers took direct strike action to protest the new direction of government policy. This strike was held in association with the telecom unions' participation in the lodging of petitions to the Supreme Court over the same matter.

Labour's organised opposition to the privatisation scheme was soundly condemned by those who argued that the economy was thereby being held to ransom by a self-interested 'labour aristocracy'. The World Bank, for example, has generally accused India's unions of 'propping up the part of the economy most in need of reform' (World Bank, 1995a: 81–2). According to bodies like the World Bank, the government's new policies were merely a rational attempt to transform a hitherto inefficient and technologically backward telecommunications service into one that met contemporary global standards. But both the strike and the petitions countered this interpretation of the government's moves by exposing the particular class interests involved in privatisation – specifically the advantages that would directly accrue to a globalising corporate sector, while objectives like job protection and employment creation, universal basic telephone access (especially in rural and non-commercial areas) and the equitable distribution of social resources (such as the radio spectrum) were threatened. Far from telecom workers being only concerned to retain obsolete and inefficient work practices of which they were the sole beneficiaries, this chapter argues their actions helped to draw public and expert attention to the wider socio-economic consequences of introducing private investment into the telecommunications sector, most obviously with regard to the issue of public access to the basic telephone service.

The telecommunications strike is of further interest to observers of the Indian labour movement in that it illustrates the role that non-union activists can play in galvanising workers to protest against the government's new liberalising efforts. In this case, it will be shown that a group of public interest advocates helped to forge organised labour's opposition to the introduction of a parallel private basic network by mitigating some of the legacies of past union strategies – namely, divisions within the labour movement arising from different party political affiliations and the dominance of the 'big men' leaders of the labour federations (see Sherlock's chapter in this volume). As in other parts of the Indian labour movement, the professional labour leadership has long performed the role of 'intermediary between workers and the state' (Rao, 1995: 251). In a situation where the wages and employment conditions of telecom workers have long been largely determined by the state, the leaders of the two largest federations covering the telecom industry were at first very reluctant to pursue the kind of political activism that a strike against government policy entails. It was the linkages that some of the larger affiliate unions forged with a group of public interest activists that were largely instrumental in circumventing the leadership's initial antipathy to protesting against the entry of private capital.

This chapter begins with a brief discussion of the history and current structure of the telecommunications sector unions. This is followed by a critical examination of the term 'labour aristocracy' as it is applied to telecom workers in India. The bulk of the chapter then examines the policy to allow the first-time entry of private capital into the basic telephone network and the union campaign that was subsequently launched against it, in concert with a group of public interest activists. In endeavouring to explain why the telecom workers took the strike action they did, attention will be paid to the processes by which a sense of commonality among the workers was transformed into collective action by the public interest advocates' efforts in countering the dominant neo-liberal account of proposed telecommunications sector restructuring.

Telecom workers and their unions

Workers in India were first drawn into the construction of a telegraph network in 1850 (Chowdary, 1992: 1). Originally built to service the needs of the East India Company, the network was soon expanded to include public traffic. In 1857, after a forty-day delay in news of the Indian 'rebellion' reaching London, the British government 'desperately sought better communications', and so immediately began to establish cable links between the two countries (Headrick, 1995: 33–4). Twenty-five years later, the first Indian telephone exchanges were commissioned in Calcutta, Madras, Bombay, Rangoon and Karachi, under licence to a British company: the Oriental Telephone Company (DoT, 1987: 1). However, it required government coordination to establish a countrywide network when newly developed technologies permitted the spread of networks intra-city, intra-state and internationally. Construction at this point was largely done by day-workers – mostly tribals recruited locally on three-month contracts to dig and erect poles as the network spread across the continent (interview with Sangal, 1997). Subsequently, the workforce grew in both number and diversity to deal with the planning, construction, operations and maintenance phases. At the same time, unions pressured the government to make long-term contract employees permanent.

One of the earliest unions in India, the Indian Telegraph Association, was formed in 1906 by Henry Barton – who also founded one of the first trade union journals, the *Telegraph Recorder*, to organise and educate workers. Seventy years later, Karnik (1978) rated telecom workers as among the best organised in the country, with a nationwide hierarchy of thousands of local units. Nowadays these units are linked to three main federations through twenty-one recognised industry unions, in all encompassing some 450,000 workers. The two biggest of the twenty-one unions – which cover more than half the unionised employees – are affiliated to the National Federation of Telecom Employees (NFTE). Besides being the largest federation, with 2,500 branches throughout the country, the NFTE is also the oldest – it traces its lineage back more than fifty years to the original united peak organisation: the Union of Posts and Telegraph Workers (Gupta, 1995: 363). Politically, the NFTE is associated through its member unions with both the Communist Party of India (CPI) and the CPI(M) – the breakaway Marxist party. Through each of these parties, it also respectively has links with two other important peak labour organisations in the non-government sector: the All-India Trade Union Congress (AITUC) and the Centre of Indian Trade Unions (CITU). The second-largest federation in the telecom industry, the Federation of National Telecom Organisations (FNTO), covers approximately another third of the unionised workforce. It was established by the Congress government to moderate the activism of telecom unions and still maintains links with the Congress Party. The smallest federation, the BTEF, has links with the Bharatiya Janata Party (BJP) (elected to govern India in 1998). The twenty-one telecom unions affiliated with these three federations are mainly run by employees on work release. By contrast, the leadership of the federations is more permanent. For example, O.P. Gupta has been General Secretary of NFTE for nearly forty years. Gupta has college credentials, while Venkataraman, General Secretary of FNTO, is an ex-telecom worker – something he deems an important asset.

Table 9.1 Indian telecommunication federations

Federation	Year established	General Secretary	Political affiliation
NFTE	1946, 1954, 1984	O.P. Gupta	CPI and CPI(M)
FNTO	1968	R. Venkataraman	Congress Party
BTEF	1977	S. Kumar	RSS/BJP

In sum, telecom workers in India are well unionised and have a history of political influence. However, the following section quashes suggestions that these workers thereby constitute a 'labour aristocracy' – a sector of the workforce whose unionisation and political influence have made them an economic elite.

A labour aristocracy?

The term 'labour aristocracy' generally denotes a stratum of workers whose relatively privileged position in the labour market leaves them isolated from the interests of the rest of the workforce. In the socialist tradition, this stratum has been said to explain the absence or weakness of a revolutionary class consciousness. Perhaps most famously, Lenin used the term against workers he regarded as 'nothing but the agents of the bourgeoisie' in that they are 'enmeshed in the fabric and institutions of bourgeois society' (Lenin, 1968: 536–7). Somewhat differently, Trotsky directed this charge at labour leaders who risk co-option through their political and economic accommodations with state and capital (Kelly, 1988: 45). Finally, sections of the intellectual left have more recently applied the term 'labour aristocracy' to some or all wage-workers in developing countries, in the belief that they are economically and politically aligned against the radical sentiments of the rural peasantry and the non-wage urban sector and so, again, are a conservative force (Fanon, 1967; Arrighi and Saul, 1968).

On the other side of the political fence, neo-liberals have also taken up the term 'labour aristocracy' – in India, specifically against public-sector workers and trade unionists (Nayar, 1990: 87; Candland, 1995: 63; Ramaswamy, 1995: 125). Here again the term refers to a relatively privileged stratum of workers, although this time the main objection lies with the labour aristocracy's perceived obstruction of the proper workings of the market. Neo-liberals take the view that laws providing job security for workers in the formal sector are a barrier to potential new entrants to the labour market from the informal sector and hence a direct cause of poverty in that sector. The World Bank, for one, has long argued that the 'protected' formal sector obstructs the efficient utilisation of labour resources across the economy (see Moser, 1978: 1,053). Accordingly, the recent actions of the telecom workers in opposing the new competitive policies are interpreted as just another attempt to defend obsolete and inefficient work practices of which they are the sole beneficiaries. While the World Bank (1995a: 80–2) has recently conceded that unions have a role to play in productivity-based bargaining with employers, the 'political' character of actions like the 1995 telecom strike is condemned for its opposition to market-enhancing reforms. In sum, the labour-aristocracy thesis 'brings strange [political] bedfellows together' (Peace, 1979: 125). Despite their different normative assumptions about the appropriate form of labour activism, socialists and liberals both use the term to denote a relatively privileged stratum of workers whose interests run counter to those of the rest of the workforce. However, as the following discussion reveals, telecom workers are hardly candidates for the title 'labour aristocracy'.

The first point to establish is that public-sector workers in the telecommunications sector in India are generally *not* highly paid. Comparisons of wages in different industries and occupations are difficult to make because they vary considerably according to the skill level of the worker, the state or region in which they work and, most importantly, in terms of the number of workers employed in one place (Rao, 1995: 241). Nevertheless, much can be gained from the simple observation that in 1995 – the year of the strike – the great majority (94 per cent) of telecom workers were clustered in the lowest public-sector salary grades, with more than half (57 per cent) at the very bottom of the scale (interview with Namboodiri, 1997). At that time, wages at the lowest end of the public-sector salary scale were generally higher than best estimates of earnings in the informal sector – in some cases, up to four times higher (*Financial Express*, 1996a: 12; Labour Bureau, 1993; *Pioneer*, 1995). But, on the other hand, such wages were still about half the amount that automobile factory workers were receiving then (Meng *et al.*, 1996: 90). When regional differences in the cost of living are taken into account, the situation for telecom workers in the largest cities (where a good deal of the network is concentrated) looks particularly grim. Accurate statistics on this matter are again difficult to obtain; however, one official survey of household expenditure patterns in the late 1980s in the largest cities – like Delhi – shows that then most telecom workers' wages were inadequate for meeting the cost of maintaining a five-person household (Chakrabarty and Pal, 1995: 27).

Second, public-sector workers are often said to have their incomes boosted by non-wage benefits like housing, health and medical schemes, and job security (Ramaswamy, 1995: 102). But, in fact, only a very small minority – less than 2 per cent – of the total telecom workforce have proper housing provided for them (*Telematics India*, 1995: 57). For the vast remainder, work-associated housing is either unavailable, unable to be used, too expensive or simply consists of tents (interviews with Sangal and Haksar, 1997). As the same situation generally applies to health care, workers usually have to pay for it themselves or go without. By contrast, it is workers in the *private* formal sector who have more opportunities to receive additional benefits in the form of bonuses, pension schemes, medical, transport and housing allowances, and so on. Available figures suggest that about 30 per cent of a private-sector employee's income may be made up of such benefits, this amount rising to as much as 80 per cent for top executives (Meng *et al.*, 1996: 95).

Third, job security in the formal sector (public and private) is something which government policy and state law have enshrined for most of the post-independence era in India (Rao, 1995: 251). However, in the Department of Telecommunications (DoT) itself, the labour federations have been party to a ban on new permanent staff since 1984. The ban was intended to tackle 'overstaffing' through natural attrition, at a time when the network was otherwise expanding (interview with Sangal, 1997). Since its introduction, new employees have mostly been appointed on a temporary or contract basis. Thus, not all workers who participated in the 1995 strike had permanent positions to protect.

A related component of the 'labour aristocracy' charge against public-sector workers is that they are inefficient because their numbers have been bloated by government job-creation schemes designed to tackle unemployment. In this regard, the World Bank (1995b: 192) has specifically claimed that the DoT was 'overstaffed' in 1987 by up to 80 per cent. However, this figure comes entirely from an inappropriate – 'chalk-and-cheese' – comparison with Singapore's very compact, advanced system, which provides 50 per cent of the population with a telephone. The Indian telecom network is spread over a much larger area (3.3 million km^2) and has higher equipment maintenance requirements because of the older technology in use. In 1994, in Singapore there were 9 workers per 1,000 lines, whereas in India there were 59 per 1,000 lines. But, by 1996, the Indian figure had already dropped to 30 workers per 1,000 lines and it was predicted that it would decline further with the rapid expansion of the network. Of interest is a Singapore University Report on business opportunities in India, which estimates that a new, high-tech basic telephone network in India would require 22 workers per 1,000 lines (Meng *et al.*, 1996: 200). This is a ratio not much different from that which is already in place.

But what of the liberal argument that protected employment is directly responsible for the economic marginalisation of large numbers of individuals in the informal sector? Critics of this position point to the dualistic and market-oriented vision that underpins it (Moser, 1978; Gerry, 1987; Portes, Castells and Benton, 1989; Breman, 1996) – the fact that the formal and informal sectors are thought to operate in a segmented fashion, with the latter often praised for its entrepreneurial vigour and development potential, in contrast to the perceived inefficiencies of the state-dominated formal sector (Gerry 1987: 114). Against this view, radicals have rejected the dualistic model by stressing the *linkages* that often exist between protected and unprotected areas of economic activity (Moser, 1978: 1,055–60; Portes, Castells and Benton, 1989). Classic among the examples used to illustrate these linkages is the use of subcontracting and outworking to deliberately avoid legislated labour standards. This alternative perspective points to a considerable amount of disguised wage-labour existing in the informal sector – labour that is not excluded from the development process, but incorporated in ways that increases its exploitation. Breman (1996: 12–14) accordingly warns that neo-liberal policy prescriptions to create a more 'flexible' labour market are likely to swell, not contract, the size of the unprotected workforce.

Finally, Peace (1979) and Pinches (1987) challenge the dualistic assumption that the benefits of formal-sector employment accrue only to the workers themselves and their immediate household. As the World Bank admits, in a labour-surplus economy like India, workers with a relatively secure income generally have to support a large extended household through its life-cycle (World Bank, 1995a: 87). But in addition, Peace (1979: 136) makes the point that wages spent in the local economy often have an important multiplier effect, to the point where equity in the community is enhanced – small-scale foodsellers and the suppliers of essential goods being also able to share in the benefits accruing from rising wages by increasing their prices.[3] Likewise, Pinches argues that the notion of impervious sectors fails to fully appreciate 'the shared or social character of work and livelihood' (Pinches, 1987: 119) and hence the ways in which the experience of wage-labour goes beyond the immediate worker and workplace to shape relations in and between households and communities. Thus these critics take to task the idea that individuals in the formal and informal sectors are atomistic competitors over scarce economic resources.

This discussion has highlighted a range of flaws in the view that public-sector telecom workers in India constitute an economic elite, isolated from the rest of the workforce. In the following sections we consider in more detail the nature of the unions' response to the proposal to introduce a parallel private basic telephone network.

Bringing in private capital

In May 1994, the government of India announced a new National Telecommunications Policy (NTP) to modernise and expand the national telecommunications network. The stated goals of this policy were twofold: (1) to upgrade the network to global standards and (2) to expand it to reach the two-thirds of the country's 600,000 villages that currently have no phones, thereby rapidly transforming one of the lowest teledensities in the world (1 phone per 100 people)[4] into a leading-edge system. At the time it was argued that private investment needed to be inducted into the system to meet the enormous cost of implementing the NTP because this was 'beyond the capacity of government funding and internal generation of resources' (DoT, 1994: 2). Competition was initially only to be permitted in the cellular phone and paging markets; however, during the implementation phase, government policy shifted so as to also allow its introduction into the basic telephone system through the private duplication of the network.[5] This was to be done by auctioning 'build and operate' licences for twenty-one regional circles, corresponding approximately to different states. In international terms, this strategy of upgrading the basic telephone system via the introduction of private capital was unusual. In advanced industrialised countries the practice has been to maintain a regulated monopoly until a near-universal service (more than 50 phones per 100 people) is reached and then to shift to competitive or contestable markets (ITU, 1995). The gradual expansion of the network is thereby achieved through cross-subsidised pricing, based on elasticities of demand (Antonelli, 1997: 41).

Three years earlier, in 1991, the Athreya Telecom Restructuring Committee had recommended that the DoT be split into six corporations – the aim being to separate the public utility from direct departmental control, enabling managerial autonomy with commercial objectives and competitive performance bench-marking between the different units (Athreya, 1993: 36). The committee further recommended that the next stage should involve selling off the whole of the DoT to the private sector, thus allowing a private monopoly to replace a public one. But this was not the option that the government eventually pursued in its 1994 policy announcement. Mody (1995) argues that this was because opposition from the telecom labour federations forced the government to take the 'middle path' of allowing a parallel private network, rather than full privatisation. Thus, she claims, the then Communications Minister, Sukh Ram, 'accommodated' the unions by negotiating 'a form of private sector that they could live with' (ibid.: 119). However, if such an accommodation was reached, it did not hold as – with the subsequent announcement to extend private competition into the basic telephone system – several large telecom unions took it upon themselves to launch protest actions, independent of their federations.

O.P. Gupta, the influential general secretary of the NFTE (the largest labour federation in the telecom industry), initially took the view that the introduction of private competition into the department's basic network was less of a problem than full privatisation. His main concern with the proposal was simply that the new technologies installed in the duplicate network might make the existing telecom workforce 'obsolete'. Therefore, he pushed the line that the government be pressured to make proper provision for the retraining of public-sector workers so that they could continue to retain employment in the new competitive environment. Gupta also held the view that greater competition would improve customer satisfaction levels. In turn, he believed this would forestall any pressures that might otherwise remain to fully privatise the industry, thus stemming even greater future job losses for the existing membership. Otherwise, the business sector was enthusiastic in its response to the NTP policy. Private subscribers also seemed happy with the promise of cheaper calls and the resolution of unexplained faults causing connection failures, dropped calls or extremely noisy lines.

The leadership of the largest telecom labour federation initially took a somewhat limited, pragmatic stance towards the government's original and modified restructuring proposals. But in subsequent months they were forced to shift ground as opposition to the new policy picked up pace, both inside and outside the organised telecom workforce. Spearheading the articulated opposition to the proposed restructuring was a group of public interest advocates made up of retired and active heads of government departments, journalists, academics, lawyers, consultants and so on. In the group, one lawyer, Nandita Haksar, donated a year of his labour to the task of preparing the briefs for the Supreme Court petitions. In addition, an information technology consultant, Prabir Purkayastha, drew together and coordinated the volunteer group of experts, including the former Chairman of the Telecom Commission and

Director General of the DoT, D.K. Sangal, who brought 'inside' experience and critical acumen to the whole process. This group of activists identified the class implications of the new policy, particularly the extent to which transnational capital would gain from the changes while workers and consumers at the lower end of the market were disadvantaged. Their analysis of the situation was made available to the telecom unions and labour organisers, who were, in turn, able to disseminate this information to rank-and-file workers across the country. Unions affiliated with the NFTE were crucial in simultaneously communicating information about the socio-economic consequences of a parallel private telephone network 'down' to mobilise the rank-and-file workforce and 'up' to the federations to force them to take action. This was achieved by cross-country tours, conferences, demonstrations, newsletters and telegrams, all designed to both inform opinion and organise activism. One invaluable asset which unions and workers in telecommunications had was their access to the national telephone network!

By January 1995, telecom workers were sufficiently concerned about the NTP to hold a number of large demonstrations and then a one-day strike over it. Following this, a national convention was organised in April by a group set up specifically for that purpose: the Door Santir Samithi. The 2,000 telecom-worker delegates who attended the convention were able to obtain still more information on the policy and to participate in decisions about further action (Namboodiri, 1995b: 42). By contrast, for much of this time the leaders of the federations were continuing to resist efforts to mount a concerted campaign. Believing that a parallel private basic network was less problematic than full privatisation, the leadership of the NFTE in particular argued that a prolonged strike would only harm the workers involved – as it has done in the past (interview with Gupta, 1997). General Secretary Gupta was well aware that such a strike would differ from the customary pattern in that, whereas 'usually the unions go on strike on economic factors', in this situation there were no economic demands being made, 'not even from the bottom rank-and-file membership' (ibid.). In a similar vein, Venkataraman (general secretary of the second largest federation, FNTO) claimed that a union's job was to protect its members and, therefore, it had 'no right to go against the government of India' (interview with Venkataraman, 1997). But so successful was the campaign that all three of the telecom federations eventually agreed to hold a countrywide, indefinite strike in mid-1995, demanding extensive public debate over the changes to the NTP, with a view to reversing proposals that were unacceptable (Namboodiri, 1995a: 11).

The petitions

The telecom unions joined with a parliamentarian and a voluntary public interest group, the Delhi Science Forum (DSF), in filing in the Supreme Court a series of petitions against the duplication of the basic telephone network. The DSF claimed to represent the 85 per cent of subscribers 'who will suffer [the consequences of] a deteriorating service' (DSF, 1995: 1). The petitions demanded that the government 'protect the national interest' by not 'surrendering to the pressure' from international and domestic companies to 'fragment' telecommunications services. In this, they covered three main issues: (1) the likelihood that the needs of rural people would not be met; (2) the corollary that the policy is principally geared to the interests of globalising corporations; and (3) the class implications of technological change. Telecommunication experts in India and overseas were already debating various financial and technical aspects of the new NTP. For example, the last public-sector managing director of British Telecom's inland operations rejected the replication of telecommunications infrastructure on the grounds that, among other things, it delays competition in services and is 'immensely expensive' (Harper, 1995: 297). However, the petitioners went beyond such criticisms in bringing public attention to the otherwise obscured socio-economic effects of the policy.

As previously stated, government had promised that its new policy would expand telephone services in the rural areas. However, the petitions observe that the system for allocating operator licences gives little priority to this outcome because the weighting allocated to a bidder's stated commitment to expand rural services was only 15 per cent, as against 72 per cent for the amount of money to be offered for the licence. As this system encouraged the tendering of very high licence fees,[6] it also saw the incentive structure further directed towards successful private operators concentrating on the high-use, high-revenue end of the market (interview with Sangal, 1997). The 8 per cent of current subscribers who generate 70 per cent of total revenue are thus favoured for 'cream-skimming' by profit-oriented private investors (Chowdary, 1995: 22). Significantly, these subscribers are concentrated in urban areas where there are very few waiting lists for phones. Not surprisingly, the petitions contained information about the outcomes of the tendering process which showed that almost half of the villages with no phones are in circles that attracted no bids whatsoever.

In sum, the petitioners argued that licensing private operators to duplicate the DoT's basic telephone network in all areas, at a time when network development remains very low, would retard rather than expand services to the rural areas (Purkayastha, 1994: 2,125). In this situation, business and affluent users in the urban and metropolitan areas would be the winners with new technologies and price discounts, whereas rural, backward and hilly areas, which need cross-subsidies to fund the network expansion, would be left to the DoT. Moreover, the loss of the high-revenue customers resulting from the effective bifurcation of the basic telephone service would severely impact on the DoT's financial ability to actually carry out their social responsibility in this area (DSF, 1995).

The petitioners argued that the government's abrogation of its public welfare responsibilities was an outcome of globalising interests lobbying for a particular configuration of high-tech communications. In one of the court petitions, D.K. Sangal argued that the Telecom Commission had been 'egged on by the large private corporations, indigenous and foreign, the latter supported by their governments and World Bank and IMF' to adopt its new policy (Sangal, 1995: 31). In this volume, Sherlock is critical of labour responses to economic liberalisation that are strongly economic nationalist in tone, on the grounds that they reproduce assumptions about 'Third World dependency'. However, there is much support for the view that recent restructuring in Indian telecommunications has been influenced – and at times forced – by events, policies and struggles outside the nation. Urey (1995: 53), for example, argues that the impetus for restructuring in the telecommunications sector particularly comes from large firms dominating the industry in advanced industrialised countries, in an environment where there is an expansion of transnational production and marketing systems. In the Indian case, she asserts, alliances between domestic and international telecommunications corporations have forced the government 'to yield authority' over the telephone system to private interests (ibid.: 76). The World Bank, in addition, has been actively pushing the privatisation of telecommunications services in developing countries since the 1980s (Kikeri and Shirley, 1992; Wellenius and Stern, 1994).

Foremost among the large firms influencing and participating in privatisation processes in the telecommunications sector are AT&T and its divested subsidiaries, the seven Regional Bell Operating Companies (RBOCs) (Horwitz, 1989: 221–3). These firms have overcome the limitations of 'regulations and the saturation of their domestic markets in the United States by increasing investment in telecommunications in developing countries' (Bagchi-Sen and Das, 1995: 85). For instance, AT&T is estimated to have ten strategic alliances in manufacturing and cellular networks in India, along with building networks for other US RBOCs (like Nynex and US West) and a national management system for the DoT. Some of the joint ventures in which AT&T is involved in India are the production of switches with Tata from 1995, producing optic-fibre cable in Pune with Finolex Cable from 1996, and installing and operating cellular networks in three circles with Birla from 1996–7 (Vajpeyi, 1995: 60–2). Significantly, of the forty licences to build and operate cellular networks in India, twenty-three went to US RBOCs and their subsidiaries, with seven going to Nynex and five to US West.

International equipment suppliers have lobbied hard to have their newest technologies seen as the solution to the problems besetting a country like India. In so doing, they have worked to undermine indigenous products through a combination of pricing strategies, credit facilitation, discrediting Indian research and development (R&D), and establishing partial local production. The transnational telecom corporations have been supported by high-profile delegations from their respective governments (in particular the United States) in putting pressure on the Indian government to sign up to new deals. Of note is the fact that each significant change to the NTP coincided with such foreign visits. On this basis, the telecom workers' activism against the government's NTP is simply the counterpoint to everyday efforts that business makes to shape government policies (directly or indirectly) through lobbying, through funding electoral campaigns and public-opinion makers, and/or through withholding or diverting investment (Korten, 1995: 141–6).

To win markets, TNCs compete using a level of technology that conflicts with the need to maximise employment in India. While some skilled workers may benefit from TNC wages and conditions, new production processes destroy labour-intensive firms, exacerbating labour's difficulties (Parikh, 1997: 130). The telecom unions are aware that rebalancing the private–public sphere in advanced industrialised countries has been accompanied by large workforce reductions, increased contracting out and decreased job security. Their concerns about the influence of global corporations are thus associated with their greater ability to use technology to displace and disorganise Indian labour.

Campaigns by TNCs to sell their equipment on the basis of technological superiority were criticised on a number of counts. First, it was argued that 'national interest' was involved in the implication that Indian technology could not deliver the goods. The government was specifically criticised for bypassing technologies indigenously designed for Indian conditions – like digital rural switches and, more recently, corDECT (a wireless in the local loop technology (WLL) to be used extensively in expanding the Indian basic networks) (*Financial Express*, 1996b). In a remarkably short period, it was pointed out, domestic manufacturers were starved of orders by over-liberalisation of the equipment market and collusive behaviour by TNCs (IETE, 1997). They are now further threatened by new import tariff reductions on fully imported equipment, lowered from 55.76 per cent to 22 per cent, while tariffs on parts used by domestic manufacturers remain unchanged at 55.76 per cent (Goyal, 1997).[7] In addition, the government was criticised for failing to negotiate 'smarter' to buy technology without compromising Indian jobs.

Technological change is normally presented to the workforce and consumers as inevitable. In this way, the government is able to circumvent its 'no exit' (no retrenchments) policy by arguing that job losses are an inevitable consequence of forces beyond their control. Thus, for example, the chairman of the Telecom Restructuring Committee, M.B. Athreya states:

> Techno-economic logic should, by and large, take its course. If cellular, paging, low orbiting satellite, iridium or some other technology is making the conventional telephone poles, cables and landlines obsolete, that new technology should be used, bypassing the landlines. High costs and obsolete jobs must not be defended.
>
> (Athreya, 1993: 37)

However, the Indian example shows that technology selection does not follow an inherent logic. Private companies are developing technologies to specifically bypass the incumbent's local monopoly. Wireless or microwave links are being used to duplicate the local loop or section so that the market for services can be accessed without having to 'pass through' the incumbent's network. In other words, certain technologies are being deployed around issues of property. The next section discusses the role that the group of public interest advocates played in galvanising worker activism by, among other things, highlighting the social nature of technology.

The role of advocates and information

In developing a four-dimensional understanding of class, Katznelson makes a distinction between shared dispositions and collective action. He makes the point that workers with 'motivational constructs' in common 'may or may not act collectively to transform disposition to behaviour' (Katznelson, 1986: 17–19) – the transition to activism must thus be separately explained in the circumstances where and when it occurs. In the case of the 1995 strike, telecom workers participated in large numbers, in part because of their already fairly well-developed sense of common identification as workers. However, it is important to emphasise that the decision to strike in this instance came only after input from a group of public interest activists had encouraged the workers to launch industrial action. The interventions of these advocates were crucial because they presented the telecom workers with information that allowed them to counter the hegemony of neo-liberal perspectives on the first-time entry of private capital. In particular, the advocates played a key role in demystifying technological upgrades, in much the way that Gramsci envisaged intellectuals might function to change the existing social order by presenting an alternative worldview (Ransome, 1992: 191).

Telecom workers were already fairly united in their own minds for several reasons. First, they shared a deep resentment towards their relatively poor public image, especially the image of themselves as inefficient and ineffective when, for many years, external factors such as inadequate training and faulty equipment had been a major cause of the unsatisfactory service. Just one example: faulty foreign-made Penta Conta switches purchased in the mid-1960s failed to connect subscribers and the DoT was forced to continue using manual operators until STD became operational in many urban exchanges in the late 1980s (DoT, 1987: 101). Mani (1995: 108) states that the Penta Conta switch technology was in the 'downward phase of its product cycle', yet – because it had been very expensive to procure – the government was locked into trying to make it work by correcting the faults. D.K. Sangal, a former director of the DoT, comments that the episode 'built up consumer agitation and dissatisfaction which persists' and caused a loss of revenue that could have been used to deal with waiting lists and new services (interview with Sangal, 1997).

But in addition to their shared identification through employment, a large proportion of telecom workers either currently work in or have shifted from rural areas, the latter group leaving family behind. For instance, the department progressively collected 100,000 unskilled workers, diggers and erectors from villages contracted to extend the cable network (ibid.). As a consequence, many have been personally affected by the poor rural infrastructure, or at least can relatively easily empathise with the needs of rural communities. In sum, not only have telecom workers had a sense of themselves sharing interests in common as workers but also, as a result of their geographical location and/or residential background, they can identify fairly well with the lot of the rural consumers of the services they provide. As they are themselves on temporary work release, union organisers tend to share these sentiments with the rank and file; yet alone, it is unlikely that this disposition would have goaded the rank and file into action. The additional factor of clarifying workers' perceptions of the particular situation at hand was provided by their interaction with the public interest advocates. It was this that solidified the workers' doubts about the effects of the new policy and allowed them to envisage an alternative outcome and so perceive that collective activism was worth pursuing.

Outcomes

The telecom strike ended abruptly on 23 June 1995 when the three federations signed an agreement with the government. According to O.P. Gupta, general secretary of the largest federation, the strike was a success because it had stimulated public debate without the participants being victimised. His view was that private entry and competition in the industry had become inevitable, hence the issue for workers and their unions was one of job protection and survival. The government came to the party on this by agreeing to the proposition that the DoT must improve workforce training to provide equivalent quality of service in order to reduce the threat of public-sector obsolescence in the face of competition from private enterprise. Other than that, no concessions were made to the broader demands of the strikers and petitioners. Unions affiliated with the federations were thus generally displeased with the outcome. They felt 'betrayed' because they had not been kept informed of the negotiations with government and because the federations had finally signed a strike-ending agreement against their wishes. Fundamental differences over union philosophy which emerged during the dispute continue. Where the unions make sharper distinctions about class interests, the federations tend towards more corporatist, reformist pragmatism. Post-strike hostility between the largest unions and NFTE General Secretary Gupta in particular remains unabated. The petitions themselves were finally transferred to New Delhi for a Supreme Court hearing in January 1996. The decision handed down on 23 February 1996 – exactly eight months after the end of the strike – was that the matter fell outside the court's jurisdiction.

However, the fact remains the telecom workers' protests provide a powerful example of organising that is not limited to narrow self-interest or workplace issues. The strike and court petitions demonstrated that, regardless of competing political affiliations or state patronage, labour in the telecommunications sector in India can be encouraged to take action over broad socio-economic issues. Significantly, they were able to commandeer government rhetoric to demand that DoT infrastructure and telecom workers be made 'fit' to compete with the new private companies. They pointed out that the government had chosen parallel private (mainly foreign) direct investment rather than the alternative of cutting expenditure, raising telecom prices, renting capital or taxing the rich to modernise and expand the telecommunications sector (interview with Rao, 1996). They also highlighted the penalty of wasted resources in building parallel basic networks, instead of modernising the existing one and expanding to the non-commercial areas. Costs and benefits were shown to be skewed as, while the costs of obsolescence and waste would be spread over all subscribers, the benefits mainly accrue to business and contiguous subscribers in metropolitan, urban and industrial nodes. Appropriation of the 'technology dividend' thus becomes a matter of corporate strategy rather than public policy (Trebing, 1995: 320). The labour-linked opposition was the first to identify the folly of putting more weight on the fee tendered by competing bidders for telecom licences, than on expansion targets, predicting that it would hinder the growth of telecommunications to rural and non-commercial users. At the same time, they indicated the job losses that would be generated by importing technologies and telecom products.

The strike and petitions caused the tendering process to be delayed nine months till the March 1996 national elections but, even with a change in government, the process of partial privatisation was not halted. Nevertheless, criticism of the policy has continued. Even the bidders were dissatisfied with the process and refused to finalise formalities to proceed in the eight basic telecom circles allocated, with the remaining thirteen circles unallotted. In December 1996, the Fifth Report of the Lok Sabha Standing Committee on Communications stated that the NTP had been inadequately planned, announced in an 'unseemly hurry' and marked by '*ad hoc*-ism and indecision' (GoI, 1996: 7, 9). Two months later, in February 1997, the experiment was universally accepted as being in 'crisis' at a special summit of the Institution of Electronics and Telecommunication Engineers that had been organised for industry, advisers and DoT management seeking solutions (IETE, 1997).

In the following two years, the impact of over-enthusiastic competitive bidding for telecom licences has confirmed the claims first raised in the petitions that such bidding was unsustainable (see Sangal, 1995) and would therefore actually deter the spread of telecommunications. Because many licensees were unable to raise finance to roll out new networks, the government was forced to make concessions – like reducing tax and import tariffs – and changes in financing arrangements (for example, public financial institutions have been pressured to change prudent lending norms). Sangal comments on the irony of the situation: where the stated aim of the NTP was to utilise the market to raise capital from the private sector to achieve certain objectives, 'it is the government which is arranging and facilitating the funds' (Sangal, 1997: n.p.).

To date, only six basic telecom licences have been issued (out of the twenty-one offered) and, after four years, only two licensees – in Madhya Pradesh and Maharashtra – have commenced network-building, adding fewer than 5,000 phone lines – none of them in villages (Bidwai, 1998; *Business Line*, 1998; Saxena, 1998). Even after the concessions, subscriber growth is low and usage is falling – licensees now owe the government more than US$500 million in unpaid fees (*India Network Special News Report*, 1998). Recognising the failure of the NTP, the Indian government is currently reviewing the policy with the aim of radically restructuring the terms of privatisation (*Economic Times*, 1999). At the same time, the government has responded to another of the strikers' demands regarding indigenous technology – being ultimately forced to retract spectrum from the Ministry of Defence's allocation to permit the use of the WLL technology developed at the Indian Institute of Technology in Chennai (Chowdary, 1998: 15). The use of indigenous corDECT technology in the new networks will improve job prospects for Indian manufacturing workers by replacing imported products at half the cost (ibid.). In short, labour activism in the mid-1990s brought public and expert attention to the defects of the policy and the class issues involved in privatisation, some of which ultimately have been recognised and become influential in modifying subsequent policies.

Notes

1   *Sangharsh* means struggle or conflict (Haksar, 1995: 16).
2   I wish to thank Nandita Haksar, D.K. Sangal, Prabir Purkayastha and all my interviewees for their immense help. Thanks also to Herb Thompson and Jane Hutchison for comments on previous drafts of this chapter.
3   Kalecki's principle, that 'workers spend what they get', is also an important determinant of total demand in the economy (Robinson, 1975: 99, 51).
4   This figure compares with the world average of 10 phones per 100 people, or 56 per 100 in Australia.
5   Competition need not entail the introduction of private capital. In China, for example, telecommunications were liberalised in 1994 by establishing two additional public-sector enterprises to compete with the incumbent (Ure, 1995: 14).
6   On average, a figure equivalent to US$208 per subscriber per year was tendered, compared to the US$80 annual subscriber fee currently charged by the DoT.
7   In China, by contrast, telecommunications policy has been used as an instrument 'to stimulate domestic equipment and components manufacturing' by insisting on technology-transfer agreements (Ure, 1995: 16).

Bibliography

Antonelli, C. (1997) 'A regulatory regime for innovation in the communications industries', *Telecommunications Policy* February: 35–45.

Arrighi, G. and Saul, J. (1968) 'Socialism and economic development in tropical Africa', *Journal of Modern African Studies* 6, 2: 141–69.

Athreya, M.B. (1993) 'Managing telecoms', *Seminar* 404 (April): 34–7.

Bagchi, A.K. (1997) 'Public sector and the political economy of Indian development', in T.J. Byres (ed.) *The State, Development Planning and Liberalisation in India*, New Delhi: Oxford University Press, pp. 298–339.

Bagchi-Sen, S. and Das, P. (1995) 'Foreign direct investment by the V.S. Bells', in B. Mody, J.M. Bauer and J.D. Straubhaar (eds) *Telecommunications Politics: Ownership and Control of the Information Highway in Developing Countries*, New Jersey: Lawrence Erlbaum Associates, pp. 85–111.

Bidwai, Praful (1998) 'India's telecom policy: Telephones before food and water', *Times of India* 30 December.

Breman, J. (1996) *Footloose Labour: Working in India's Informal Economy*, Cambridge: Cambridge University Press.

Business Line (1998) 'Big strides in telecom policy', 28 December.

184   *Patricia Cahill*

Byres, T.J. (1997) 'State, class and development planning in India', in T.J. Byres (ed.) *The State, Development Planning and Liberalisation in India*, New Delhi: Oxford University Press, pp. 36–81.

Candland, C. (1995) 'Trade unionism and industrial restructuring in India and Pakistan', *Bulletin of Concerned Asian Scholars* 27, 4: 63–78.

Chakrabarty, G. and Pal, S.P. (1995) *Human Development Profile of the Indian States*, National Council of Applied Economic Research (NCAER) Working Papers, New Delhi: NCAER.

Chowdary, T.H. (1992) *The Indian Telegraph Act, 1885*, Hyderabad: Centre for Telecom Management and Studies (CTMS).

—— (1995) Untitled article, *Journal of the CTMS* August.

—— (1998) 'Indian Telecom: A year's harvest', *Journal of the CTMS* July: 15.

DoT (Department of Telecommunications) (1987) *Forty Years of Telecommunications in Independent India*, Delhi: DoT.

—— (1994) *National Telecommunications Policy*, Delhi: DoT.

DSF (Delhi Science Forum) (1995) Petitions, General Submission and Annexures (court documents).

Economic Times (1999) 'New telecom policy by March 31: Jaswant', 8 January.

Fanon, Frantz (1967) *The Wretched of the Earth*, Harmondsworth: Penguin.

Financial Express (1996a) 'Minimum wage for unorganised labour at Rs32 per day mooted', 24 February.

—— (1996b) 'Analog devices launches corDECT system', 25 July.

Gerry, Chris (1987) 'Developing economies and the informal sector in historical perspective', *Annals AAPSS* 493 (September): 100–19.

GoI (Government of India) (1996) *Fifth Report, Eleventh Lok Sabha Standing Committee on Communications*, New Delhi: Lok Sabha Secretariat.

Goyal, Arun (1997) 'Telecom equipment duty cut to 22 the most vital tariff change', Export-Import Notes in *Economic Times* 14 May.

Gupta, O.P. (ed.) (1995) 'TeleLabour: Brief summary of DoT's Instructions for Guidance of Branch Secretaries', *Journal of NFTE*.

Haksar, N. (1995) 'The problem', *Seminar* 419 (May): 12–16.

Harper, J.M. (1995) 'The case against competing infrastructures', *Telecommunications Policy* 19, 4: 285–98.

Headrick, D.R. (1995) 'Public–private relations in international telecommunications before World War II', in B. Mody, J.M. Bauer and J.D. Straubhaar (eds) *Telecommunications Politics: Ownership and Control of the Information Highway in Developing Countries*, New Jersey: Lawrence Erlbaum Associates, pp. 31–49.

Horwitz, R.B. (1989) *The Irony of Regulatory Reform: The Deregulation of American Telecommunications*, New York: Oxford University Press.

IETE (Institute of Electronics and Telecommunication Engineers) (1997) *Roundtable Summit*, New Delhi.

India Network Special News Report (1998) 'India panel sees new telecom policy in February', 6 (17 December).

ITU (International Telecommunications Union) (1995) *World Telecommunication Development Report*, Geneva: ITU.

Karnik, V.B. (1978) *Indian Trade Unions: A Survey*, Bombay: Popular Parkashan.

Katznelson, I. (1986) 'Working-class formation: Constructing cases and comparisons', in Ira Katznelson and Aristide R. Zolberg (eds) *Working-Class Formation: Nineteenth Century*

Patterns in Western Europe and the United States, Princeton: Princeton University Press, pp. 3–39.

Kelly, J. (1988) *Trade Unions and Socialist Politics*, London and New York: Verso.

Kikeri, S.J. and Shirley, M. (1992) *Privatization: The Lessons of Experience*, Washington, D.C.: World Bank.

Korten, D.C. (1995) *When Corporations Rule the World*, London: Earthscan.

Labour Bureau (1993) *Indian Labour Statistics*, Delhi: Ministry of Labour.

Lenin, V.I. (1968) *Lenin: Selected Works*, Moscow: Progress Publishers.

Mani, Sunil (1995) 'Technology import and skill development in a microelectronics-based industry: The case of India's "Electronic Switching Systems" ', in A.K. Bagchi and R. Samaddara (eds) *New Technology and the Workers' Response: Microelectronics, Labour and Society*, New Delhi: Sage Publications, pp. 98–122.

Meng, T.T., Meng, A., Williams, J.J. and Zutshi, R. (eds) (1996) *Business Opportunities in India*, Singapore: Prentice Hall.

Mody, Bella (1995) 'State consolidation through liberalization of telecommunications services in India', *Journal of Communication* 45, 4 (Autumn): 107–24.

Moser, Caroline (1978) 'Informal sector or petty commodity production: Dualism or dependence in urban development?', *World Development* 6, 9–10: 1,041–64.

Namboodiri, V.A.N. (ed.) (1995a) 'Organise sit-in/tools down/pens down/strike on 23rd January 1995', *Telecom 2: Organ of the All India Telecom Employees Union Class III*, February.

—— (1995b) 'All India Convention against Telecom privatisation', *Telecom 5: Organ of the All India Telecom Employees Union Class III*, May.

Nayar, B.R. (1990) *The Political Economy of India's Public Sector: Policy and Performance*, Bombay: Popular Prakashan.

Parikh, Kirit S. (ed.) (1997) *India Development Report*, Delhi: Oxford University Press.

Peace, A. (1979) 'The Lagos proletariat: Labour aristocrats or populist militants?', in H. Goulbourne (ed.) *Politics and State in the Third World*, London: Macmillan, pp. 124–41.

Pinches, M. (1987) 'All that we have is our muscle and sweat: The rise of wage labour in a Manila squatter community', in M. Pinches and S. Lakha (eds) *Wage Labour and Social Change*, Monash Papers on Southeast Asia no. 16, Clayton: Centre of Southeast Asian Studies, Monash University, pp. 103–36.

PIRG (Public Interest Research Group) (1994) *Alternative Economic Survey 1993–94*, New Delhi: PIRG.

Portes, Alejandro, Castells, Manuel and Benton, Lauren A. (eds) (1989) *The Informal Economy: Studies in Advanced and Less Developed Countries*, Baltimore: Johns Hopkins University Press.

Purkayastha, P. (1994) 'New telecom policy: Rushing in where angels fear to tread', *Economic and Political Weekly* August: 2,125–7.

Ramaswamy, E.A. (1995) 'Organized labour and economic reform', in P. Oldenburg (ed.) *India Briefing: Staying the Course*, London: M.E. Sharpe, pp. 97–128.

Ransome, Paul (1992) *Antonio Gramsci: An Introduction*, London: Harvester Wheatsheaf.

Rao, J. Mohan (1995) 'Capital, labour and the Indian State', in Juliet Schor and Jong-Il You (eds) *Capital, the State and Labour: A Global Perspective*, Aldershot and Brookfield: Edward Elgar, pp. 238–81.

Robinson, Joan (1975) *Collected Economic Papers*, 2nd edn, vol. 3, Oxford: Basil Blackwell.

Sangal, D.K. (1995) 'Basic telephone services, new telecom policy and its implications: A critique', unpublished mimeo.

—— (1997) 'Confess and get going', *Economic Times* 9 April.

Saxena, Neeraj (1998) 'Telecom: Still on hold but tone is clear', *Financial Express* 31 December.

Srinivas, A. (1995) 'Women staff bear the brunt in electronics sector/Administrators, industry evade minimum wage issue', *Pioneer* 7 March.

Telematics India (1995) August.

Trebing, H.M. (1995) 'Privatization and the public interest: Is reconciliation through regulation possible?', in B. Mody, J.M. Bauer and J.D. Straubhaar (eds) *Telecommunications Politics: Ownership and Control of the Information Highway in Developing Countries*, New Jersey: Lawrence Erlbaum Associates, pp. 309–27.

Ure, J. (1995) *Telecommunications in Asia: Policy, Planning and Development*, Hong Kong: Hong Kong University Press.

Urey, M. (1995) 'Telecommunications and global capitalism', in B. Mody, J.M. Bauer and J.D. Straubhaar (eds) *Telecommunications Politics: Ownership and Control of the Information Highway in Developing Countries*, New Jersey: Lawrence Erlbaum Associates, pp. 53–84.

Vajpeyi, R. (with Das, S. and Voice Team) (1995) 'Problems and complaints of users', *Telematics India* September.

Wellenius, B. and Stern, P. (1994) *Implementing Reforms in the Telecommunications Sector: Lessons from Experience*, Discussion Paper 192, Washington, D.C.: World Bank.

World Bank (1995a) *World Development Report 1995: Workers in an Integrating World*, New York: Oxford University Press.

World Bank (1995b) *Bureaucrats in Business: The Economics and Politics of Government Ownership*, New York: Oxford University Press.

Interviews

Gupta, O.P., NFTE General Secretary (January/February, 1996; February, 1997).

Haksar, N., lawyer for the petitioners (January/February, 1996; February, 1997).

Namboodiri, V.A.N., E-3 Union General Secretary (January/February, 1996; February, 1997).

Rao, K.A., President of the National Confederation of Officers' Associations of Central Public Sector Undertakings (January/February, 1996; February, 1997).

Sangal, D.K., former Director General of the DoT (January/February, 1996; February, 1997).

Venkataraman, R., FNTO General Secretary (February, 1996).

10 Class and national identity

The case of Filipino migrant workers

Michael Pinches[1]

Working-class organisation and consciousness often take on unexpected and ambiguous forms. In this chapter, I examine some of the class-based practices of Filipino overseas contract workers, focusing in particular on the links between class and ethnicity. While an analytical distinction between class and ethnicity may be useful (Eriksen, 1997: 35–7), I reject the common argument or assumption (Lloyd, 1982: 81–2; De Guzman, 1993: 42–52; Buendia and Tigno, 1998: 10) that one form of consciousness or organisation is necessarily exclusive of the other.[2] I argue here that the particular class experiences of Filipino migrant workers tend to find expression in assertions of ethnic or national solidarity.[3] There may be limitations and ambiguities embedded in the class ethnicity of Filipino overseas workers, but I argue that these should not be overdrawn and that class struggles are necessarily rooted in, and expressed through, particular cultural and political relations. I further suggest that, in contrast to ideologies of proletarian universalism, a powerful feature of ethnic identification among Filipino workers is that it connotes a valued social existence apart from the world of capital and commodified labour power. More significant than the possible limitations of ethnic consciousness on the class practices of Filipino overseas workers, is the fact that overseas employment offers the chance of limited upward social mobility and thus tends to engender a preparedness to tolerate hardship and abuse.

In this chapter I seek to address a problem in much of the literature on class in industrialising Asia: the tendency to ignore the lives of workers beyond the workplace, the trade union or the political party. Outside these arenas, the qualities through which workers are constituted and constitute themselves – their cultural practices, social attachments and personhood – tend to be trivialised, reduced to productive relations or viewed as impediments to the achievement of working-class unity (Katznelson, 1986; Pinches and Lakha, 1987; Perry, 1996). In the industrial relations literature especially, there is a strong tendency to see trade unions as the only true or effective expression of worker agency and organisation.[4] At very least, this simply overlooks the practices of large numbers of workers who are not unionised and who are often not in areas of employment where formal unionisation is viable. In some of the more abstract literature, there is even a tendency to reify the identity of workers in much the same way as does capital – that is, in terms only of their commodified labour power.

Just as there are dangers in assuming that trade unions are the only genuine forms of working-class organisation, so too there are dangers in measuring class consciousness through the universal language of the intelligentsia.[5] Popular working-class sensibilities and critiques of capital are much more likely to be expressed through the ordinary, idiosyncratic, often ambiguous and metaphorical language of the local (Nash, 1979; Taussig, 1980; Ong, 1987; Pinches, 1992). This not only acknowledges the importance of cultural setting, but also the fact that proletarian life is not totally circumscribed by class (Katznelson, 1986; Crompton, 1993: 18).

An obvious difficulty in expanding the study of class from the workplace arena into the wider terrain of sociality, culture and everyday life is that one encounters much that is not simply about class, and indeed the concept of class itself becomes increasingly blurred and ambiguous. However, as I hope to show here, any study of workers that ignores or underplays this wider terrain, seriously limits both our empirical understanding of class and the analytical efficacy of the concept itself. Thus, while it would be fallacious to adopt the reductionist position that local, ethnic or national loyalties are simply expressions of class interest, it would be equally fallacious to suppose that such loyalties are anathema to class. Indeed, it should be evident in this study that the universal category 'proletariat' or 'working class' is only useful as an abstraction and that workers, necessarily, are differentiated into varied historically, culturally and politically constructed groups or relations which, nonetheless, may be largely understood as expressions of class.

The remainder of the chapter is divided into five sections. While the arguments and material presented draw on a range of empirical studies of Filipino overseas workers, they focus in particular on my own fieldwork among migrant workers and their families in the Visayan Area – a poor neighbourhood in Tatalon, Manila. In the first section, I introduce the phenomenon of Filipino overseas contract labour and outline the pattern of recruitment and social organisation of migrant workers in the above neighbourhood. The second section considers the common ethnic and institutional controls used to subordinate Filipino overseas contract workers. The third section examines the preparedness of most overseas Filipino workers to endure these controls as part of a strategy of escaping class degradation in the Philippines. The fourth section explores some of the ways in which Filipino overseas workers nonetheless resist the subordination and abuse entailed in most overseas employment, in particular through their assertions of ethnic solidarity. The final section problematises the relationship between class and ethnicity among Filipino overseas workers, focusing in particular on the subversive, class-based constructions of Filipino ethnic or national identity. A short conclusion follows.

Filipino overseas workers and the Visayan Area, Tatalon

In the early 1980s an advertisement on Philippine television featured a smiling Filipino worker flying home by magic carpet over the modern skyscrapers of Manila's well-to-do Makati district. Gathered closely around him were a new radio-cassette player, toys and other gifts for his family, mementos of the new wealth that had become available to Filipino workers in the Middle East. Once on the ground, the man is greeted by his excited wife and children as he enters his spacious, newly furnished house. Produced at a time when the Philippines' economic crisis contrasted sharply with growing prosperity in the region, the images in this advertisement convey something of the importance that had become attached to overseas contract work, as a source of both private wealth and national development. Only after a period of exile from the comforts of home and family, it seemed, could ordinary Filipinos expect to enjoy prosperity, and only by drawing on the wealth of other nations could the Philippines itself prosper. On one hand, these images speak clearly of the way in which Filipino workers have been caught up in the processes of globalisation; on the other, they assert the enduring attachment of these workers to a national homeland.

Though the mid-1990s brought a change in the economic fortunes of the Philippines relative to many of its neighbours (Pinches, 1999), the promise of a better life still propels large numbers of Filipinos to overseas work sites. Unable to find comparable employment or remuneration in the Philippines, a growing number of Filipino workers have spent many years overseas as contract employees. Indeed, the Philippines is now reported to be Asia's largest labour-exporter and the world's second largest (Tigno, 1997: 2), with nearly 2,000 contract workers leaving the country every day for overseas destinations (Karp, 1995: 43). Over 4 million Filipinos are employed overseas on a temporary basis: most on three-month to two-year contracts, the remainder as illegal aliens (Ball, 1996: 70; Alegado, 1997: 23; Tigno, 1997: 2–3; Gonzalez, 1998: 36). Labour exports have become the Philippines' largest source of foreign exchange: they were a major factor behind the country's improving economic growth in the early to mid-1990s and have operated as a significant brake on the effects of the regional economic crisis in the late 1990s.[6]

The present exodus from the Philippines began in the mid-1970s with the deployment of male construction workers to Saudi Arabia and other countries in the Middle East on large, oil-funded, infrastructure projects (Birks and Sinclair, 1980; Arnold and Shah, 1986).[7] As these projects were completed and as local middle-class affluence grew, more diverse areas of service employment opened up for Filipino workers in the Middle East, including domestic service and nursing for women (Smart, 1986; Stalker, 1994: 240; Ball, 1996). Since the mid-1980s, the flow of workers leaving the Philippines has expanded into other parts of Asia, primarily into the newly industrialising countries (NICs) of Hong Kong, Malaysia, Singapore, South Korea and Taiwan, and more recently into Japan. While significant numbers of Filipino men have found jobs in construction, manufacturing and services within the region, the shift to employment of

Filipinos in Asia is most remarkable for the predominance of women workers –
almost exclusively in domestic service (in Hong Kong, Malaysia, Singapore and
Taiwan) and entertainment (Japan). Today, the Middle East accounts for just
over half of all Filipino contract workers (Tigno, 1997: 5) and there are slightly
more Filipino women than men working abroad (Gonzalez, 1998: 40; *Business
Weekly*, 6 May 1998: 20).[8] While a growing minority of Filipinos are employed as
salaried professionals in the same countries (Demery, 1986: 33; Gonzalez, 1998:
48), they have generally lived apart and assumed a less public profile.

There are few people, communities or localities in the Philippines that have
not been touched in some way by the overseas exodus of workers over the past
two decades (see Jackson, 1997). Like many urban neighbourhoods and villages
throughout the Philippines, the Visayan Area – a poor residential community in
the former squatter settlement of Tatalon, Manila – has been transformed by the
phenomenon of overseas contract work. The people of the Visayan Area have
been living with the phenomenon of labour migration for over half a century.
The great majority are first- or second-generation migrants from the Visayan
Islands in the central Philippines, most having come to Manila from provincial
villages and towns in search of a better life and livelihood (Pinches, 1987; 1989).[9]
The local networks of mutual help and moral obligation built up in this
neighbourhood – as generations of relatives, friends and neighbours have
assisted one another to migrate and to find housing and work – have been
crucial to the more recent migration of many of them overseas, confirming a
general pattern explored elsewhere in the Philippines (Lindquist, 1993).

In 1979, when I first worked in Tatalon, the Visayan Area had only 12 of its
1,000-odd people employed overseas: all were men – half worked in elevator
installation and other areas of building construction in the Middle East, the
other half were merchant seamen. This changed markedly over the following
few years. By 1983, the number of overseas workers in the community had more
than trebled to about one in seven employed adults: nearly all were men, the
great majority employed on construction sites in the Middle East. By 1991, when
the Visayan Area itself had more than doubled in size, the number of overseas
workers had risen to seventy-five – still about one in seven employed adults.
While the single largest number continued to be those employed in construction
work in the Middle East, there had been substantial diversification into other
countries and occupations. Many new overseas workers from the Visayan Area
got jobs in Singapore, Hong Kong, Malaysia, South Korea and Brunei: most of
them were women in domestic service. Women now represented over a quarter
of all overseas workers from the neighbourhood. By early 1999, there had been a
further increase in the number of women from the Visayan Area leaving for
employment elsewhere in Asia – in some cases replacing husbands or sons who
could no longer find jobs overseas. This time, the greatest increase was in those
going to Japan to work as entertainers.

While some families had failed in their attempts to find overseas employment
or else had not pursued the possibility, in other cases several family members
over one or more generations were employed outside the Philippines. In some

instances, men who had been overseas for many years had retired to be replaced by their sons, often in the same occupation. Some men had remained out of the country for well over a decade, only returning every year or so for a vacation. Similar patterns now appear to be unfolding among women overseas workers from the community. Although there are some ways in which the overseas work-experience of people in the Visayan Area is distinctive, it is noticeable that the broad workplace and occupational patterns of overseas employment that have unfolded in this locality over the past two decades follow closely those described above for the Philippines as a whole.[10] Before looking more closely at the practices, organisation and consciousness of Filipino overseas workers, it is necessary to consider something of the controlling institutions and ideologies they have to contend with.

Ethnic repression and state regulation

International labour migration is a facet of globalisation, but it is crucial to an understanding of migrant workers to recognise that their movement occurs between nation-states differentially placed within the global arena, each embarking on separate projects of nation-building and national development. From the vantage point of both sending and receiving nation-states, the value of migrant workers lies in their contribution to such projects. But in the very act of breaching state territorial boundaries, the migrant worker also poses a threat to national integrity and so is the subject of considerable anxiety and repression, especially in host countries. Thus it is fundamental to the experience of Filipino overseas workers that they are not just workers, but workers whose identities and citizenship are founded in the Philippines. Their encounter is not only with capital, it is also with contending nation-states. The harsh institutional and cultural restraints imposed on Filipino and other overseas contract workers suggest a form of unfree labour bordering on bondage or slavery (Cohen, 1985; David, 1991: 15; Karp, 1995: 43; Hing, 1996; Tyner, 1996: 87; Hugo, 1997: 279).

The massive exodus overseas of Filipino contract workers since the 1970s has largely been orchestrated by the Philippine state as a programme of economic development and political control (see Battistella and Paganoni, 1992; Alegado, 1997; Gonzalez, 1998). While most workers are deployed through private agencies, the Philippine government has been active in promoting and overseeing the recruitment, screening, training and monitoring of overseas workers. It has also sought to control the flow of workers' wages, requiring that they be remitted through the Philippine banking system. Apart from the benefit of the considerable state-revenue exacted through various fees associated with these controls and activities, overseas employment has offered a succession of Philippine governments a lucrative source of national income and foreign exchange, as well as a partial solution to unemployment and social unrest.

The most obvious way in which Filipino overseas contract workers contribute to the national development programmes of foreign nation-states is in solving the problem of labour and skill shortages. The massive infrastructure and construction projects in the oil-rich Gulf countries would not have been possible without overseas contract workers, who significantly outnumber the local workforce (Stalker, 1994: 241). The official stance on the ethnic identities of overseas workers in these countries has been largely an instrumental one: Southeast Asians, including Filipinos, not only offer cheap labour, but they seem to be preferred to South Asians and Arab workers from neighbouring countries because they are perceived as more culturally distinctive, hence more easily isolated and controlled, and less inclined to overstay (Smart, 1986: 9).[11] Beyond the pursuit of national economic development, there is also a sense in which the family autocracies ruling the Gulf countries have sought to elevate the political and cultural integrity of their dominions by counterpoising them to the 'secondary' serving societies made up of ethnically degraded foreign workers (see Humphrey, 1990: 2–3).

This latter aspect of overseas contract work does not only apply to Filipino construction workers in the Middle East; it is even more apparent in the case of Filipino women employed in domestic service and entertainment. The demand for Filipino domestic servants in the industrialising countries of Asia and the Middle East has been partly generated by the absorption of local urban poor and peasant women into industrial and other non-domestic employment. But it has also resulted from the expansion of the middle classes, and the growth of female white-collar and professional employment. Intrinsic to the employment of Filipino domestic servants in these countries is their place as status-markers for their middle-class and elite employers (Humphrey, 1990: 4; Wong, 1996: 90; Chin, 1997: 353, 372; Ozeki, 1997: 678). Having Filipinos and other foreigners do work that is seen as servile and demeaning not only enhances the social standing of the middle class, but also the national identity of the broader populace, now released into less servile and supposedly more productive occupations. As domestic service in many countries has become synonymous with Filipinos, so has this stigmatised Filipino ethnic identity. Similarly, the entry of Filipino women into entertainment and prostitution in Japan has been partly founded on the shift of local women out of these activities into what is seen locally as more respectable employment. But it is also based in the growing affluence and sexual leisure activities of Japanese men, already linked to the Philippines through sex tours in the 1970s (Ishi, 1996: 151). Again, as Filipino women have been concentrated in this industry, the occupational stigma associated with it has been read into the ethnic and gender identities of Filipino women, implicitly elevating Japanese national and female gender identities in the process (Hosoda, 1996: 169; Tyner, 1996).

Working within societies in which ethnic ideologies are well established, Filipino workers have not only become identified with lowly work: they have also been devalued by ethnic wage hierarchies that see them paid less than local citizens and expatriate Europeans or Americans, even if they perform the same jobs (CIIR, 1987: 81; David, 1991: 15; De Guzman, 1993: 24; Margold, 1995: 287–88; Shu-Ju, 1996: 118). In part, the rationale for this concerns the relative economic status of different migrants' countries of origin. In many host countries in the Middle East (Humphrey, 1990: 10; Shah, Al-Qudsi and Shah, 1991) and Asia (Stalker, 1994: 77; Margold, 1995: 286–8; Ishi, 1996: 153; Constable, 1997: 38–9; Lowe, 1997), these inequalities and ethnic prejudices are articulated around ideas of racial or cultural inferiority. In Japan, Filipino entertainers are even distinguished from each other on the basis of skin colour: the fairer-skinned or more mestizo-looking receive better treatment and higher pay (Ballescas, 1992: 69) – a practice in keeping with the experience of many workers in the Philippines itself. In Malaysia, where it would be difficult to distinguish Filipino workers from locals on the basis of 'race' or skin colour, the divide seems to be articulated around a quasi-racial distinction between foreigner and national (Chin, 1997).

While Filipino and other foreign workers are valued for their labour service and the effect their presence has in elevating local national identities, they are also seen as a threat that needs to be tightly controlled.[12] Thus, segregation into work camps, residential enclaves or particular spaces within a single dwelling (in the case of domestic workers) is common practice, as is the segregation achieved through various distancing rituals in social interaction (Birks and Sinclair, 1980: 110–12; Humphrey, 1990: 2–4; Hing, 1996: 43; Ozeki, 1997: 682–3, 691). For many local citizens, Filipino and other foreign workers are unwelcome strangers, whose only valid identity is that of the obedient worker. Although Filipino contract workers have received some support – paternalistic and otherwise – from local citizens (Constable, 1997: 103–5; Ozeki, 1997: 686–9), they have also encountered widespread hostility, disrespect and abuse, expressed in reference to their ethnic or 'racial' identities – often from their employers, but also from officials, journalists and others (Arcinas, Bautista and David, 1986: 42; Nobuki, 1988: 58; Ventura, 1992: 62; TWF, 1995; Margold, 1995: 276; Shu-Ju, 1996: 114; Lowe, 1997). Much of this centres on the challenge overseas workers seem to pose to the existing cultural, social and political integrity of the host society. Thus, Filipino workers are commonly stereotyped in public discourse and the local media as sexually immoral, untrustworthy, lazy, unhygienic, noisy, aggressive and criminally inclined (Margold, 1995: 292; Tyner, 1996: 77; Chin, 1997; Constable, 1997: 36, 58; Lowe, 1997). These degrading images tend not only to excuse the harsh and arbitrary treatment often meted out to Filipino workers, but also tend to make this treatment appear necessary.

Filipino workers are formally contained by the limited residence periods stipulated in their work contracts or by the precariousness of their status as illegal aliens (David, 1991; Chin, 1997: 371). But they are also the subject of various other intrusive controls aimed at limiting their participation in the host society. In Singapore, Taiwan and Malaysia, for example, Filipino maids have to undergo regular pregnancy tests and, should they become pregnant, are immediately deported (Shu-Ju, 1996: 117; Wong, 1996: 93; Chin, 1997: 371). In Singapore, they are prohibited from marrying local men (Wong, 1996: 93). In Japan, Filipino workers may marry locals but, if they are separated or widowed, they are normally required to leave – even if their marriages have produced children (Ishi, 1996: 155). In Saudi Arabia and other major employer-countries in the Middle East, Filipino male workers are prohibited from having contact with local women, from gambling, drinking alcohol, possessing Christian religious symbols and conducting Christian ritual activities – all of which are valued features of ordinary male life in the Philippines (Arcinas, Bautista and David, 1986: 42; De Guzman, 1993: 15–16; Margold, 1995). Visayan Area workers complain that such restrictions are far more lax when it comes to the activities of Americans or Europeans employed in managerial or professional positions in the Middle East.

Some of the tightest legal restraints placed on Filipino overseas workers are codified in the contracts they sign. In many countries, these expressly forbid union membership or strike activity, prohibit workers from changing employer without first leaving the country, and offer workers little legal opportunity for redress should their employers contravene the conditions of the contract. Where workers have to live with the constant threat of deportation, jail or income loss should they break their contracts, employers often do so with impunity (CIIR, 1987: 81–2; Constable, 1997: 132–3). Domestic workers are particularly vulnerable: any dispute with their employers being seen by authorities in many countries as a private matter (Humphrey, 1990: 14; Shu-Ju, 1996: 116). In Singapore and Taiwan, employers are free to terminate the employment of their domestic servants at any time, requiring them to leave the country immediately (Shu-Ju, 1996: 116). Only in Hong Kong are domestic servants offered any significant protection by state labour laws, but even here it is difficult for workers to exercise their legal rights and obtain fair treatment (Shu-Ju, 1996: 116–17; Constable, 1997: 125–54). Like most domestic servants, Filipino entertainers in Japan are excluded from any rights under the country's labour laws, in this case because their formal identity as cultural entertainers precludes them from being classified as workers (Ballescas, 1992: 52).

Not only are employers and labour recruiters relatively unrestrained by labour laws and work contracts: many of them flagrantly replace the original contracts, requiring their newly arrived workers to accept lower wages and less attractive conditions (Arcinas, Bautista and David, 1986: 43–5; CIIR, 1987: 82; Ballescas, 1992: 78–80). Filipino domestic workers in Hong Kong are often forced to sign new contracts in which recruiting agents or employers set out an array of idiosyncratic conditions – specifying such things as required washing, grooming, speech and eating practices (Constable, 1997: 80–1, 87–8). Most of these are a direct affront to Philippine cultural practices and identity. Filipino entertainers arriving in Japan often discover that their services have been subcontracted out through a chain of agencies or syndicates, and that prostitution – rather than dancing or singing – is the main condition of their employment (Ballescas, 1992: 55). Not content with the tight legal and contractual restraints imposed on migrant workers, employers frequently establish further leverage and authority by confiscating their workers' passports and other documents until such time as they no longer want their workers' services (CIIR, 1987: 81; Stalker, 1994: 243–4; Hosoda, 1996: 172; Chin, 1997: 363).

Notwithstanding differences between particular employers, occupations, industries and countries of employment, the class experiences of nearly all Filipino overseas contract workers are inextricably bound to their treatment as tightly controlled, ethnically degraded aliens. This treatment arouses resentment and opposition, a subject I examine shortly, but most of the time it is tolerated. In order to understand why, it is necessary to see how the very engagement of Filipino workers in overseas employment is, in large part, a reaction to the class-based indignities they experience at home.

Escaping class at home

Despite the hardships of offshore employment, what is perhaps most striking about Filipino overseas workers – from the Visayan Area and elsewhere (Hing, 1996: 50; Hosoda, 1996: 173; Aguilar, 1999: 100) – is their apparent general satisfaction with the experience. On the face of it, this seems simply to reflect the fact that the great majority earn substantially higher wages than they can in the Philippines. Indeed, most commentators explain the migrant exodus from the Philippines as an outcome of poverty (David, 1991: 13), unemployment (Karp, 1995: 42) or economic need (Ballescas, 1992: 23), while migrants themselves commonly explain it in terms of the need to earn more income (Arcinas, Bautista and David, 1986: 25) – usually citing their obligations to their families (Ballescas, 1992: 24, 117–23; Constable, 1997: 185).

However, these explanations are insufficient because they gloss over the social, relational and cultural context within which would-be migrants act. International and interregional inequalities in wealth are certainly part of the equation but, as seems to be true for migrants generally, Filipino overseas workers do not tend to come from the most impoverished backgrounds: they have relatively high levels of formal education (Teodosio, Jimenez and Smart, 1983: 32; Arcinas, Bautista and David, 1986: 11; Constable, 1997: 78); in rural areas, they often come from wealthy village families (Pertierra, 1994: 72–5); and they are commonly already employed in the Philippines (Teodosio, Jimenez and Smart, 1983: 43; Ballescas, 1992: 26). Moreover, as Aguilar (1999: 111) argues, the citing of family obligations often conceals the fact that individual migrants largely make their own choices. These are often based on a desire to escape oppressive family relations, to acquire interpersonal legitimacy or to undergo a transformative experience akin to pilgrimage (ibid.: 111–14; see also Tacoli, 1996).

A closer look at the desire for more money also reveals that migrant workers are not simply looking to alleviate poverty, but to address class and other social sources of discontent in the Philippines. As I have argued elsewhere (Pinches, 1991; 1992), the major preoccupation and source of discontent among people in the Visayan Area is not with material hardship *per se*. Rather it is with the demeaning and degrading way in which they feel they are treated by members of the Philippine middle classes and elite, and the fact that material hardship is a central condition of this treatment. As one returning overseas worker from the Visayan Area put it:

To have a good future, it's best to sacrifice first by working abroad … I really think it is good if you have money, because if you don't have money in the Philippines, people will look down on you. They will not respect you.

For many workers from the Visayan Area and elsewhere in the Philippines (Pertierra, 1994: 55–6; Aguilar, 1999: 131), the stigmatisation and abusive work relations often experienced in overseas employment are little different from what is experienced at home. Though most workers also complain about loneliness and separation from family and friends, overseas work offers them the chance for an experience beyond the reach of old oppressors. Most importantly, it promises the money they believe will bring long-term respect – if not for themselves, then for their children – through improved consumer status, better education and small-business investment. Thus, for workers in the Visayan Area and many other such communities, overseas employment represents an attempt to escape the degradation of class in the Philippines through a strategy of upward social mobility. Though success is usually limited and may necessitate an endless succession of overseas contracts, many are clearly prepared to take the gamble (cf. Aguilar, 1999).

The upward mobility response to class degradation is primarily an individual or family-centred strategy, rather than one that emphasises class solidarity (Pinches, 1991; 1992). Nonetheless, it evidences important collective elements – notable in the mutual help networks through which overseas workers find employment (Ballescas, 1992: 34–7; Lindquist, 1993; Goss and Lindquist, 1995; Hugo, 1997: 280–2; Nagasaka, 1998a) or through which, for example, they may circulate and share passports (Ballescas, 1992: 122). Indeed, in the case of the Visayan Area and many other urban neighbourhoods, the interpersonal networks employed to mutual advantage in obtaining overseas employment continue a pattern already established in the social mobility sought through rural–urban migration (Pinches, 1987). Moreover, the networks and cooperative practices that characterise the Visayan Area have been crucial in establishing particular employment niches for those living in or connected to the neighbour-hood. Thus, the mainstay of male employment in the community for over fifty years has been the installation and servicing of elevators (Pinches, 1989). While Visayan Area men are now positioned in a wide range of jobs overseas, the great majority got their initial contracts in this industry and did so on the basis of work experience and contacts in the Philippines. And just as most women from the neighbourhood who had migrated from the Visayas to Manila first found jobs in domestic employment (Pinches, 1987), so have most of the community's current generation of women followed a similar path to overseas work in domestic service.[13]

Individual strategies of upward social mobility do not only evidence impor-tant collective elements in job recruitment and worker aspirations, but may also entail collective class consequences – as was the case in the mass exodus of workers from one elevator company, Fujitec. Many of the Visayan Area men employed in the elevator industry had relatively secure jobs and earned higher wages than most others in their neighbourhood, but they were particularly critical of the way in which they were treated by some of the companies for which they worked. At the same time as overseas work opportunities were expanding in the early 1980s, Fujitec's management had gained a reputation for being unusually harsh and punitive. Amid heightening conflict, one after another of the Visayan Area workers in the company resigned to find work in the Middle East or in other local elevator companies. Over a period of twelve months, all of the Visayan Area workers had left, along with a number of others. This walkout by experienced workers caused Fujitec serious losses in contracts and profits, an outcome the workers themselves took some pleasure in having inflicted.

The satisfaction that most overseas migrant workers express on their return to the Philippines reflects the fact that the majority do assume greater respectability and status among their relatives and peers. In part, this is associated with their new worldliness, but it is mainly a measure of their conspicuous consumption (cf. Aguilar, 1999: 119–28). Like other neighbourhoods in Manila and elsewhere in the Philippines where there are substantial numbers of overseas workers, the Visayan Area now includes many new, relatively expensive houses, fitted out with various electrical appliances and modern furnishings. Through these dwellings and other consumer wealth, overseas workers and their families enjoy significantly heightened local status and, measured against their past circumstances and the continuing poverty of many of their neighbours, see themselves as having been successful. As is the case elsewhere (Nagasaka, 1998b), they sometimes attract further approval and respect through conspicuous gift-giving. What many returning workers do not fully anticipate is the local resentment that often accompanies their new-found wealth and respectability (Pinches, 1992), and the fact that most among the Filipino middle class and elite continue to look down on them. Overseas contract workers thus commonly find themselves in an ambiguous position on their return to the Philippines. Their status achievements may have set them apart from other workers but, as workers themselves, they are still often maligned by other nationals.

Combating class abroad

The prospect of heightened social standing and increased respect at home provides a major impetus for Filipino workers to endure the apparently short-term hardships, abuses and loneliness of an overseas work contract (cf. Constable, 1997: 180–201). Migrant workers often describe this endurance as an act of sacrifice (*sakripisyo*) that will either allow them or their children to enjoy a better future (cf. Rugkasa, 1997). Thus, in addition to decorating their living quarters with various mementos to remind themselves of home, many Filipino workers in the Middle East display new consumer items or large dollar signs in their rooms to inspire them to harder work and greater sacrifice (De Guzman, 1993: 33–4, 49). Many workers see the self-discipline entailed in their work abroad as a gamble or challenge that may or may not pay off (Ballescas, 1992: 130; Aguilar, 1999).

However, Filipino migrant workers do not simply impose a self-discipline of compliance while they are employed overseas; they often also engage in overt and covert forms of resistance. Clearly there are significant differences in the employment and living conditions facing Filipino overseas workers, and some workers have more reason or opportunity to rebel than others. Yet their shared class experiences as tightly controlled, ethnically degraded aliens, have engendered among Filipino overseas workers common patterns of defiance centred, in particular, on their identity as Filipinos. I begin with the stories of Lina and Dodong, two workers from the Visayan Area, whose experiences and responses exemplify those of many overseas contract workers from the Visayan Area and elsewhere in the Philippines.

Lina is a single mother in her early thirties. Like many returning overseas workers, she says you must have great inner strength (*palakasan ng loob*; *matirang matibay*) to work abroad. Lina was employed in Hong Kong as a domestic worker for a professional couple with one young child. She had no difficulty with the tasks she had to perform, but complained bitterly about the way she was treated – particularly by the husband. Rarely was Lina paid on time and, even then, she often had to argue at length before she received her money. Sometimes she was refused permission to take her weekly day off and, when she was allowed to do so, her employers insisted she return early, though Lina knew both restrictions contravened the conditions of her contract. More than anything, Lina resented the husband's frequent insults and accusations that she was dishonest, stole their food or used the phone when they were away. Lina says she tried to convince the couple of her innocence, but they would not listen, the husband sometimes responding that she was just a 'stupid Filipino'. Once, Lina says, she retorted, saying that he too was stupid, and then responded to his heightened rage by pointing out that he now too knew what it was like to be described that way. Lina became increasingly frightened that her boss would harm her. At the time, she says, many Filipinos in Hong Kong were worried that they might suffer the same well-known fate of Delia Maga and Flor Contemplacion, two Filipino maids killed in Singapore. At night Lina locked herself in her room with a knife under her bed.

The one respite to this came on Sundays, Lina's usual day off, when she would join thousands of other Filipino domestic workers in a virtual take-over of Hong Kong's Central District. Lina looked forward to this opportunity to be with fellow Filipino and Visayan workers. Here they had an opportunity to shop together, to enjoy Filipino food, to speak in their own regional languages, to attend mass in Tagalog, to exchange news from home and to arrange to send gifts to their families. Here Lina could escape the controls of her employers and the loneliness of their apartment, and she could freely discuss the problems she was having. Some months into her stay Lina became friends with a group of fellow Filipino domestic workers who were having similar experiences to hers. Most Sundays they would meet to offer each other moral support and tactical advice on how best to deal with their employers. Lina says this not only helped give her the courage to endure the way she was being treated, but also some ideas about how to combat that treatment.

After one year Lina decided to leave her employers, despite having another year of her contract to complete. The couple said they would not let her go and refused to return her passport. But Lina would not give way and threatened to report them to the Philippine embassy. After some weeks of argument Lina was given her passport and moved out. Having broken her contract, she was now legally required to return to the Philippines, but instead went into hiding in a rented apartment with some other Filipino maids who had also left their original employers, or overstayed their visas. For the remaining twelve months, Lina worked for other employers on a daily basis. She says she enjoyed this period of her stay in Hong Kong because she now had some independence: she could cook Filipino food every day, go shopping and spend more time talking and joking with other Filipinos, sometimes about the victories they had over their employers.

One of Lina's neighbours in the Visayan Area was Dodong, who had been a contract worker in the Middle East for many years. When he started, Dodong was married with three children; by the end of his last contract he had another child but, under the strain of his absences overseas, he and his wife had separated. All of Dodong's overseas contracts were in construction, mainly in elevator installation, his earlier line of employment in Manila. He was one of the workers to resign from Fujitec in the hope of better employment overseas. Like Lina, Dodong left his first job in Saudi Arabia after the first year of a two-year contract, in his case because he was forced to accept a lower wage than had been originally agreed. While his wage was higher than his income in Manila, he did not think it compensated for the long absence from his family and friends. Back in the Philippines, Dodong applied for and was offered a better contract with another company. Over the following years he spent in the Middle East, Dodong gained more skilled and more highly paid jobs. He was able to acquire many consumer valuables, build a new house in Tatalon and send his children to good schools. Yet Dodong continued to encounter problems.

While he generally found the work itself easy, like Lina, he resented the way he was treated. Once he badly injured his leg at work and was told to take leave without pay until he recovered. Believing this to be unfair, Dodong continued to turn up to work in order to qualify for his wages, but managed to spend most of the time resting until he was well. Three months into his second contract in Saudi Arabia, Dodong and his fellow workers discovered that the subcontractor employing them was not remitting their wages to their families at home. After complaining to management and being told they could not be paid until the job was complete, all of the workers – most of them Filipinos – went on strike. Each morning they would clock on, but then return to their barracks and play cards, watch television or listen to music. Despite the illegality of the strike and threats to jail or deport them, Dodong and his fellow workers refused to budge for three weeks. They were eventually able to transfer to another work-site and subcontractor, who ensured that their wages were sent home.

Like other men from the Visayan Area, Dodong says the major problems he encountered in the Middle East were the hostility and intolerance of the Arab managers, officials and general populace, and the strict limitations placed on the activities of foreign workers. According to Dodong: 'The Arabs are always angry towards us Filipinos; they see us as low people and are always trying to provoke us.' Dodong resented having to accept lower pay than the few Arabs employed at his construction sites, saying: 'They only work as sweepers and just sleep when they feel like it; they don't have the skills of the Filipino.' Like other Visayan Area workers returning from the Middle East, Dodong reflects on his experiences by recounting a variant on the oft-told story of the Filipino worker driving a car or walking the streets. An Arab driver crashes into him, but it is the Filipino who is thrown into jail, the explanation from the Arab police or officials being that if the Filipino worker had stayed at home, the collision would not have taken place.

Although Dodong continued to experience mistreatment and homesickness, this seemed less difficult to cope with the longer he stayed away, largely because of the friendships he formed with fellow Filipino workers. Sometimes Dodong was even able to spend time with friends from the Visayan Area who were employed in the same city or country. Working and living together enabled Dodong and other Filipino men to reconstruct something of their life in the Philippines, in much the same way as Lina and her friends did in Central District, Hong Kong. They could speak in Tagalog or Visayan, play basketball, sing and play Filipino songs, eat Filipino dishes and celebrate such events as Christmas and Philippine Independence Day. If they worked in or near a large city, they could also spend time with Filipino women workers. Dodong and his friends took risks in trying to maintain their Philippine lifestyle. Though it was forbidden, some of them participated in Catholic religious ritual using Bibles, rosary beads and other such objects smuggled into the country. Often they held secret gambling sessions and, though they enjoyed the non-alcoholic beer that was openly available, some of them secretly produced their own alcoholic drink, *sadike* (see also De Guzman, 1993: 16).

One lunchtime the police came to Dodong's work-site in Saudi Arabia to charge him and some of his workmates with illegally manufacturing alcohol. At their trial the men protested that they were not doing anyone any harm and that, for men, drinking alcohol was Philippine custom. Nevertheless, they were found guilty and sentenced to sixty lashes and six-months gaol, after which they were deported. This had been Dodong's most lucrative contract, but now he was forced to forego all of the savings and valuables he had kept with him and return home empty-handed.

Though peculiar in some respects, Lina's and Dodong's stories resonate with those told by other overseas workers from the Visayan Area and elsewhere in the Philippines. They tell not only of hardship and sacrifice, but also of defiance. Lina's and Dodong's principal responses to abuse and subordination, like those of many other Filipino overseas contract workers, could be described as informal 'everyday resistance' (Scott, 1986; Pinches, 1992; Constable, 1997: 166–78).

Despite their contractual obligations and income loss, both Lina and Dodong abandoned employers who mistreated or deceived them, just as countless other Filipino overseas workers have abandoned their employers (Arcinas, Bautista and David, 1986: 42–3; Humphrey, 1990: 15; Ballescas, 1992: 70; De Guzman, 1993: 26). And, like Lina, large numbers of other Filipino workers have found ways to stay overseas illegally in order to improve their livelihoods (David, 1991: 17; Ballescas, 1992: 86; Ventura, 1992; Wong, 1996: 94–5; Ozeki, 1997: 685). Many, like Dodong, have also engaged in 'foot dragging' (Chin, 1997: 364–5). The stories of other Visayan Area workers reveal a range of similar practices, also noted in other studies, like resisting the dress-codes set by employers (Constable, 1997: 173), mocking and joking about employers behind their backs or through deliberate miscommunication (ibid.: 169–76), and damaging employers' property (Chin, 1997: 365).

Most of these actions avoid direct confrontation (cf. Scott, 1986), but just as Lina was prepared to argue and exchange insults with her employer, so too have other Filipino workers – as seems to be reflected in their widespread reputation overseas for assertiveness (Humphrey, 1990: 11; Margold, 1995: 277; Shu-Ju, 1996: 119; Constable, 1997: 35). And while Lina fortunately did not have to use the knife she kept under her bed, many employers of Filipino workers would have heard the widely publicised story of sixteen-year-old Sarah Balabagan in the United Arab Emirates who killed her employer after he raped her in 1994 (see *Asiaweek*, 29 September 1995: 42–3).

While many of the above 'everyday' practices are carried out by individuals, it is also apparent that they commonly draw on the support of fellow Filipino workers. Indeed, practices of mutual help among overseas Filipino workers are widely remarked on (Arcinas, Bautista and David, 1986: 42–3; Nobuki, 1988: 60–1; Constable, 1997: 170–2) and might sometimes be best understood as an informal, covert kind of trade unionism. This is evident, for example, in Hong Kong where employers with a bad reputation among domestic workers have great difficulty finding employees (Ozeki, 1997: 685). According to Dodong: 'The most important thing when you go to work abroad is you should help each other, because we are all Filipinos there and we all suffer.' In some cases, overseas Filipino workers have acted collectively and overtly in confronting employers or state authorities with specific demands, despite the severe sanctions that can be brought to bear on such actions. While the strike in Saudi Arabia in which Dodong participated is a rare occurrence, others have also been noted (De Guzman, 1993: 46). In the more liberal environment of Hong Kong, organised rallies by Filipino and other foreign workers have been relatively common (Constable, 1997: 164–6). In a few cases, Filipino overseas workers have even been able to openly form trade unions, such as the Asian Domestic Workers Union in Hong Kong (ibid.: 2), Kalabaw in Japan (Nobuki, 1988: 60) and the Alliance of Filipino Workers in Italy (Anonymous, 1989: 23).[14]

It is crucial to an analysis of these various work-based practices and the wider class agency of Filipino overseas workers, to examine the ways in which workers conceptualise their labour experiences and spend their time away from work.

What most angered both Lina and Dodong was that, beyond the labour they provided, they were not recognised or respected as human beings. Their needs and desires were considered unimportant or dangerous, they were distrusted, their voices were ignored, and they were insulted and abused for no apparent reason. Angered by similar experiences, many Filipino overseas workers complain of being treated like cattle, dogs and slaves (Arcinas, Bautista and David, 1986: 42; Nobuki, 1988: 58; Margold, 1995: 275, 288; Chin, 1997: 363). Like them, Lina and Dodong refused to accept this treatment. When Lina commented to her boss in the midst of one of their arguments that he now knew what it was like to be insulted, she was asserting the same principle of human equality as were the two Filipino entertainers, quoted by Ballescas (1992: 74, 125), who said the only difference between themselves and their Japanese customers and co-workers were clothes and language (cf. Jayawardena, 1968). And just as Dodong defiantly declares that Filipino workers are more skilled than Arabs, so do some overseas Filipino domestic workers assert – against prevailing local prejudice – that their jobs are honourable (Silverman, 1995: 48; Constable, 1997: 161).

These sorts of statements highlight the presence among Filipino overseas workers of ideas and values that depart from the dehumanising ideologies and practices with which they have to contend. And just as ethnic degradation is integral to the manner in which Filipino migrant workers are exploited and controlled, so is the positive assertion of Filipino identity integral to the way in which they have defended themselves.

Ethnicity and class

In one sense, Filipino overseas contract workers simply bring with them a store of cultural resources and dispositions they call upon to deal with the new circumstances under which they work and live. It might hardly seem surprising that they seek each other out, assist each other and enjoy, where possible, a way of life that is familiar to them. Thus one may interpret the collective life of the worker barracks in the Middle East, the Sunday festivities in Hong Kong and Singapore, or the underground in Japan's Kotobuki (Ventura, 1992), as simply the cultural world of displaced Filipinos. Looked at more closely though, this life takes on a more proletarian and subversive character.

First, the collective Filipino life discussed here is almost exclusive to contract and illegal wage-workers. And it is not simply the fact that they dominate numerically. Wealthy Filipinos employed overseas as salaried professionals, or visiting on business or as tourists, are loath to be confused with Filipino workers. They both avoid and are embarrassed by the latter's public displays of cultural identity and have developed various strategies aimed at distinguishing and distancing themselves from Filipino contract workers (Aguilar, 1996: 120–3). Filipino contract workers have little or no contact with middle-class or elite Filipinos while overseas, and generally assume all the Filipinos they see are workers like themselves.

Second, Filipino overseas workers are selective in the way in which they on and act out their shared ethnicity. More important than the self-consci nationalist symbolism of the Philippine state and intelligentsia is the perfoɪɪɪ- ance of popular everyday Philippine culture, played out in conversation, humour, dress, culinary tastes and popular Catholic religious observance. Although Filipino officials, labour recruiters, journalists, and even some migrant workers themselves, have attempted to invoke Philippine national pride in urging overseas workers to abandon their boisterous public behaviour and cooperate more with their employers, this has had little effect.[15] Moreover, it is the collective cultural life that Filipino workers construct, mainly outside work hours, that enables them to find the social, moral and tactical support necessary to resist, confront or leave their employers, to hide from state authorities and, less often, to mount strikes or protest rallies. The link between Filipino identity and class agency is evident in the names Filipino contract workers have generally adopted for the few unions and other such bodies they have been able to form overseas.[16]

Third, even for the many Filipino workers who do not directly challenge their employers or join overt protest rallies, the positive collective display of Philippine cultural practice is a powerful symbolic defence against the degrading practices and ideologies encountered at work and in everyday life. Thus, in their barracks and on outings during their days off, Filipino construction workers in the Middle East together assert a cultural dignity and humanity denied them in the wider host society. In doing so, many are prepared to flout prohibitions on alcohol, gambling and Christian religious practice. Through such practices as renaming attractive landmarks after familiar counterparts in the Philippines (De Guzman, 1993: 14, 17), they also achieve a certain symbolic colonisation over a landscape in which they are otherwise denied cultural recognition. It is significant that the most structurally disempowered and individuated workers – those in domestic service – are the ones who are responsible for the largest and most publicly visible displays of camaraderie and popular Philippine cultural life, the most open and celebrated in Hong Kong's Central District and Singapore's Lucky Plaza. Here, at least fleetingly, an important inversion takes place: the silenced become vocal, the invisible are seen and (to the chagrin of many local citizens) a prestigious part of the city is taken over by strangers bearing a culture they are normally denied (see Constable, 1997: 166–70). On such occasions, Filipino workers from the Visayan Area and elsewhere may assert their particular regional traditions and affiliations. However, in the overseas context, it is the overarching sense of national identity that predominates.

Much of the collective behaviour of Filipino overseas workers may start in a realm of 'pre-reflective' lived culture (Pertierra, 1997: 187–90) adapted from the Philippines. However, as it is practised overseas in the midst of racism, cultural disjuncture, workplace discipline and state repression, it has taken on a more self-conscious, politicised form. This transformation is evident, for example, in Dodong's indignant defence of his alcohol use as an integral part of his Philippine identity and is present in countless exchanges in which Filipino workers insist on the value of their cuisine, dress-sense or language (for example, Margold, 1995: 277). Philippine culture and ethnicity become the vehicle through which Filipino overseas contract workers constitute themselves against the conditions of their wage labour and ideological repression.[17] Following Cohen (1985) and Jenkins (1997), the significance of Philippine ethnicity among overseas workers is not to be found so much in the presence of particular cultural practices or traditions, but rather in the relational or contextual settings in which they are found. In this case, these are settings in which the dehumanisation of Filipino workers as the mere carriers of labour-power is coterminous with their degradation as uncultured, ethnic inferiors. The way in which most overseas Filipino contract workers respond to this by positively asserting Philippine cultural practice and ethnic identity should therefore be read as class-based and counter-hegemonic.

However, there remain two ways in which assertions of Filipino ethnic identity might be seen to undermine class consciousness. The first concerns relations between fellow workers who claim or are attributed with different ethnic identities. It is true that Filipino overseas workers generally display a stronger sense of solidarity among themselves than they do with workers of other nationalities. In part this is because of linguistic and other cultural barriers, but it is also a consequence of the ways in which employers, labour recruiters and state authorities have segmented their labour markets along ethnic lines. Like many other Filipino workers, Dodong and Lina had little opportunity to spend time with or get to know non-Filipino workers. Yet Filipino and non-Filipino workers often meet and, in the Middle East especially, spend time working side by side. Evidence on the quality of their relations is mixed. While Arcinas, Bautista and David (1986: 52) report that relations between Filipino and Arab workers are generally good, De Guzman (1993: 44) notes that Filipino workers engage in a degree of divisive ethnic stereotyping. Dodong's negative remark on the skills and work habits of Arab workers, quoted earlier, also evidences the kind of divisiveness ethnic consciousness may generate among workers. Yet Dodong associated Arab ethnicity most with employers and officials, and generally spoke well of the Pakistani, Indian, Thai and Korean workers he came across. Indeed, in the strike Dodong participated in, Filipinos and Pakistanis worked and organised together. Lack of contact and cooperation with workers of other national backgrounds may reflect the extent to which particular lines of work are exclusive to one ethnic group – as in Hong Kong, where over 90 per cent of domestic servants are Filipinos (Ozeki, 1997: 678). Yet, even here, Constable (1997: 158–9) notes a degree of shared class consciousness based on common experience among some Filipino and local Chinese servants, and it is also notable that both Filipino and non-Filipino workers participate in Hong Kong's Asian Domestic Workers Union.

There is no doubt that ethnicity may significantly impede worker unity and consciousness (Smith, 1985), but this cannot simply be assumed. Moreover, when it is remembered that there are significant organisational and geopolitical constraints on the activities of most employers and business enterprises, as well

as on the logistics of working-class action, it becomes clear that the impc
of national or ethnic divisions among workers is often exaggerated. What
shown here is that ethnic or national identities may be powerful vehicles t... ...
which working-class sentiments and agency find expression, notwithstanding
certain ambiguities in relation to workers who may be looked on as ethnic
outsiders. But even here it is important to note that ethnic identity is not fixed or
absolute; rather it is negotiated and, to some degree, selectively invoked
depending on circumstance and the social relations at hand. In this case, the
principal Other of Filipino ethnic identity comprises employers and state
officials, not fellow workers, with whom such distinctions appear less pressing.[18]

The second way in which ethnicity might be seen to inhibit the class consciousness and agency of Filipino overseas contract workers concerns their
shared national identity with the Philippine middle class and elite. Given the
virtual absence of Filipino capitalists and salaried professionals from many
overseas settings in which Filipino workers are employed, it might be argued that
this is not always an issue. However, as I have argued, the consciousness and
agency of Filipino overseas workers is rooted not only in their experiences
overseas, but also in their continued attachment to the Philippines, both while
they are away and when they return home. In recent years the heightened
politicisation of the hardships associated with overseas employment appears to
have welded the identity of Filipino overseas workers to that of all Filipinos.[19]
This seemed particularly evident in the widespread outrage over the conviction
and execution in 1995 of the Filipino maid, Flor Contemplacion. In what was
widely believed among Filipinos to be a trumped-up double murder charge,
Singaporeans were held responsible, not only for silencing Contemplacion and
one of her alleged victims, fellow Filipino maid Delia Maga, but also for
dismissing with equal contempt the respectable voices of President Ramos and a
team of Filipino legal and forensic experts seeking to have either the conviction
or the sentence overturned.[20] The appearance of all of this was that class
differences between overseas contract workers and other Filipinos had given way
to feelings of national solidarity in the face of foreign abuse. Moreover, in
response to criticisms of neglect, the Philippine government has also sought to
symbolically forge such a unity by declaring Filipino overseas workers 'our
modern-day heroes' and 'ambassadors of goodwill' (Tigno, 1997: 12), and by
instigating such events as 'the month of overseas Filipinos' (Asis, 1992: 74).

However, much of this is superficial and misleading. At the same time as some
middle-class nationalists were agitating for better state protection of Filipino
overseas contract workers, others (as noted above) were seeking to cultivate
among those workers a self-imposed discipline that would see them comply with
the tastes and dictates of foreign employers in the name of Philippine national
pride. Indeed, the indignation that middle-class and elite Filipinos expressed over
the Flor Contemplacion execution, generally concerned the way in which their
own identities were sullied through their association with Filipino workers
(Pertierra, 1992: xv; Aguilar, 1996: 125–6). On their overseas shopping, business
and holiday trips, many were enraged by foreigners who treated them in the

same way they treated Filipino labourers and domestic workers – as racial and class inferiors. The treatment of Filipino political leaders by Singaporean authorities during the Flor Contemplacion case compounded this further. While drawing on some of the same national symbols as Filipino overseas contract workers, the elite and middle class are principally concerned with distinguishing themselves and their Philippine national identity from what they too ultimately regard as the lowly position of the Filipino worker.

The nationalist, anti-Singapore sentiments that surfaced over the Contemplacion case were more evident in the Visayan Area among those who had not worked overseas.[21] For the neighbourhood's overseas contract workers, such labels as 'new national hero' rang hollow against their experiences with most elite and middle-class Filipinos. Though Lina threatened to call on the authority of the Philippine embassy in Hong Kong during her conflict with her employer, she did not pursue it. Indeed, overseas workers from the Visayan Area generally ridicule Philippine embassy officials for their lack of genuine interest in the welfare of Filipino workers, and are similarly scathing of Filipino labour recruiters and companies contracting overseas. Though their responses are mixed, a number of workers in the Middle East complain of the mistreatment they experienced at the hands of Filipino superiors overseas. One worker told the story of an abusive Filipino supervisor on a construction site in Saudi Arabia. Afraid of what the local authorities might do should this worker and his friends confront their supervisor at work, they waited until they were on the flight back to the Philippines before beating him up.

Filipino overseas workers returning to find jobs at home, where most would prefer to work, encounter the same lack of generosity and support from wealthy Filipinos that had embittered them in the past. Moreover, the experience of better wages overseas only serves to make many workers even more disgruntled with local employers when they return home. In their general encounters with rich and middle-class Filipinos, returning overseas contract workers notice little change. While they have more spending power and assume greater consumer status in the eyes of their peers than they did before, the established middle class and elite still tend to look on them as people who may have new money, but who lack the taste and refinement to know how to use it.

The heightened attachment to a national homeland that develops among Filipino contract workers seems to find clear expression in the spontaneous cheer that usually erupts as aeroplanes departing overseas work sites touch down in the Philippines. Yet as the urgency and power of that attachment – founded in the class experiences of overseas employment – fades, it tends to give way to more localised sentiments within the Philippines. For Filipino contract workers overseas, Philippine national identity is primarily a vehicle of class empowerment, but at home its content, performance and meaning lies mainly in other hands. At home, different patterns of class identity and action tend to re-emerge, in some cases having a parallel logic to overseas nationalism in assertions of local regional or ethnolinguistic attachment (cf. Pinches, 1991; 1992).

Conclusion

For many Filipinos, the opportunity to work overseas as contract labourers has significant appeal, not least because it offers the promise of an escape from the degradation of class relations in the Philippines. Hoping that more money and worldly experience will bring new opportunities and respectability at home, Filipino overseas workers celebrate their release from local hardships and indignities, at the same time steeling themselves for periods of sacrifice and self-discipline abroad. Notwithstanding this resolve and the heightened vulnerability that goes with overseas contract labour, Filipino workers respond to the class degradation they encounter overseas with varied forms of resistance – individual and collective, concealed and open. What most distinguishes this resistance is the extent to which it relies on, invokes and celebrates the national identity of Filipino contract workers themselves. While this may appear unremarkable and counterproductive to the development of class consciousness or class action, I have argued in this chapter that the reverse is largely true.

The accelerating processes of globalisation, exemplified in the increased movement of labour across national boundaries, have not resulted in a simple playing out of capital and labour on a world stage. Two things are left out of this equation. The first is the unequal and contentious system of nation-states within which migrant workers are defined not just as sources of labour-power, but also as the carriers of particular national identities and statuses. These are intrinsic to the class experiences of Filipino overseas contract workers and, in particular, to their degradation either as ethnically inferior aliens or as beings whose personhood, beyond employment, is seen to be of no consequence. The way in which Filipino overseas workers utilise and assert their shared national identity may suggest a certain unreflective pragmatism but, as I have shown, it also evidences significant class-based action, shaped by and directly opposed to this degradation. The Filipino identity that is fashioned or refashioned through the experience of overseas workers is an identity invested with significant working-class content.

The second thing left out of a simple capital versus labour equation is the fact that Filipino workers bring to overseas employment dispositions and modes of self-consciousness that have been formed by and are rooted in particular social, cultural and spatial settings, related to (but not synonymous with) the Philippine nation-state. The attachments and self-identities that Filipino overseas contract workers inject into their assertions of national or ethnic honour, have less to do with the elite nationalism of the Filipino state or intelligentsia than with a world of lived popular culture, largely embedded in particular localities and interpersonal histories. What is significant about the positive assertions of these attachments and identities overseas is that they humanise workers, not just in the face of racism or ethnic prejudice, but in the face of commodified labour. They pronounce and celebrate what the wage-labour/capital relation denies: that workers possess a social and cultural being that is inseparable from their labour-power. In this sense, the ethnic or national consciousness of Filipino overseas contract workers may go more critically to the heart of capitalism and class than has hitherto been recognised.

Filipino overseas contract workers simultaneously engage in different nationally constructed systems of class at home and abroad. They variously respond to the experiences of degradation that come with these systems by seeking escape or by engaging in combat. While one response may limit or compromise the other, and while neither have brought dramatic structural change to the collective lives of Filipino workers, these forms of worker agency and resistance should not be overlooked or trivialised.

Notes

1 I wish to thank Jane Hutchison, Myrna Tonkinson and Cheryl Lange for their helpful comments on earlier drafts of this chapter.
2 Staniland (1985: 176–81) makes the same point. That class and ethnic (or 'racial') identities may overlap is evident, for example in Jayawardena (1968), Leggett (1968) and Miles (1989: 99–131), yet rarely has the character of this overlap been fully explored or analysed.
3 In this chapter I use the terms 'ethnic identity' and 'national identity' interchangeably to refer to a shared sense of Filipino identity. Though the term 'national identity' conventionally implies a higher level of politicisation than does 'ethnic identity', the distinction remains blurred and problematic (see Eriksen, 1993; Jenkins, 1997: 142–7). However, this is not a point I develop in the chapter.
4 Often this is simply implicit in the research focus, and in the equation of 'organised labour' with trade unionism; see, for example, Frenkel (1993).
5 For a discussion of some of the problems here, see Metcalfe (1988: 126–36) and Katznelson (1986).
6 The growing dependence of the Philippine economy on the remitted wages and salaries of overseas workers is evident from the fact that these contributions totalled US$15.6 billion in the period 1992–7, up from US$5.5 billion in the previous five-year period, 1986–91 (Tiglao 1997: 40). Expected remittances in 1998 were US$6 billion (*Philippine Star*, 17 October 1998: 14).
7 The Philippines has a long history of large-scale overseas labour migration, mainly to North America (see CIIR, 1987; Gonzalez, 1998: 25–33). This has undoubtedly contributed to the readiness of many in the current generation to leave.
8 Although the regional economic crisis has precipitated a moderate overall drop in the numbers of Filipinos leaving for overseas employment, the pattern has been highly uneven: while there has been significant drop in those leaving for the Middle East and Asian countries badly affected by the crisis, there has been a parallel increase in those leaving for Japan and Taiwan (*Manila Standard*, 24 August 1998: 4; *Philippine Star*, 12 October 1998: 38).
9 By far the single largest concentration of contemporary overseas migrants come from Metropolitan Manila (Teodosio, Jimenez and Smart, 1983: 33; Jackson, 1997: 42) but, according to one study, the majority of this number were born elsewhere in the Philippines (Teodosio, Jimenez and Smart, 1983: 33).
10 The same is true, for example, in the coastal town of Malinaw (Lindquist, 1993), though in other cases there is a heavy reliance on specific occupations or places of employment (for example, Nagasaka, 1998a).
11 But see Birks and Sinclair (1980: 32) and Demery (1986: 23–4).
12 Programmes of labour training and recruitment aimed at replacing foreign workers with local citizens in the Middle East (De Guzman, 1993: 26; Buendia and Tigno, 1998: 8) have so far had only limited success and reveal how dependent these countries are on foreign labour.

13 Because of these sorts of histories, some local Philippine communities hav associated with particular occupations or places of employment overseas. ple, the district of Santa Rosa in the town of Alaminos, Laguna province, is kn locally as a place of overseas domestic workers, mainly employed in Italy and Spain – hence the community's nickname, 'Italian village' (Karp, 1995: 44). See also Naga saka (1998a).

14 Some Filipino overseas workers, individually and collectively, have benefited from the legal advice, material resources and organising capacity of sympathetic non-governmental organisations which have been quite active in countries like Hong Kong and Japan, as well as in the Philippines itself (Ballescas, 1992: 10; De Guzman, 1993: 3; Ishi, 1996: 156; Constable, 1997: x–xi).

15 Constable (1997: 185–7) says that in Hong Kong such exhortations, commonly expressed in the popular magazine *Tinig Filipino*, come from Filipino migrants them-selves. This may be, but the manner and tone of the statements quoted suggest that they come from that small section of the overseas Filipino workforce that has been drawn from the educated middle class in the Philippines. It is also noteworthy that these statements reproduce the very stereotypes of Philippine workers that offend the middle class and elite in the Philippines itself (Pinches, 1991).

16 Hence the United Filipinos in Hong Kong (Constable, 1997: 164–6), Kalabaw in Japan (Nobuki, 1988: 60) and the Alliance of Filipino Workers in Italy (Anonymous, 1989: 23).

17 While some Christian Filipino workers in the Middle East have converted to Islam, this has apparently been for instrumental reasons (Arcinas, Bautista and David, 1986: 42; De Guzman, 1993: 36). Conversely, Mindanao Muslims – associated with a strong separatist tradition in the southern Philippines – appear more likely to identify as Filipinos as a consequence of their working experiences in the Middle East (Lacar, 1994: 448).

18 This point is further amplified by Ozeki (1997: 682), who found that the only situation in which the Hong Kong Chinese apparently abandoned their racist stereo-types of Filipinos was when they associated with them as work colleagues.

19 This has come about mainly through the agency of influential middle-class activists and sections of the nationalist intelligentsia, critical of the Philippine government's inadequate overseas welfare provisions and lamenting, in general, the exodus of Filipino workers as a breach in the national community and an indictment of the nation's leaders (see David, 1991; Ballescas, 1992: 11; Aguilar, 1999: 132). Forced to respond to these criticisms, the Philippine government has assumed a more protective stance towards overseas workers (Gonzalez, 1998: 124–8).

20 For fuller treatment of these events, see May (1997), Rafael (1997) and Hilsden (2000).

21 The demand for jobs in Singapore did not wane during this time and, though they had the opportunity to return to the Philippines, most Filipino workers in Singapore decided to remain.

Bibliography

Aguilar, F. (1996) 'The dialectics of transnational shame and national identity', *Philippine Sociological Review* 44, 1–4: 101–36.

—— (1999) 'Ritual passage and the reconstruction of selfhood in international labour migration', *Sojourn* 14, 1: 98–139.

Alegado, D. (1997) 'The labor export industry and post-1986 Philippine economic development', *Pilipinas* 29: 19–38.

Anonymous (1989) 'Filipino workers in Italy', *Pinoy Overseas Chronicle* VII, 2: 22–3.

Arcinas, R., Bautista, C. and David, R. (1986) *The Odyssey of the Filipino Migrant Workers to the Gulf Region*, Quezon City: Department of Sociology, College of Social Sciences and Philosophy, University of the Philippines.

Arnold, F. and Shah, N. (eds) (1986) *Asian Labor Migration: Pipeline to the Middle East*, Boulder: Westview.

Asis, M. (1992) 'The overseas employment program policy', in G. Battistella and A. Paganoni (eds) *Philippine Labor Migration: Impact and Policy*, Quezon City: Scalabrini Migration Center, pp. 68–112.

Ball, R. (1996) 'Nation building: The globalization of nursing – The case of the Philippines', *Pilipinas* 27: 67–91.

Ballescas, M. (1992) *Filipino Entertainers in Japan: An Introduction*, Quezon City: Foundation for Nationalist Studies.

Battistella, G. and Paganoni, A. (eds) (1992) *Philippine Labor Migration: Impact and Policy*, Quezon City: Scalabrini Migration Center.

Birks, J. and Sinclair, C. (1980) *International Migration and Development in the Arab Region*, Geneva: International Labour Organization.

Buendia, R. and Tigno, J. (1998) *The Resurgence of Nationalism and Ethnicity in Post-Industrialism: Migration in Asian Context*, paper presented at the Workshop on Migrations in Contemporary Southeast Asia, Institute of Southeast Asian Studies, Singapore, 2–3 January.

CIIR (Catholic Institute for International Relations) (1987) *The Labour Trade: Filipino Migrant Workers Around the World*, London: CIIR.

Chin, C. (1997) 'Walls of silence and late twentieth century representations of the foreign female domestic worker: The case of Filipina and Indonesian female servants in Malaysia', *International Migration Review* 31, 2: 357–85.

Cohen, A. (1985) *The Symbolic Construction of Community*, London: Tavistock.

Constable, N. (1997) *Maid to Order in Hong Kong: Stories of Filipina Workers*, Ithaca: Cornell University Press.

Crompton, R. (1993) *Class and Stratification*, Cambridge: Polity Press.

David, R. (1991) 'Filipino workers in Japan: Vulnerability and survival', *Kasarinlan* 6: 9–23.

De Guzman, A. (1993) ' "Katas ng Saudi": The work and life situation of the Filipino contract workers of Saudi Arabia', *Philippine Social Sciences Review* 51, 1–4: 1–56.

Demery, L. (1986) 'Asian labor migration: An empirical assessment', in F. Arnold and H. Shah (eds) *Asian Labor Migration: Pipeline to the Middle East*, Boulder: Westview, pp. 17–46.

Eriksen, T. (1993) *Ethnicity and Nationalism: Anthropological Perspectives*, London: Pluto Press.

—— (1997) 'Ethnicity, race and nation', in M. Guibernau and J. Rex (eds) *The Ethnicity Reader: Nationalism, Multiculturalism and Migration*, Cambridge: Polity Press, pp. 33–42.

Frenkel, S. (ed.) (1993) *Organised Labour in the Asia-Pacific Region: A Comparative Study of Trade Unionism in Nine Countries*, Ithaca: ILR Press.

Gonzalez, J. (1998) *Philippine Labour Migration: Critical Dimensions of Public Policy*, Singapore: Institute of Southeast Asian Studies.

Goss, J. and Lindquist, B. (1995) 'Conceptualizing international labor migration: A structuration perspective', *International Migration Review* 29, 2: 317–51.

Hilsden, A. (2000) 'The Contemplacion fiasco: The hanging of a Filipino domestic worker in Singapore', in A. Hilsden, M. McIntyre, V. Mackie and M. Stivens (eds) *Gender Politics and Human Rights in the Asia-Pacific*, London and New York: Routledge.

Hing Ai Yun (1996) 'Foreign maids and the reproduction of labor in Singapore', *Philippine Sociological Review* 44, 1–4: 33–57.

Hosoda, N. (1996) 'Filipino women in the Japanese entertainment industry', in J. Lele and W. Tettey (eds) *Asia – Who Pays for Growth?*, Aldershot: Dartmouth Publishing, pp. 163–77.

Hugo, G. (1997) 'Asia and the Pacific on the move: Workers and refugees, a challenge to nation states', *Asia Pacific Viewpoint* 38, 3: 267–86.

Humphrey, M. (1990) *Class, Ethnicity and Nationality: The Politics of Labour Regulation in Arab -States, the Case of Domestic Workers in Jordan*, paper presented at the Asian Studies Association of Australia Conference, Griffith University, Brisbane, 2–5 July.

Ishi, Y. (1996) 'Forward to a better life: The situation of Asian women married to Japanese men in Japan in the 1990s', in G. Battistella and A. Paganoni (eds) *Asian Women in Migration*, Quezon City: Scalabrini Migration Center, pp. 147–64.

Jackson, R. (1997) 'The regional sources of overseas Filipino workers', *Pilipinas* 29: 39–48.

Jayawardena, C. (1968) 'Ideology and conflict in lower class communities', *Comparative Studies in Society and History* 10: 413–46.

Jenkins, R. (1997) *Rethinking Ethnicity: Arguments and Explorations*, London: Sage.

Karp, J. (1995) 'Migrant workers: A new kind of hero', *Far Eastern Economic Review* March 30: 42–5.

Katznelson, I. (1986) 'Working class formation: Constructing cases and comparisons', in I. Katznelson and A. Zolber (eds) *Working Class Formation: Nineteenth-Century Patterns in Western Europe and the United States*, Princeton: Princeton University Press, pp. 3–41.

Lacar, L. (1994) 'Culture contact and national identification among Philippine Muslims', *Philippine Studies* 42: 431–51.

Leggett, J. (1968) *Class, Race and Labour: Working Class Consciousness in Detroit*, London: Oxford University Press.

Lindquist, B. (1993) 'Migration networks: A case study in the Philippines', *Asian and Pacific Migration Journal* 2, 1: 75–104.

Lloyd, P. (1982) *A Third World Proletariat*, London: Allen & Unwin.

Lowe, C. (1997) 'Negotiating meaning across cultures: Interpersonal communication between the Filipino domestic workers in Hong Kong and their Hong Kong employers', *Pilipinas* 29: 77–88.

Margold, J. (1995) 'Narratives of masculinity and transnational migration: Filipino workers in the Middle East', in A. Ong and M. Peletz (eds) *Bewitching Women, Pious Men*, Berkeley: University of California Press, pp. 274–98.

May, R. (1997) 'The domestic in foreign policy: The Flor Contemplacion case and Philippine–Singapore relations', *Pilipinas* 29: 63–76.

Metcalfe, A. (1988) *For Freedom and Dignity*, North Sydney: Allen & Unwin.

Miles, R. (1989) *Racism*, London: Tavistock.

Nagasaka, I. (1998a) 'Kinship networks and child fostering in labor migration from Ilocos, Philippines to Italy', *Asian and Pacific Migration Journal* 7, 1: 67–92.

—— (1998b) *Giving a Feast in the Homeland Village: International Migration and Traditional Feasts in the Ilocos Region, Philippines*, paper presented to the Population Movement in Southeast Asia: Changing Identities and Strategies for Survival conference, National Museum of Ethnology, Osaka, 17–19 September.

Nash, J. (1979) *We Eat the Mines and the Mines Eat Us: Dependency and Exploitation in Bolivian Tin Mines*, New York: Columbia University Press.

Nobuki, F. (1988) 'Holding out against discrimination and exploitation: Filipino laborers', *Kaibigan Migration Folio* 1, 1: 57–62.

Ong, A. (1987) *Spirits of Resistance and Capitalist Discipline: Factory Women in Malaysia*, Albany: University of New York Press.

Ozeki, E. (1997) 'Migration frontier of Filipino women: Ethnic relations of Filipina domestic helpers with Chinese employers in Hong Kong', *Tonan Ajia Kenkyu (Southeast Asian Studies)* 34, 4: 676–95.

Perry, E. (1996) 'Putting class in its place: Bases of worker identity in East Asia', in E. Perry (ed.) *Putting Class in Its Place: Worker Identities in East Asia*, Berkeley: Institute for East Asian Studies, University of California.

Pertierra, R. (1992) *Remittances and Returnees: The Cultural Economy of Migration in Ilocos*, Quezon City: New Day Publishers.

—— (1994) 'Lured abroad: The case of Ilocano overseas workers', *Sojourn* 9, 1: 54–80.

—— (1997) *Explorations in Social Theory and Philippine Ethnography*, Quezon City: University of the Philippines Press.

Pinches, M. (1987) 'All that we have is our muscle and sweat: The rise of wage labour in a Manila squatter community', in M. Pinches and S. Lakha (eds) *Wage Labour and Social Change: The Proletariat in Asia and the Pacific*, Clayton: Centre of Southeast Asian Studies, Monash University, pp. 103–40.

—— (1989) 'Sending people up: Industrial structure and primordial sentiments in the making of Philippine elevator workers', *Anthropological Forum* 6, 1: 7–26.

—— (1991) 'The working class experience of shame, inequality and people power in Tatalon, Manila', in B. Kerkvliet and R. Mojares (eds) *From Marcos to Aquino: Local Perspectives on Political Transition in the Philippines*, Quezon City: Ateneo de Manila University Press, pp. 166–86.

—— (1992) 'Proletarian ritual: Class degradation and the dialectics of resistance in Manila', *Pilipinas* 19: 67–92.

—— (1999) 'Entrepreneurship, consumption, ethnicity and national identity in the making of the Philippines' "new rich" ', in M. Pinches (ed.) *Culture and Privilege in Capitalist Asia*, London and New York: Routledge, pp. 275–301.

Pinches, M. and Lakha, S. (eds) (1987) *Wage Labour and Social Change: The Proletariat in Asia and the Pacific*, Clayton: Centre of Southeast Asian Studies, Monash University.

Rafael, V. (1997) ' "Your grief is our gossip": Overseas Filipinos and other spectral presences', *Public Culture* 9: 267–91.

Rodriquez, E. (1996) 'Net social benefits of emigration from the perspective of the source country: Do overseas Filipinos really benefit the Philippines?', *Philippine Sociological Review* 44, 1–4: 137–61.

Rugkasa, J. (1997) *Sacrifice and Success: The Meaning of Migration in a Filipino Local Setting*, Oslo: Department and Museum of Anthropology, University of Oslo.

Scott, J. (1986) 'Everyday forms of peasant resistance', *Journal of Peasant Studies* 13, 2: 5–35.

Shah, N., Al-Qudsi, S. and Shah, M. (1991) 'Asian women workers in Kuwait', *International Migration Review* 25, 3: 464–86.

Shu-Ju Ada Cheng (1996) 'Migrant women domestic workers in Hong Kong, Singapore and Taiwan: A comparative analysis', in G. Battistella and A. Paganoni (eds) *Asian Women in Migration*, Quezon City: Scalabrini Migration Center, pp. 109–22.

Silverman, G. (1995) 'Mothers to the world', *Far Eastern Economic Review* March 30: 48.

Smart, J. (1986) 'Worker circulation between Asia and the Middle East', *Pacific Viewpoint* 27, 1: 1–28.

Smith, W. (1985) 'A Japanese factory in Malaysia: Ethnicity as a management ideology', in K. Jomo (ed.) *The Sun Also Sets: The Lessons in Looking East*, Petaling Jaya: Insan.

Stalker, P. (1994) *The Work of Strangers: A Survey of International Labour Migration*, Geneva: ILO.

Staniland, M. (1985) *What is Political Economy? A Study of Social Theory and Underdevelopment*, New Haven: Yale University Press.

Tacoli, C. (1996) 'Migrating "for the sake of the family"? Gender, life course and intra-household relations among Filipino migrants in Rome', *Philippine Sociological Review* 44, 1–4: 12–32.

Taussig, M. (1980) *The Devil and Commodity Fetishism*, Chapel Hill: University of North Carolina Press.

Teodosio, V., Jimenez, C. and Smart, J. (1983) *Working Abroad*, Manila: Institute of Labour and Manpower Studies.

Tiglao, R. (1997) 'Global view', *Far Eastern Economic Review* June 19, 40–4.

Tigno, J. (1997) 'Ties that bind: The past and prospects of Philippine outmigration', *Pilipinas* 29: 1–18.

TWF (Tenagita Women's Force) (1995) 'Abuse, torture and dehumanized treatment of migrant workers at detention centers', *Asian Migrant* 8, 4: 114–16.

Tyner, J. (1996) 'Constructions of Filipina migrant entertainers', *Gender, Place and Culture* 3, 1: 77–93.

Ventura, R. (1992) *Underground in Japan*, London: Jonathan Cape.

Wong, D. (1996) 'Migrant women domestic workers in Hong Kong', in G. Battistella and A. Paganoni (eds) *Asian Women in Migration*, Quezon City: Scalabrini Migration Center, pp. 87–108.

Name index

Subject index